LEGENDARY LOCALS

OF

SAN FRANCISCO'S RICHMOND, SUNSET, AND GOLDEN GATE PARK

CALIFORNIA

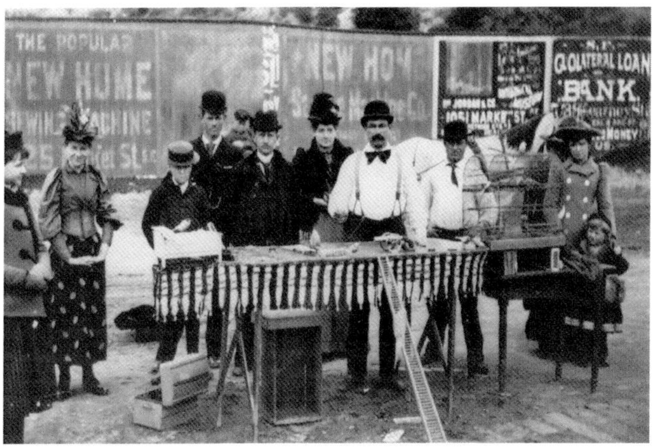

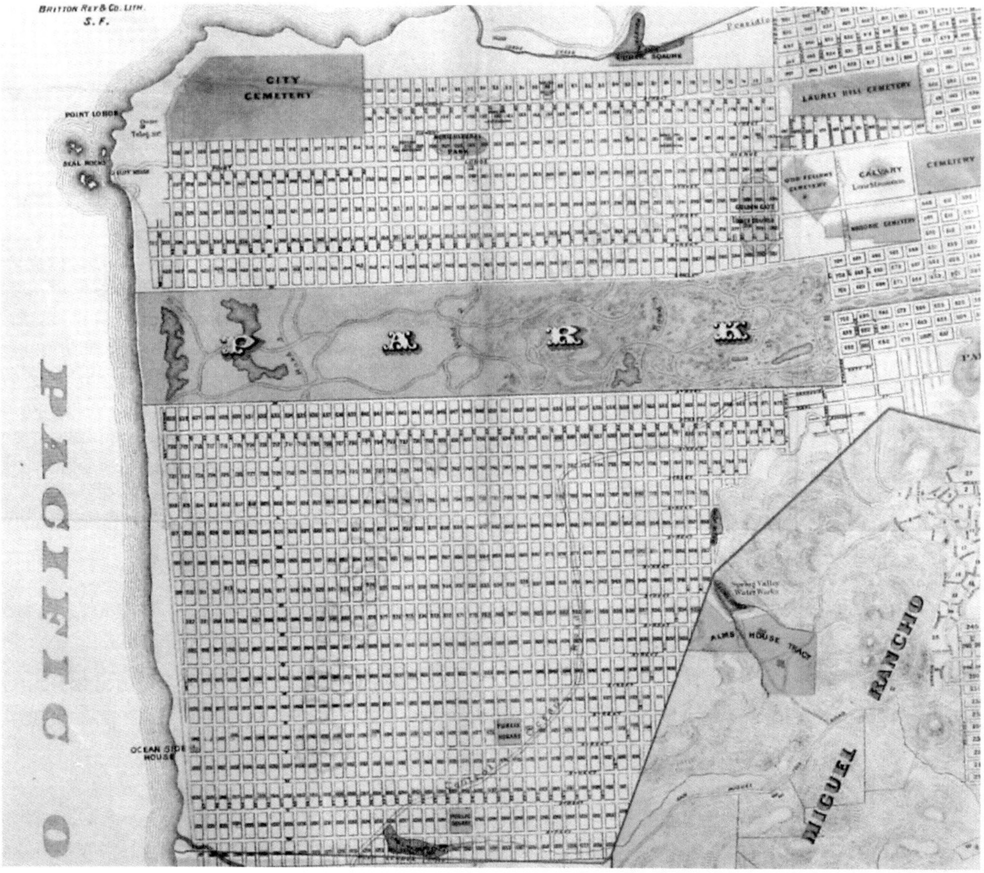

Outside Lands Map
In 1866, the areas that became the Richmond District, the Sunset District, and Golden Gate Park became part of San Francisco. This is the first map showing how the future park and neighborhoods would look. (Courtesy Dennis Minnick.)

Page 1: Johnnie-the-Birdman Williams
For more than 20 years, John Williams entertained visitors to Ocean Beach and the Cliff House. For more information, see page 106. (Courtesy Marilyn Blaisdell.)

LEGENDARY LOCALS

OF

SAN FRANCISCO'S RICHMOND, SUNSET, AND GOLDEN GATE PARK

CALIFORNIA

LORRI UNGARETTI

LEGENDARY LOCALS

ISBN 978-1-4671-0177-6

Legendary Locals is an imprint of Arcadia Publishing
Charleston, South Carolina

Printed in the United States of America

Library of Congress Control Number: 2014937843

For all general information, please contact Arcadia Publishing:
Telephone 843-853-2070
Fax 843-853-0044
E-mail sales@arcadiapublishing.com
For customer service and orders:
Toll-Free 1-888-313-2665

Visit us on the Internet at www.arcadiapublishing.com

Dedication

To John Freeman, for his historical knowledge and his help and support; and to other local historians who love discovering and sharing San Francisco history

On the Front Cover: From left to right:
Remo del Tredici, violin maker (Author's photograph; see page 78), Noah Griffin, performer (Courtesy Noah Griffin; see page 90), Josephine Cole, teacher (Courtesy Bancroft Library, University of California, Berkeley; see page 45), Barbara Eden, actress (Courtesy Tangible Dreams Entertainment; see page 89), Ellen Kieser, owner of Kieser's Colonial (Courtesy Ellen Kieser; see page 111), Amy Meyer, conservationist (Courtesy Amy Meyer; see page 55), Anton LaVey, founder of the Church of Satan (Courtesy the Church of Satan, photograph by Nick Bougas; see page 72), George Burns and Gracie Allen, actors (Courtesy Jack Tillmany; see page 91), William Gee, dentist (Courtesy the Gee family; see page 58).

On the Back Cover: From left to right:
Paul Kozakiewicz, publisher of the *Sunset Beacon* and the *Richmond Review* (Author's photograph; see page 62), Sarah Bacon, Richmond blogger (Courtesy Sarah Bacon; see page 63).

CONTENTS

ACKNOWLEDGMENTS

No one ever writes a book like this alone. Many people have been especially helpful, and I thank all the people who shared their time with me, told me about their lives, and gave me photographs to use. In addition, I would like to thank the following people and groups who helped me learn about the legendary locals who should be included: the Abraham Lincoln High School Alumni Association, Tammy Aramian, John Barry, Cammie Blackstone, Marilyn Blaisdell, Jeffrey Burns of the Archdiocese of San Francisco archives, John Carlson, Robert Cherny, Maria Cunningham of St. Anne's Home, Roy Diner (and Christopher and Patty), Bruce Eng, John Freeman, Linda Fries, David Gallagher, Phil Gangi, Greg Gee, Kathleen Gee, Peter H. Gilmore, Judy Harter, Inge Horton, Tom Jackson, Patricia Kaussen, David Kiehn, Paul Kozakiewicz, Woody LaBounty, Brendan Lange of the San Francisco Botanical Garden, Angus MacFarlane, Kathleen Manning, Bruce Moore, Jimmy O'Keefe, Eva Ong, Annabelle Marsh Piercy, Christopher Pollock, Megan Prelinger, Rick Prelinger, Michael Randolph (for William "PoPsie" Randolph), Paul Rosenberg, Bill Rosetti, Dewey Rosetti, San Francisco History Center at the San Francisco Public Library, St. Anne's Home/Little Sisters of the Poor, Lorraine Scullion, Robin Stamps, Frank Sternad, Jack Tillmany, Harold Tuchfeld, and Joss Wilson.

If I have overlooked anyone, please forgive me.

INTRODUCTION

This book is about three distinct areas—the residential Richmond and Sunset Districts, separated by Golden Gate Park—that were once considered the western desert of San Francisco. At one time, much of this land was inaccessible sand dunes, and many people believed it was uninhabitable. Over time, however, visionary people moved sand, created a great park, constructed roads, laid water and sewage lines, and built houses in the Richmond and Sunset Districts, creating "suburbs" within the city limits of San Francisco. Most of these changes met with resistance, as many people did not believe these areas could become habitable. Even today, many people still have no appreciation for the rich history of the west side of the city.

How did these neighborhoods evolve? The Richmond District's development began first, with the building of a toll road to the Cliff House and beach recreation in 1863. Development did not immediately follow the toll road, however. From the late 1850s into the mid-1860s, the city decided to move all burials to this far margin of the city, and four cemeteries were established at the eastern boundary of the Richmond District. Residential building west of the cemeteries came slowly but increased once Golden Gate Park was established in the 1870s. People displaced by the 1906 earthquake and fire began to migrate to the Richmond District; as the area became more desirable for development, the cemeteries were moved out of San Francisco.

The Sunset District was the last of the three areas to develop. In the 1880s, a rail line to Ocean Beach, on the south side of Golden Gate Park, opened the area to transportation and to development of the nearby property. The aftermath of the 1906 earthquake further boosted development along that corridor and south into the Parkside. From the 1920s through the 1940s, builders extended streets and built houses in the central Sunset, creating cohesive neighborhoods quite different from the older, developed areas in the eastern part of the city. The early residents of these new neighborhoods would develop special bonds as pioneers of this in-city suburb.

How was this part of San Francisco discovered and developed? Much of San Francisco is built atop sand. The deepest sand is on the western side of the city, washed in from the south and from the Pacific Ocean. For many years, this edge of the city was uninhabited and composed entirely of sand dunes with some low-growing plants.

San Francisco was once far smaller than it is now. All areas outside the city limits were called "Outside Lands" and controlled by the federal government. In 1851, San Francisco was growing and wanted the entire upper peninsula to be part of the City and County of San Francisco, so the city took the US government to court for these lands. The case went through the courts for 15 years. In 1866, the US Supreme Court declared that San Francisco was entitled to the additional land.

With the final decision giving more land to San Francisco, city leaders had to decide what to do with the Outside Lands, especially in the inaccessible western areas. A Committee on Outside Lands recommended the creation of a huge park. The land set aside for Golden Gate Park changed from sand dunes to trees, meadows, and paths within a decade, starting in 1870. Building continued in the Richmond District, and it began in the Sunset District in the early 1900s.

Although the term *Outside Lands* originally referred to all lands outside the original city limits, Outside Lands has come to mean the west side of San Francisco. This book shows some of the famous, infamous, and unsung heroes who made or are making a difference in the development of two residential neighborhoods and one large park in the Outside Lands.

The variety of legendary locals in this book attests to the thousands of people who have chosen to live in or contribute to these far-west regions of San Francisco.

Charles Williams and Jack

Charles Williams, shown here second from the left with his dog Jack, hunted rabbits in the Sunset dunes in 1915. Within 30 years, a complete neighborhood with houses, schools, stores, and other amenities had replaced the dunes. (Courtesy Ada and Charles Williams family.)

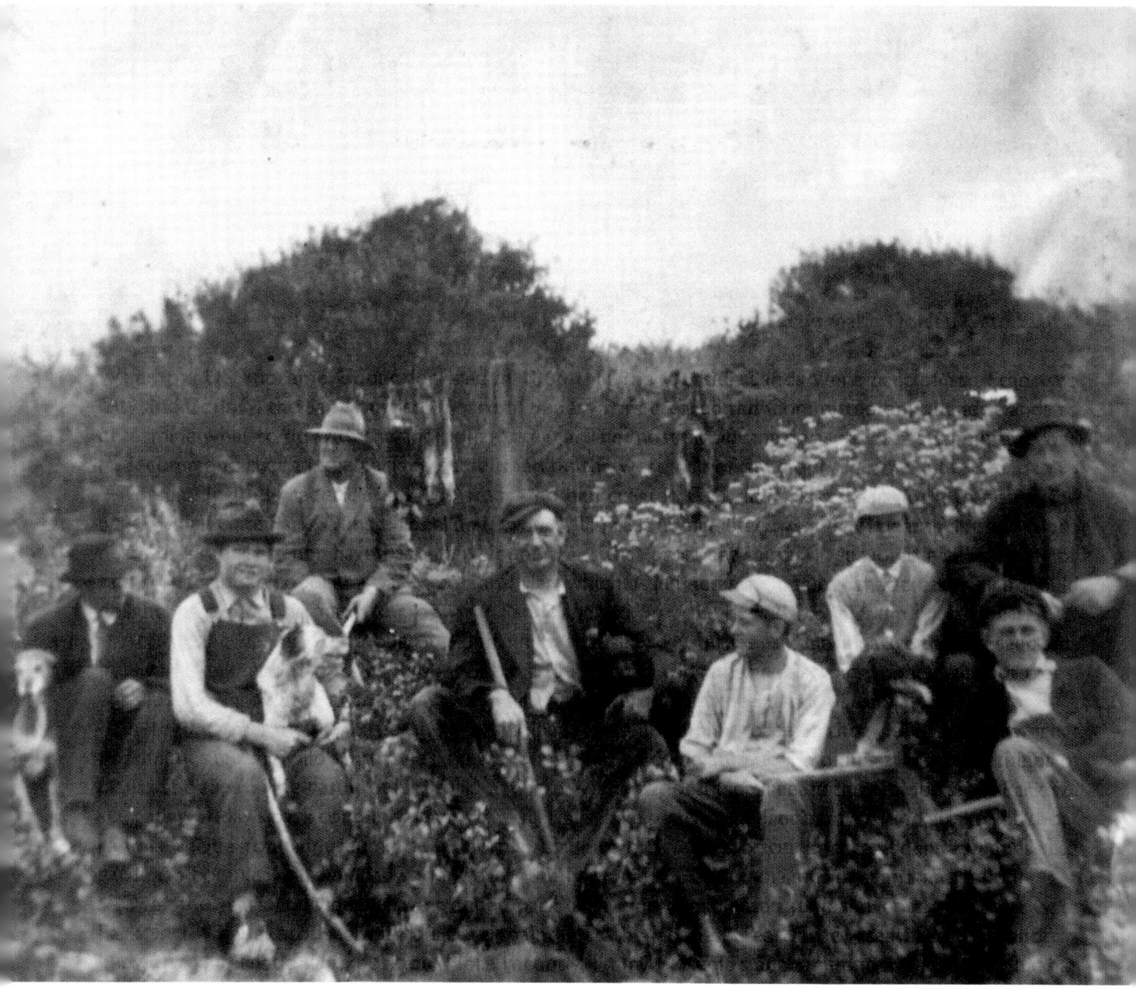

CHAPTER ONE

Golden Gate Park

When the US Supreme Court declared in 1866 that the Outside Lands were part of San Francisco City and County, the San Francisco Board of Supervisors created the Committee on Outside Lands to determine what to do with the additional acreage. The most significant decision of the committee was to recommend that a large park be established on the west side of the city.

The city invited Frederick Law Olmsted, who had created Central Park in New York, to design the new Golden Gate Park. Olmsted declined, saying, "There is not a full-grown tree of beautiful proportions near San Francisco, nor have I seen any young trees that promised fairly . . . It would not be wise nor safe to undertake to form a park upon any plan which assumed as a certainty that trees which would delight the eye can be made to grow near San Francisco."

Actually, he was right. Although it is difficult to believe today, tall trees are not native to San Francisco. In pictures taken in the 1800s, Mount Sutro and Mount Davidson, for example, appear without trees, with just low-growing plants. Today, these hills are covered with trees.

In 1870, San Francisco hired engineer William Hammond Hall to design the park. Hall saw great possibilities for the wild sand dunes; he was convinced he could "tame" the dunes and grow all kinds of plants and trees. The result of his work, and later work by John McLaren, is the Golden Gate Park we see today. Today's park contains meadows, waterfalls, bike paths, a children's playground, a lake with boat rentals, the de Young Museum, the California Academy of Sciences, bison, a rose garden, a Japanese tea garden, a botanical garden, redwood groves, the National AIDS Memorial Grove, and more.

Over the years, individuals have planned park areas and coordinated special events in Golden Gate Park. In 1893, Makoto Hagiwara built and maintained the Japanese Tea Garden for the 1894 California Midwinter International Exposition. More recently, Jimmy O'Keefe's annual Jimmy's Old Car Picnic has attracted families to the park to enjoy picnics and look at vintage cars.

At the same time, advocates have worked to protect the natural beauty of the park. John McLaren, the park's superintendent for more than 40 years, worked to keep the park a place of refuge from city life. Other advocates, such as Raymond Clary and Katherine Howard, have fought for preserving and protecting the beauty of the park.

This chapter also highlights the San Francisco Zoo, technically south of the Sunset District but still a popular destination for residents of the Sunset District and other areas. Herbert Fleishhacker established the zoo and Fleishhacker Pool in the 1920s. Today, Jacqueline Jencek lives her dream by working with animals in the zoo.

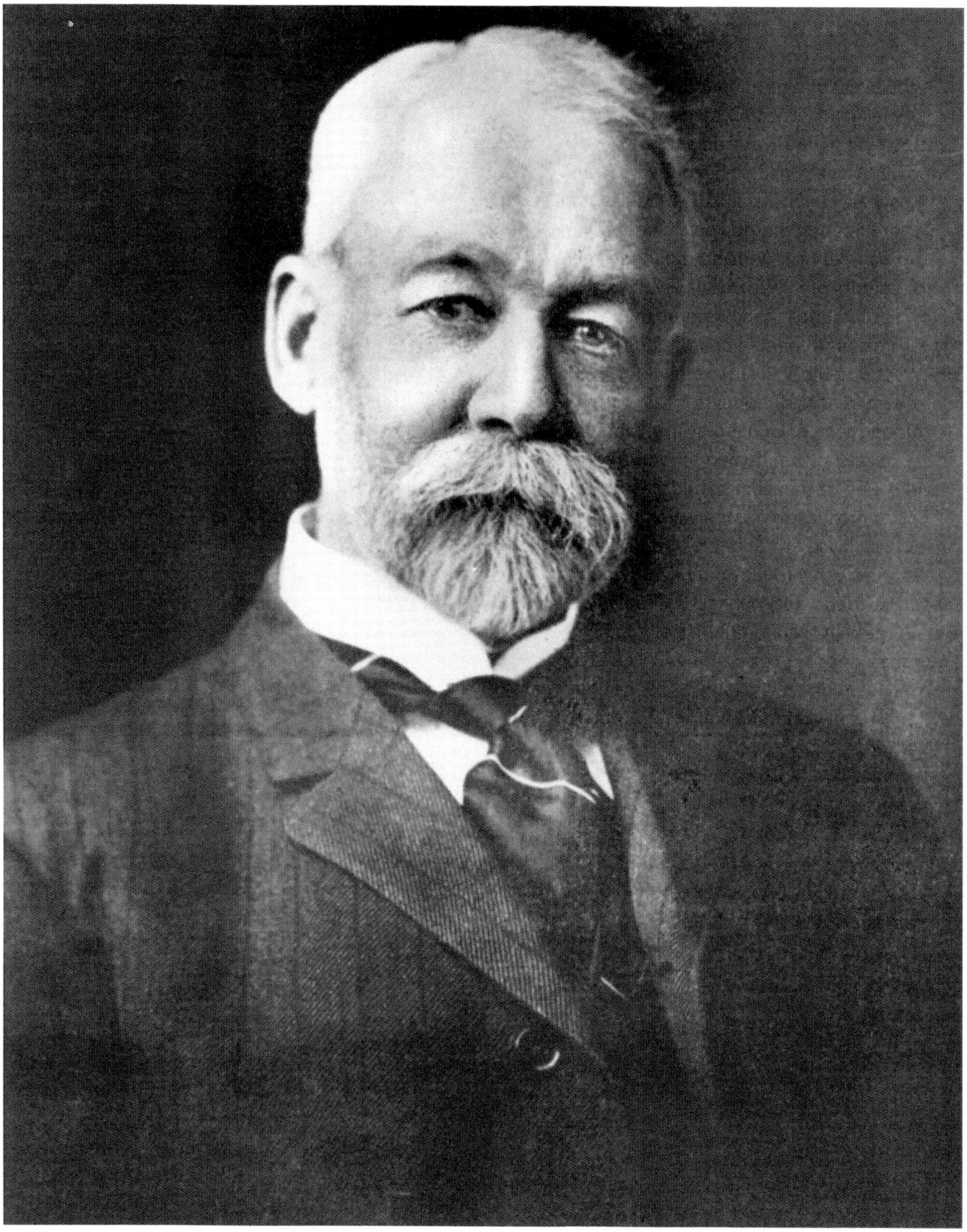

The Park's First Designer

When San Francisco leaders decided to build a large park in San Francisco, they set aside 1,013 acres (later 1,017) of undeveloped sand dunes and appointed 24-year-old engineer William Hammond Hall to design the park. Some people were dubious that anything could be made out of the windy sand dunes in the Outside Lands, but Hall made it work. He started designing the park in August 1870 and was superintendent until 1876. In 1886, he returned as an interim superintendent and was responsible for hiring a new superintendent, John McLaren (see facing page). Today, it is hard to believe that less than 150 years ago, before William Hall worked on it, the entire area now called Golden Gate Park was sand dunes and scrub brush. (Courtesy San Francisco History Center, San Francisco Public Library.)

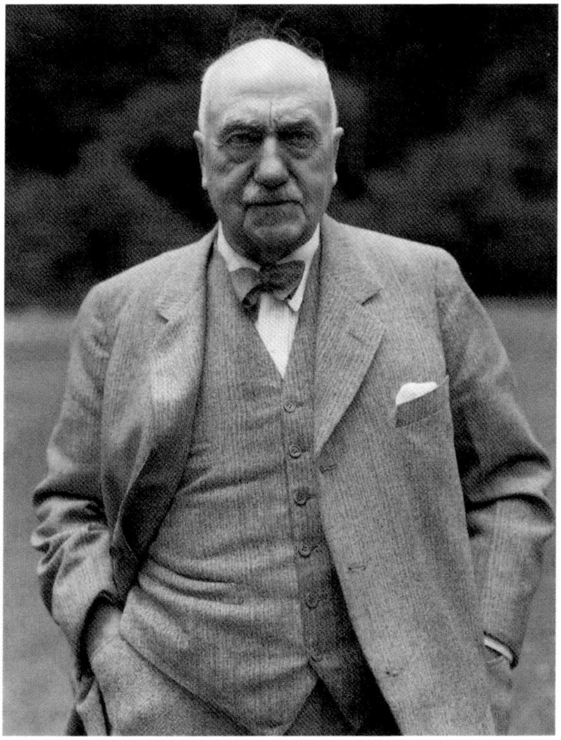

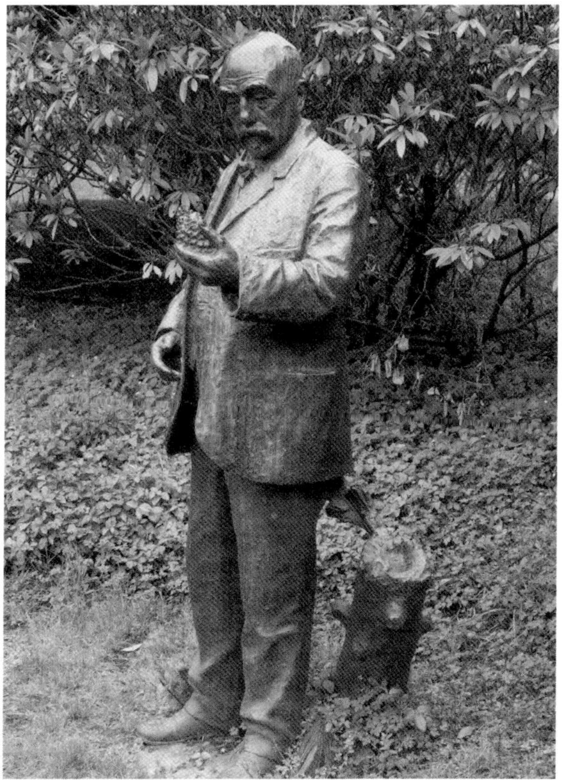

Memorable Park Superintendent

John McLaren made Golden Gate Park what it is today. Born in Scotland in 1846, he studied horticulture at the Edinburgh Royal Botanical Gardens. After immigrating to the San Francisco Bay Area, John became superintendent of Golden Gate Park in 1887, at the age of 27. He held this position for more than 50 years. His goal was to keep the park a "sylvan retreat" from the business of city life. He also hated statues; whenever a statue was donated to the park, he planted bushes around to keep it out of sight. Ironically, for John's 65th birthday, the City of San Francisco gave him a life-size statue of himself, created in 1911 by bronze artist M. Earl Cummings. The "gift" remained in its original packaging until John died. Today, the statue stands in the John McLaren Memorial Rhododendron Dell. (Above, courtesy Marilyn Blaisdell; below, author's photograph.)

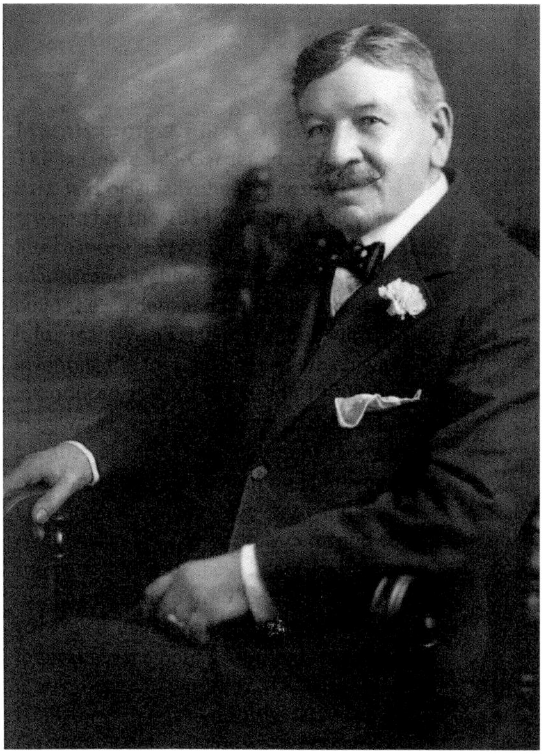

Land Speculator and Park Fair Promoter

Known as cofounder and publisher of the *San Francisco Chronicle*, Michael H. de Young was born in 1849 in St. Louis. His family moved to San Francisco when he was a boy. Later, Michael was vice president of the commission for the Chicago Columbian World Exposition, or World's Fair, of 1893. He lobbied for bringing some exhibits from that fair to San Francisco and helped organize the 1894 Midwinter Fair in Golden Gate Park. Part of his motivation for the Midwinter Fair might have been to attract people to buy land he owned in the Sunset and to establish a museum to house his collection. Two attractions from the 1894 fair still stand in the park: the De Young Museum, rebuilt in 2005, and the Japanese Tea Garden (see opposite page). Michael died on February 15, 1925. (Left, courtesy San Francisco History Center, San Francisco Public Library; below, from *Midwinter Fair and Sunset Scenes*, 1894.)

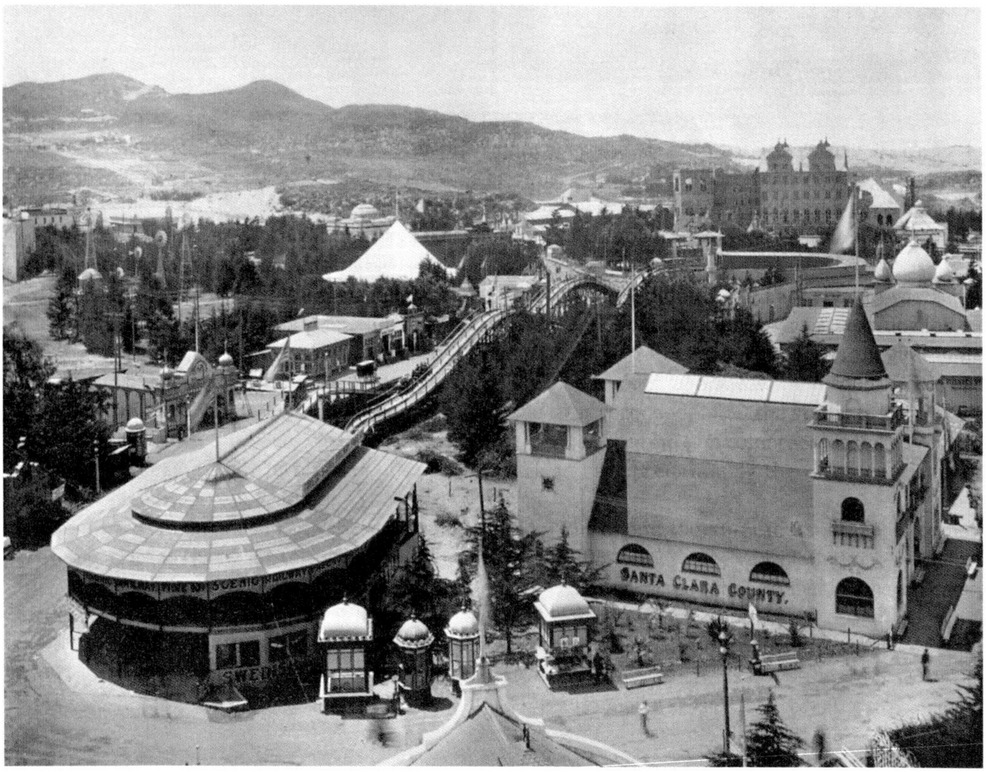

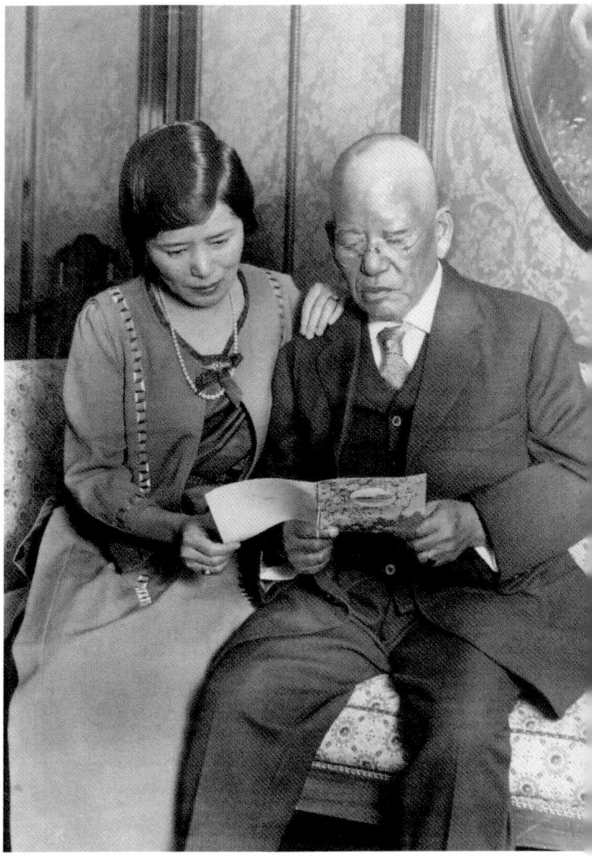

Maintaining a Place of Beauty

The Japanese Tea Garden in Golden Gate Park was originally the Japanese Village, created for the 1894 California Midwinter International Exposition. Makoto Hagiwara, a landscape architect born in 1854, helped build the garden, and his family maintained it for many years. He is credited with inventing the fortune cookie, which was introduced at the 1894 fair. In 1900, the Hagiwaras were forced out of the park because of anti-Asian sentiment. They then opened a Japanese garden on H Street (now Lincoln Way) between Seventh and Eighth Avenues. In 1907, the family returned to the park. Makoto, shown here in 1924 with his daughter, died in 1925, and his family took over maintenance of the park until the federal government sent them to a Japanese internment camp in 1942. The Hagiwara family never returned to the Japanese Tea Garden. (Right, courtesy San Francisco History Center, San Francisco Public Library; below, from *Midwinter Fair and Sunset Scenes*, 1894.)

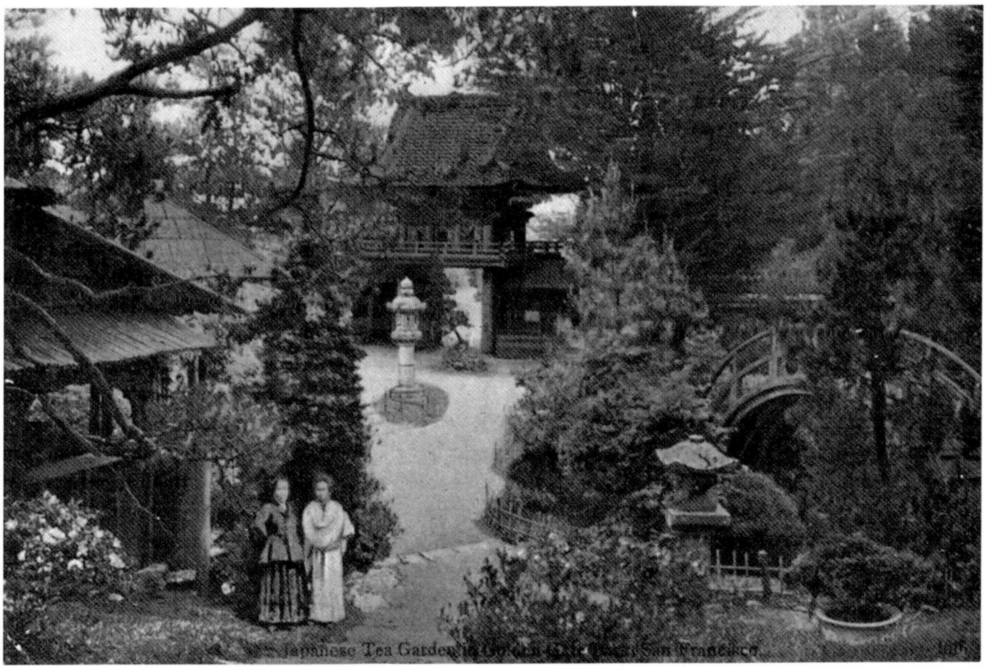

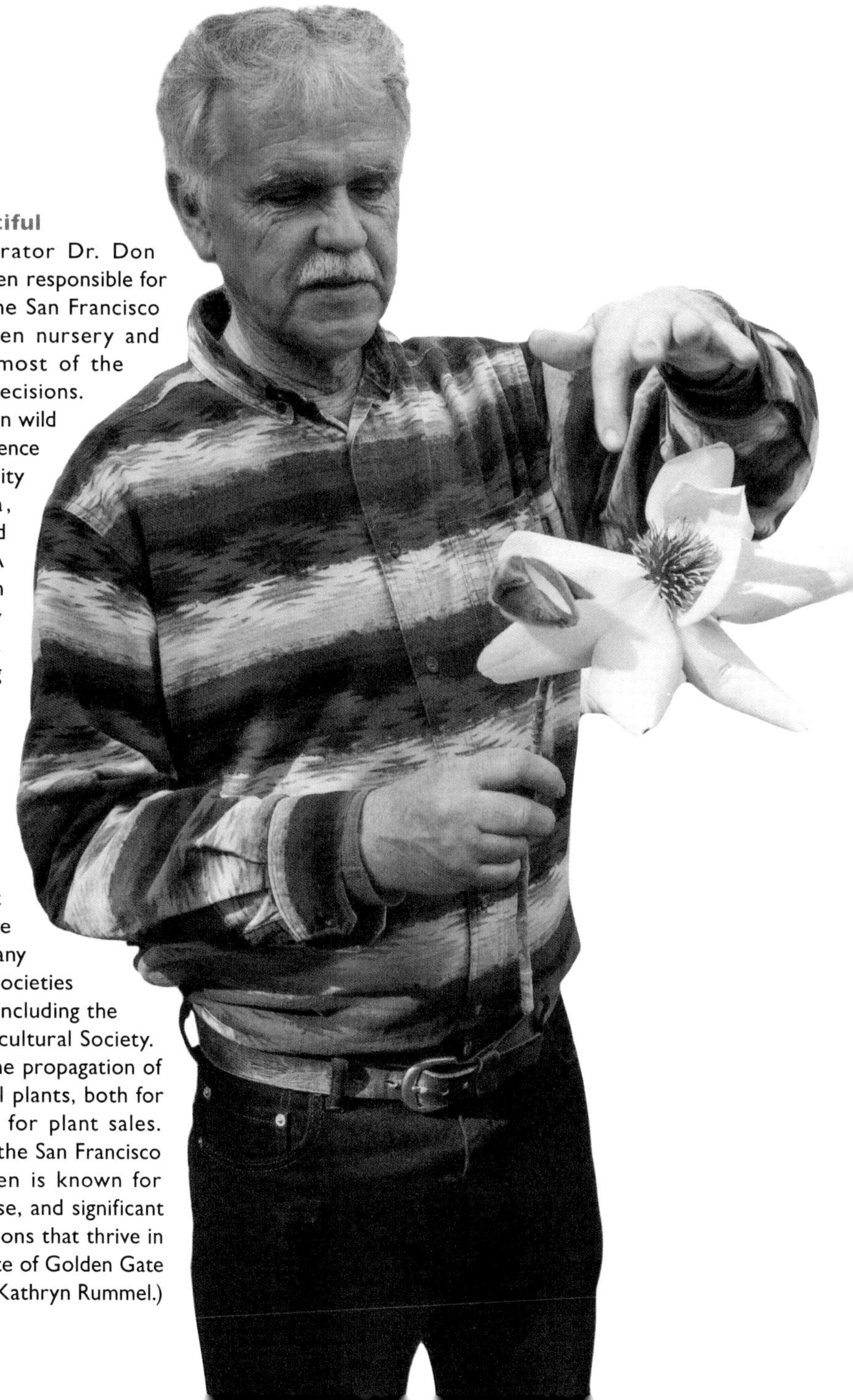

Keeping the Garden Beautiful
Since 1984, curator Dr. Don Mahoney has been responsible for operations of the San Francisco Botanical Garden nursery and involved with most of the garden design decisions. He holds a PhD in wild lands resource science from the University of California, Berkeley, and both MS and BA degrees from the University of Nebraska. Don is a leading horticulture expert, has taught classes in horticulture and botany at the garden, and has given numerous talks throughout the Bay Area. He has served on many boards of plant societies and nonprofits, including the California Horticultural Society. He supervises the propagation of rare and unusual plants, both for the garden and for plant sales. Thanks to Don, the San Francisco Botanical Garden is known for its unique, diverse, and significant botanical collections that thrive in the unique climate of Golden Gate Park. (Courtesy Kathryn Rummel.)

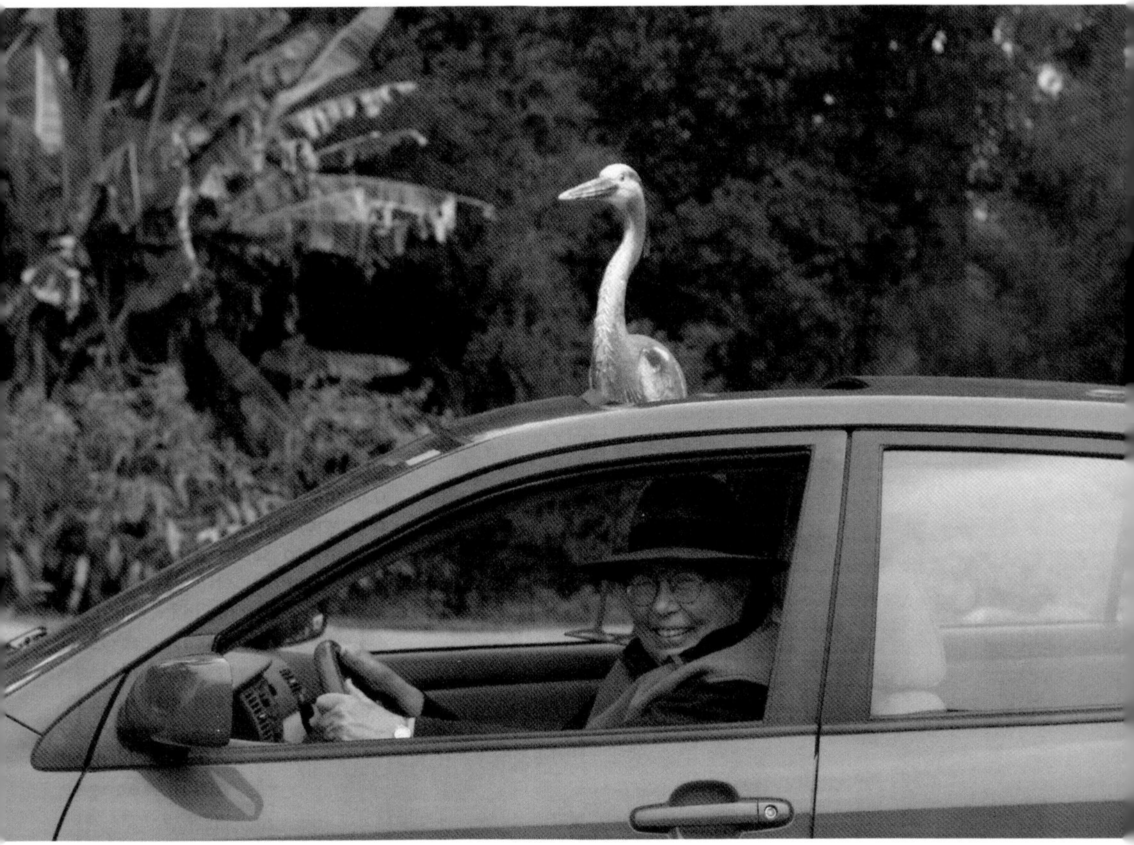

The Heron Lady

Richmond District resident Nancy DeStefanis is known as the "Heron Lady of Golden Gate Park." After she discovered a pair of nesting Great Blue Herons at Stow Lake more than 20 years ago, her life was never the same. Previously a social justice attorney, in 2000 Nancy founded San Francisco Nature Education, a nonprofit organization that takes underserved students from kindergarten through fifth grade out in nature to observe local birds.

It started in June 1993. While walking around Stow Lake in Golden Gate Park, Nancy spotted an enormous bird fly into a nest atop a Monterey cypress tree. "The experience was so exciting for me, I kept coming back," she says, and she later learned that her 1993 heron sighting was the first in San Francisco's history. In 1995, she co-wrote the song "My Blue Herons" ("a squawk and squeak from each little beak will lead you to My Blue Herons"), which she later recorded. Now the students learn to sing it every year before they visit the Stow Lake herons. In 1996, she and her volunteers installed raccoon collars on every tree on Heron Island to prevent chick and egg predation by the raccoons that swam over in search of food. It worked!

Nancy started an annual local bird-calling contest for third- and fourth-graders. Students come in costume, singing, calling, or screeching like their birds. In 2005, Nancy received a Jefferson Award from the American Institute for Public Service. More recently, Nancy raised funds to install a heron cam at Stow Lake, the first in California, so that children could watch at home.

To date, more than 10,000 students have visited Stow Lake. "They become mini experts on the birds of San Francisco," says Nancy. "When a child says to me after a field trip, 'It was the best day of my life' and goes back home and recycles, that's the only reward I need," Nancy says. (Courtesy Autumn Sartain.)

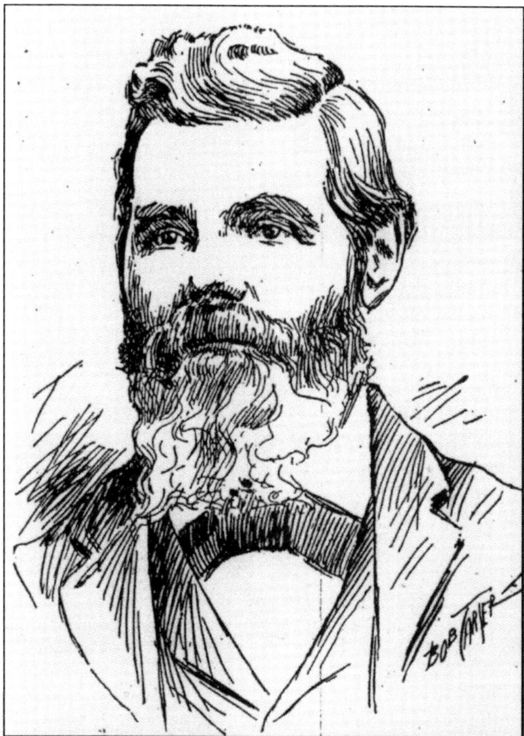

A View of Surrounding Areas
Thomas U. Sweeney moved to San Francisco in 1852 and lived on the corner of Seventh Avenue and Judah Street. In 1900, the *San Francisco Call* newspaper said he was "a firm believer in the improvement of Strawberry Hill, Golden Gate Park . . . [because] . . . of the beautiful view to be obtained from it." He donated $11,000 to create the Park Panorama on Strawberry Hill, and Sweeney's Observatory was built in 1891. Visitors climbed up to the second level and saw a 360-degree view of the surrounding areas. The observatory collapsed in the 1906 earthquake and was never rebuilt. Now the trees at the top of Strawberry Hill make it impossible to see the sweeping views that people once saw from Sweeney's Observatory. (Left, from *San Francisco Call*, January 25, 1900; below, courtesy Jaci Pappas, photograph by Fernando Cortez Ruggles.)

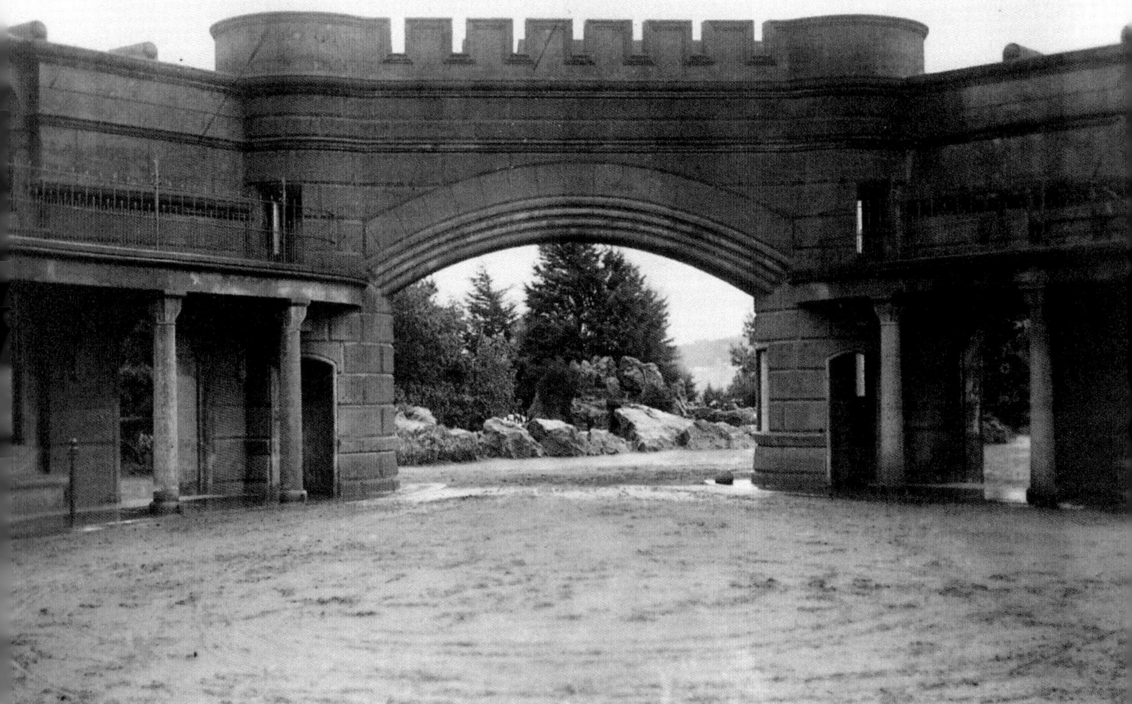

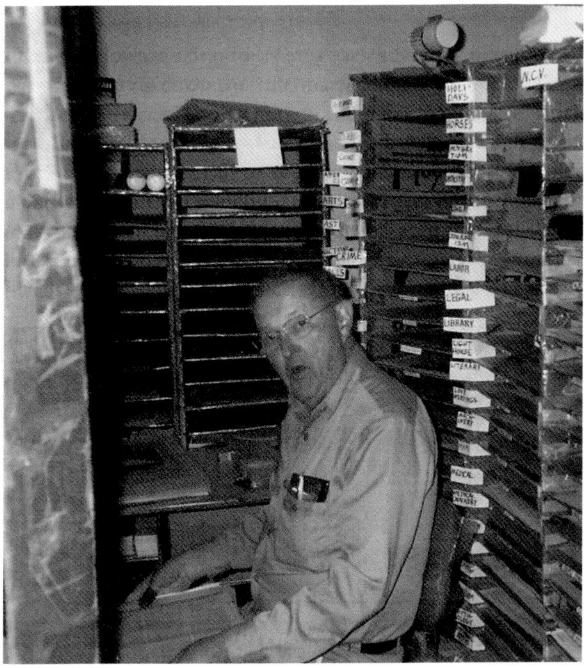

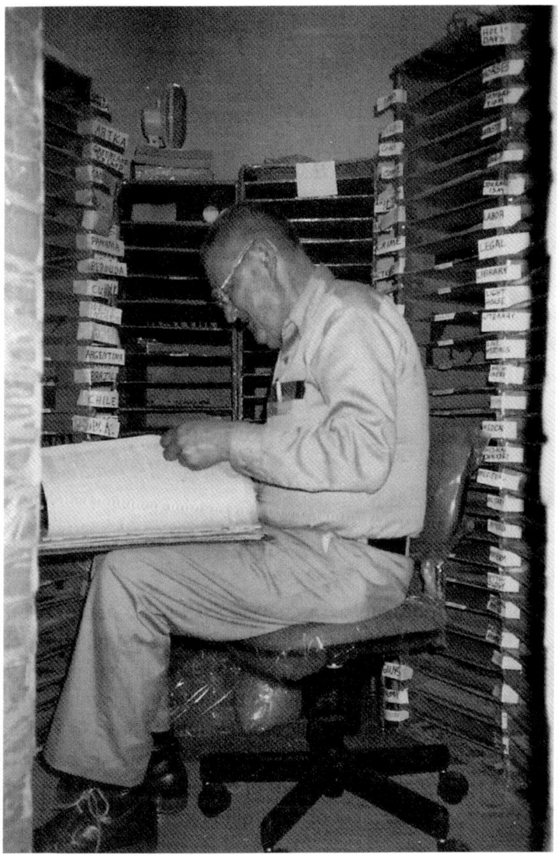

The Historical Guardian of the Park

Ray Clary was born in 1914 in Ohio. He came to San Francisco during World War II, and, after the war, he asked the local library for books on the history of Golden Gate Park. Since there were none, he wrote two books titled *The Making of Golden Gate Park*, one covering the park from 1865 to 1906 and the other from 1906 to 1950. Ray gave tours of the park to college students and gave presentations at local libraries. Newspaper columnist Herb Caen wrote that San Francisco needed more Ray Clarys and called him a "historian, gadfly, good guy, wizeguy and my kinda guy. In short, a curmudgeon, a sourpuss with a heart of gold, a man who knows and loves San Francisco — especially Golden Gate Park." When Ray died in 1992, his friends scattered his ashes on the park's Strawberry Hill. (Courtesy Kathleen Manning.)

Park Advocate

Katherine Howard's first foray into park advocacy occurred when the Recreation and Park Department proposed cutting down the 100-year-old trees in Golden Gate Park's music concourse to make way for a garage. Katherine, shown here in the music concourse, worked with others to have the area declared a city landmark, and the trees were saved. As a resident of the Richmond District and later the Sunset District, Katherine began to see her role as protecting Golden Gate Park for future generations. She helped to form the Golden Gate Park Preservation Alliance and SF Ocean Edge, opposing building a water treatment factory as well as a seven-acre artificial turf soccer field on the park's natural parkland. "The public needs to be informed of what's happening with our parks, so that they can hold their elected officials responsible for protecting our precious park heritage," Kathy insists. (Author's photograph.)

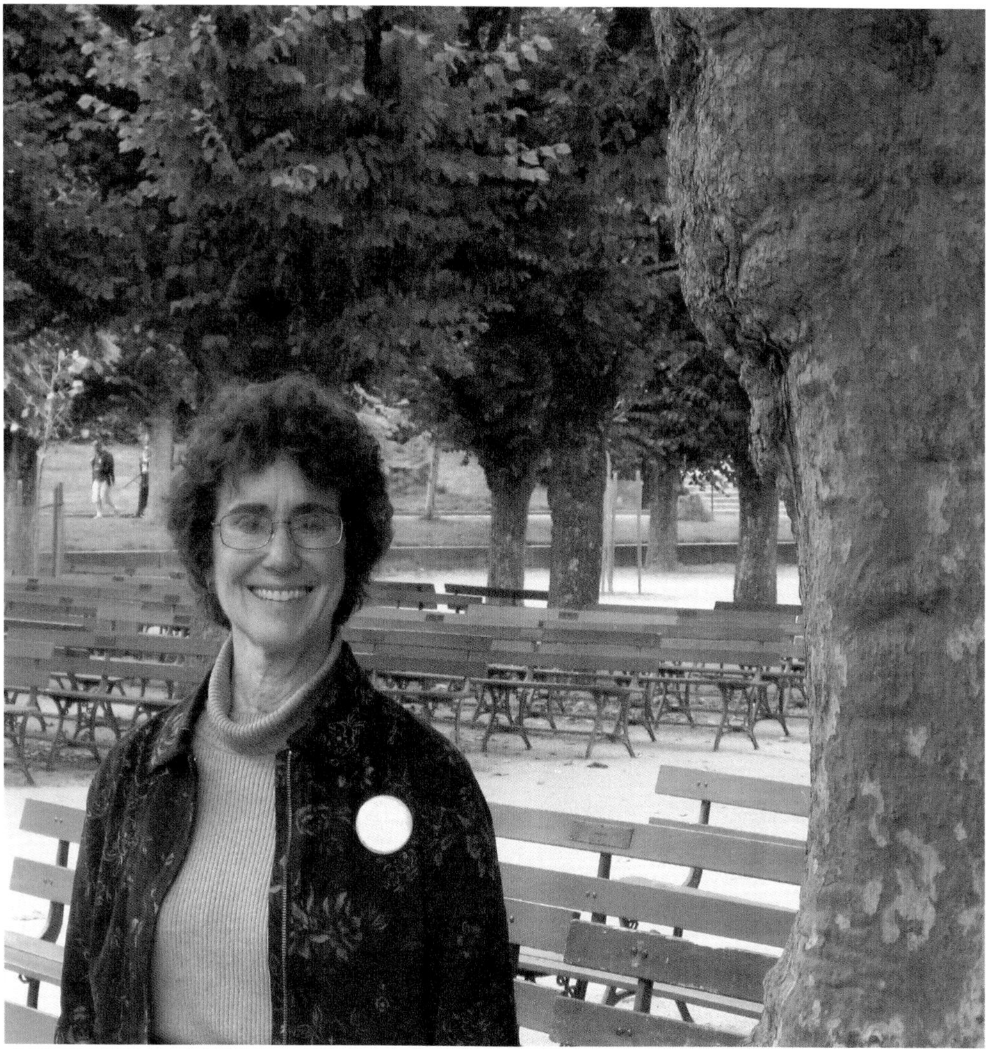

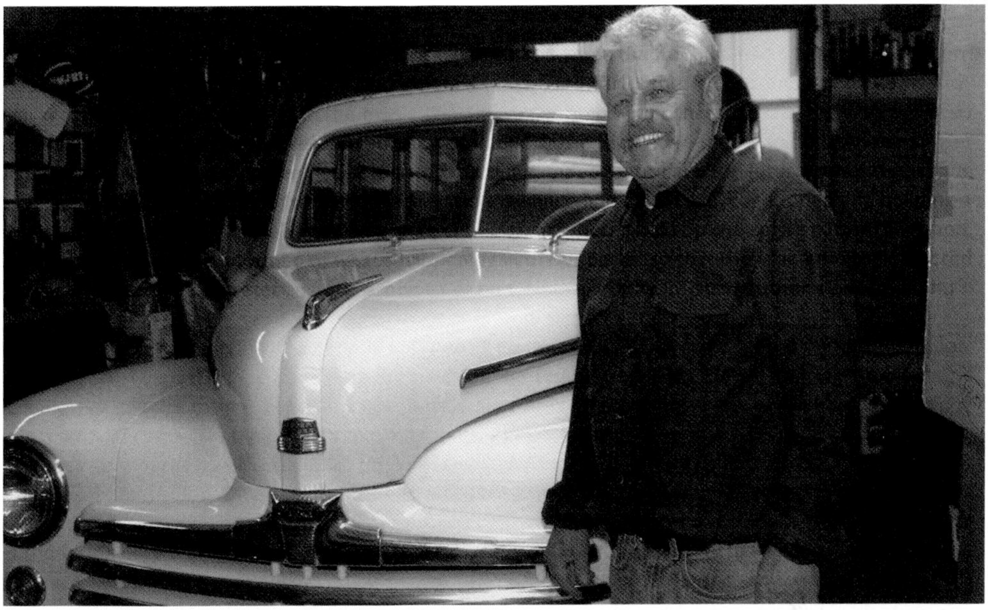

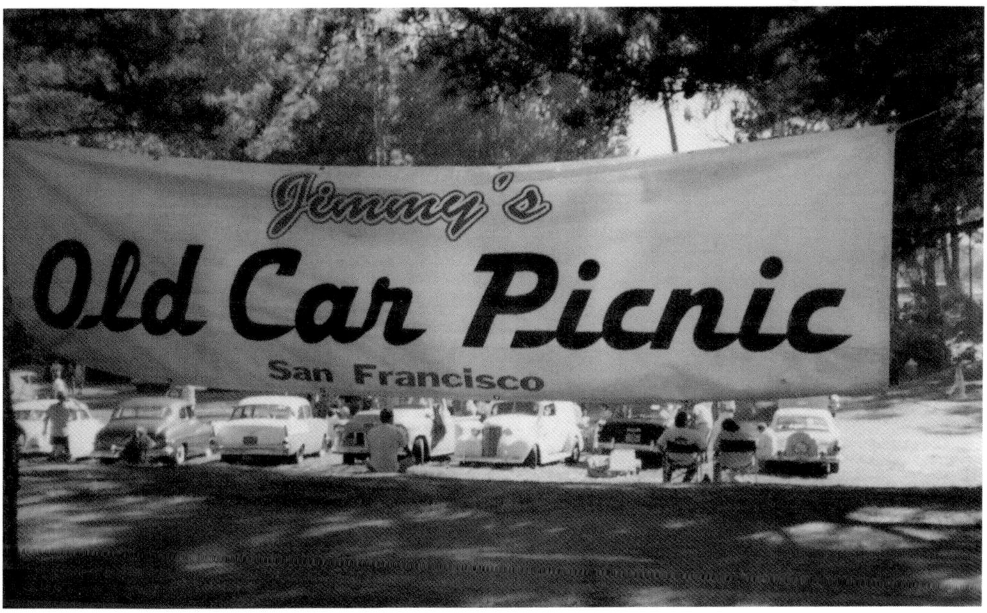

A Personal Public Reunion

Sunset native James "Jimmy" O'Keefe, a former Golden Gate Park gardener, graduated from Lincoln High School in 1965. A classic car fan, Jimmy started "Jimmy's Old Car Picnic" in 1988 as a birthday get-together for friends and family. The picnic became an annual event that celebrated its 25th anniversary in 2013. A fundraiser for programs that serve the developmentally disabled, the picnic has attracted hundreds of cars and thousands of spectators from all over California. People with old cars pay a fee to exhibit them; attendees visit free of charge. Not just a classic car day, the picnic has become a unique San Francisco event and a reunion of sorts for many people who grew up in the city. People who attended the picnic as children now bring their children. (Above, courtesy Philip Liborio Gangi; below, courtesy Jimmy O'Keefe.)

Banker Who Gave to the City

Herbert Fleishhacker never lived in the Outside Lands, but his contributions were huge to the children who grew up there, especially in the Sunset District. Born in San Francisco on November 2, 1872, Herbert was a successful banker, civic leader, and philanthropist. In his early career, he worked in his father's paper business as a salesman and founded a lumber company in Oregon. It was after he returned to San Francisco that he became a successful banker. He married May Belle Greenbaum on August 9, 1905, and the couple had three children.

Herbert is remembered for his development of the land just south of the Sunset District, near the beach. He built Fleishhacker Pool, which opened in 1924. At the time, Fleishhacker was the largest outdoor pool in the world. It was 1,000 feet by 150 feet and held 6.5 million gallons of ocean water pumped in from the Pacific Ocean just over a nearby bluff. The pool was so large that lifeguards patrolled it in rowboats (see facing page). It closed in 1971, and it has since been filled in and covered by the zoo's parking lot. When Herbert's mother, Delia, died in 1925, he and his brother built the Delia Fleishhacker Mother's Building as a tribute to her. The building stands empty now, but, for many years, mothers with young children could rest while their older children romped in the nearby playground. As San Francisco's park commissioner, Herbert helped develop the Herbert Fleishhacker Zoo in 1929. Some animals were moved to the site from Golden Gate Park, while Herbert and other benefactors donated others. Animal exhibits were built in the 1930s as part of a federal Works Progress Administration project. The photograph on the facing page features zookeepers in the 1930s. In 1941, Herbert suggested a new name, and now the much-larger site is called San Francisco Zoo. (Below, courtesy San Francisco History Center, San Francisco Public Library; facing page above, courtesy San Francisco History Center, San Francisco Public Library; facing page below, courtesy San Francisco Zoo.)

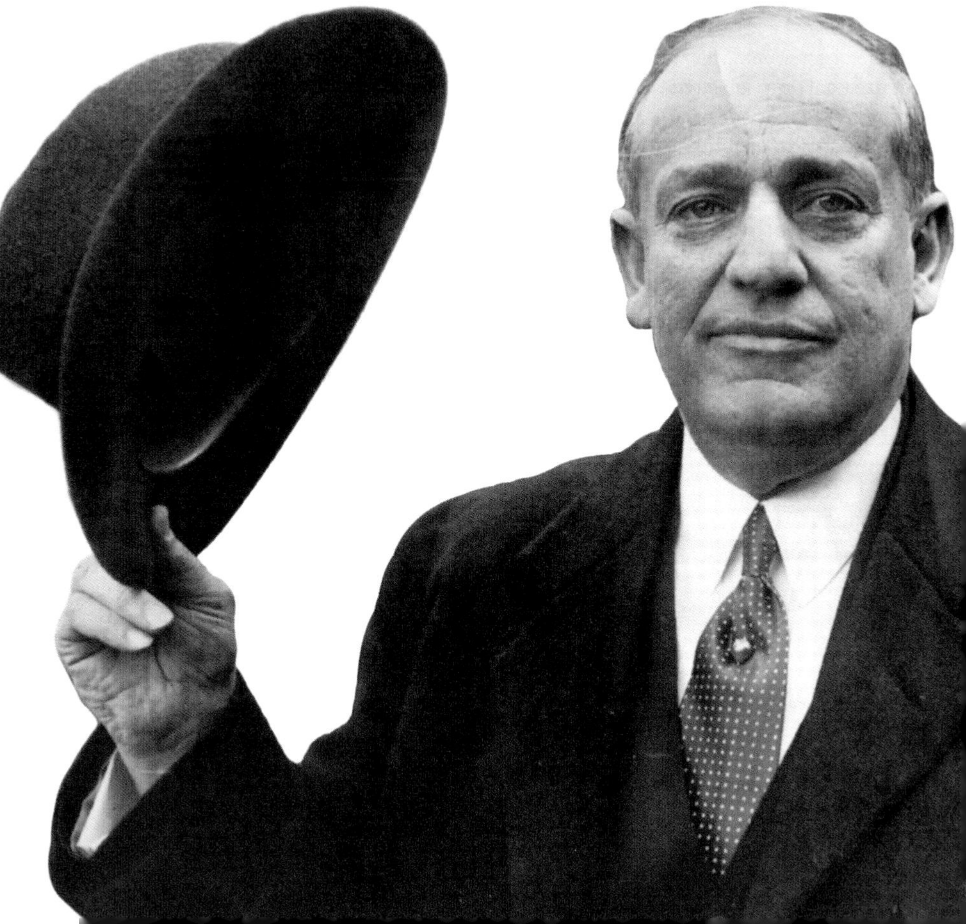

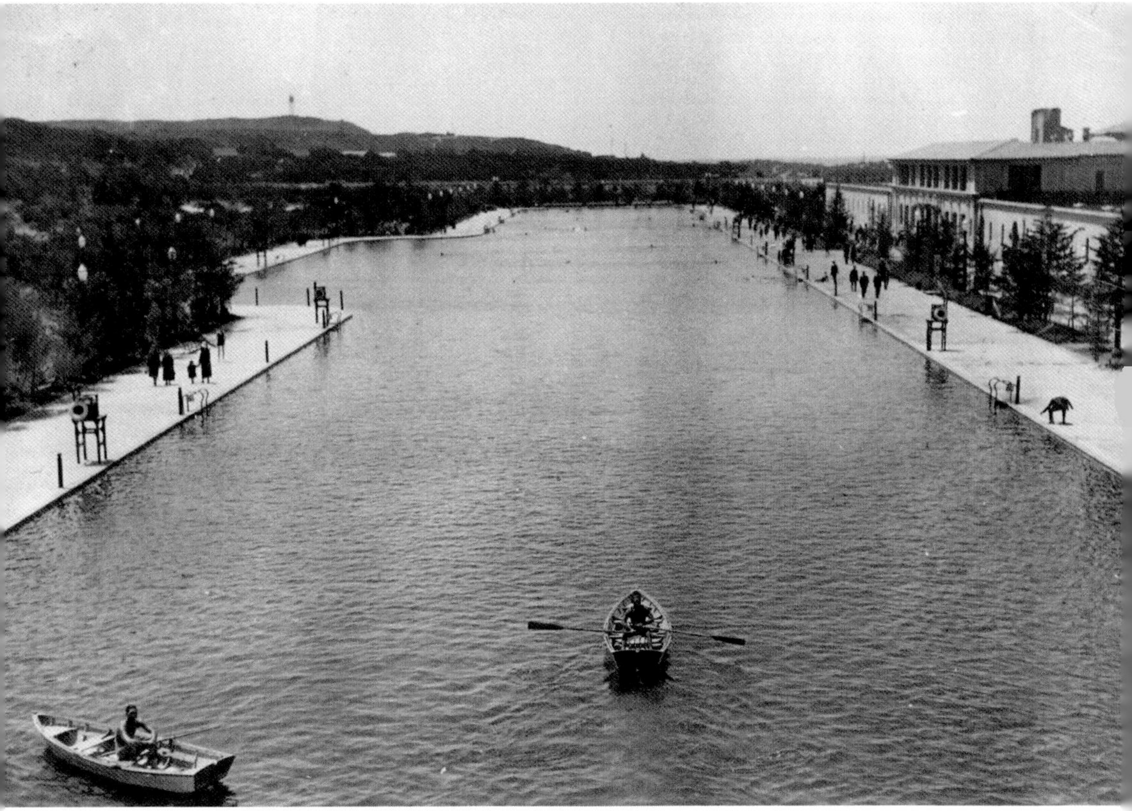

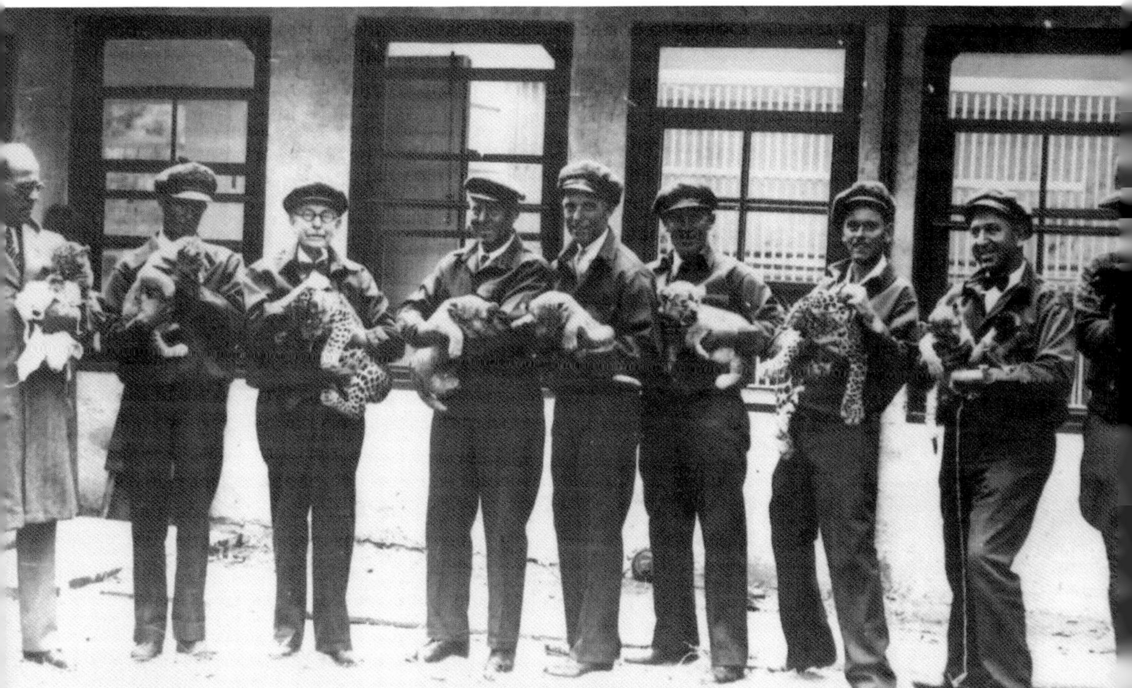

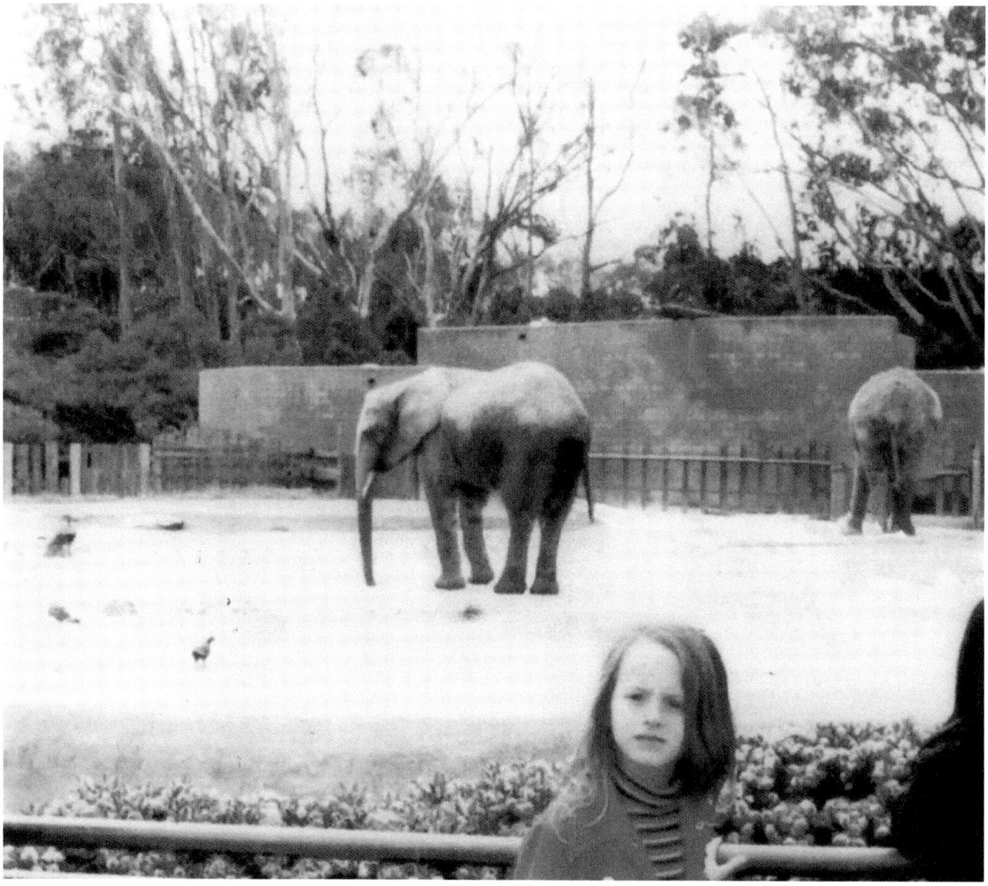

Living Her Childhood Dream

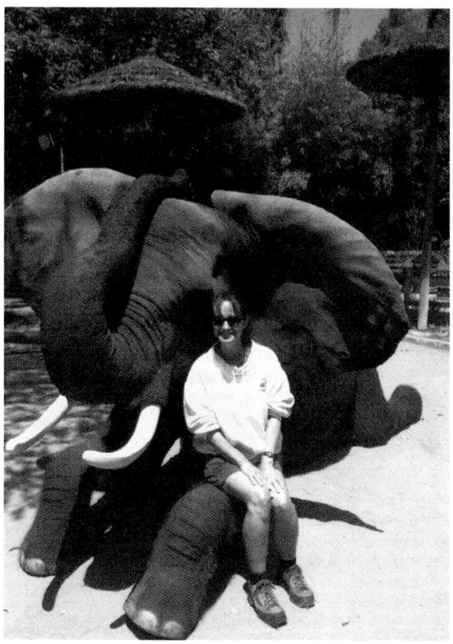

Raised on Twenty-ninth Avenue in the Sunset, Jacqueline (Hansted) Jencek went to St. Anne's Grammar School and Mercy High School. "From the time I was a young child," Jacqueline, shown above in second grade, says, "I knew I wanted to work with exotic animals." In high school, Jacqueline volunteered as a "penguin recorder" at the San Francisco Zoo. While attending San Francisco State University, she worked at Sunset Veterinary Hospital and the San Francisco Zoo Hospital. Jacqueline received her veterinary doctorate from University of California, Davis. After working outside San Francisco for seven years, she returned to the San Francisco Zoo as staff veterinarian, and, in 2007, she was appointed chief of veterinary services. She currently provides relief work at both the Zoo and at Six Flags Discovery Kingdom. Having cared for more than 300 different species, she considers herself "Jacqui of all trades." (Courtesy Jacqueline Jencek.)

CHAPTER TWO

History Lovers

San Francisco has many groups and individuals who thrive on learning about and sharing the city's history, and there are many ways of recording history. Ada Williams's husband saved his stories from 80 to 100 years ago and told them to his wife, who put them in *Parkside Pranks and Sunset Stunts*, the first book ever written about life in the Sunset District. More recent historians, like John Freeman, learn an interesting story or detail about San Francisco history and decide to research and learn more about it. More often than not, we all benefit from John's research, because he and other local historians love to write about and tell others what they have learned.

Then, there are the people who record history visually, by whatever method is available at that time, so it can be saved for posterity. Jesse Brown Cook and Treu Hecht took photographs but also reproduced photographs by other people so we would not lose them. Our current photograph collector is Marilyn Blaisdell, who, over the years, has collected thousands of historical images and, unlike many of us, is organized enough to make it clear where each picture is stored. Richmond District resident Rick Prelinger digitizes home movies and professional films so that this personal record can be preserved among our historical documents. Other historians, like Brewster Kahle, have moved into the 21st century and are collecting and storing all kinds of digital information.

This book recognizes the many ways people have preserved past history in the Richmond and Sunset Districts and Golden Gate Park, as well as those who are preserving the history we are making today.

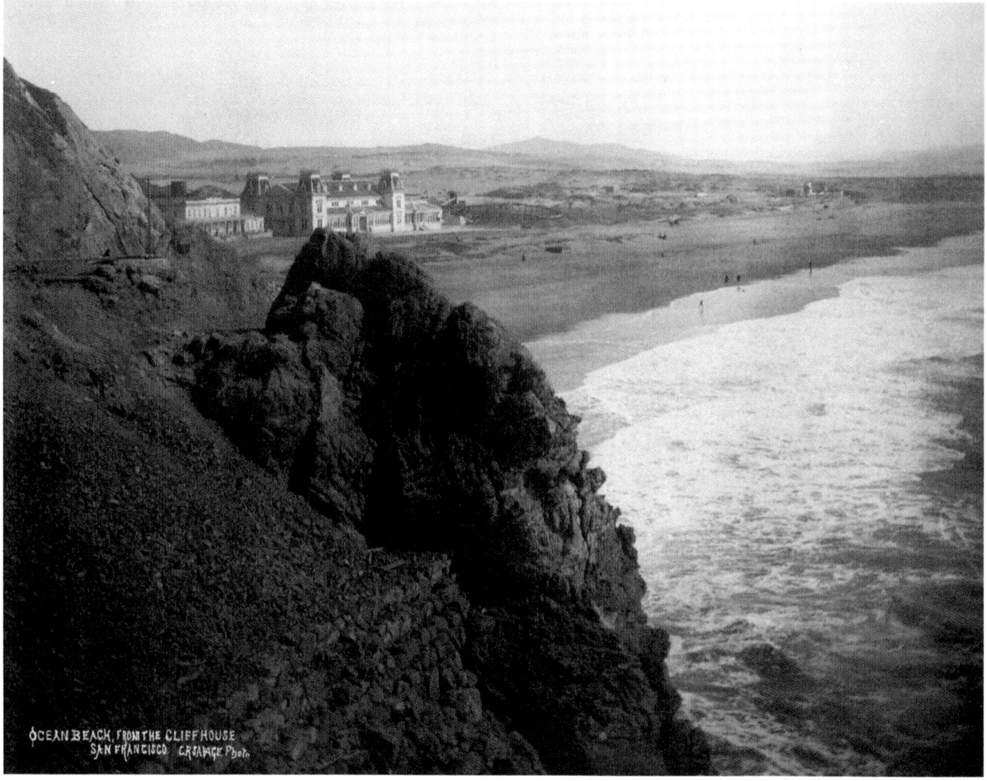

Preserver of the Photographic Record

Treu Ergeben Hecht, whose given names translate as "steadfast" or "loyal," was born in May 1875 on the island of Tahiti. His father was Austrian and his mother was Czech. The family immigrated to America about 1878 and settled in San Francisco. Starting as a photograph printer and retoucher at age 18, Treu worked for R.J. Waters until 1902. By the 1910 census, he was listed as married to Jennie, an English woman who immigrated in 1893. They had no children.

Treu's residence, and business address, 430 Thirty-fifth Avenue, remained constant from 1898 until his death in 1937. Following the 1906 earthquake, the logo on his quake-damage photographs read "T. E. Hecht, 35th Ave. Nr. Pt. Lobos." In 1918, he was working for Cardinell-Vincent Co., at 577 Market Street. Beginning in 1925, he ran his own commercial photography business, remaining there for the rest of his career.

Hecht supplemented his income by making reproductions of San Francisco pre-quake images taken as far back as the 1850s. He had not taken many of these photographs, but he helped future generations see rare views. Few original negatives of the old city survived the devastation of the 1906 earthquake and fire. In the absence of original negatives, Hecht made copy negatives from surviving prints and his own negatives taken prior to April 1906. The photograph above, taken from the Cliff House, shows the sand dunes in the area that would become the Richmond and Sunset Districts. On the facing page, the photograph above shows Market Street between Third and Fourth Streets in 1865. The image below on the facing page shows Sacramento and Polk Streets after the 1906 earthquake and fire. Many of Treu's own photographs and preserved images by others are now stored with the San Francisco Public Library, the Bancroft Library, the Society of California Pioneers, and the California Historical Society. (Above, courtesy Marilyn Blaisdell; facing page photographs, courtesy Frank Sternad.)

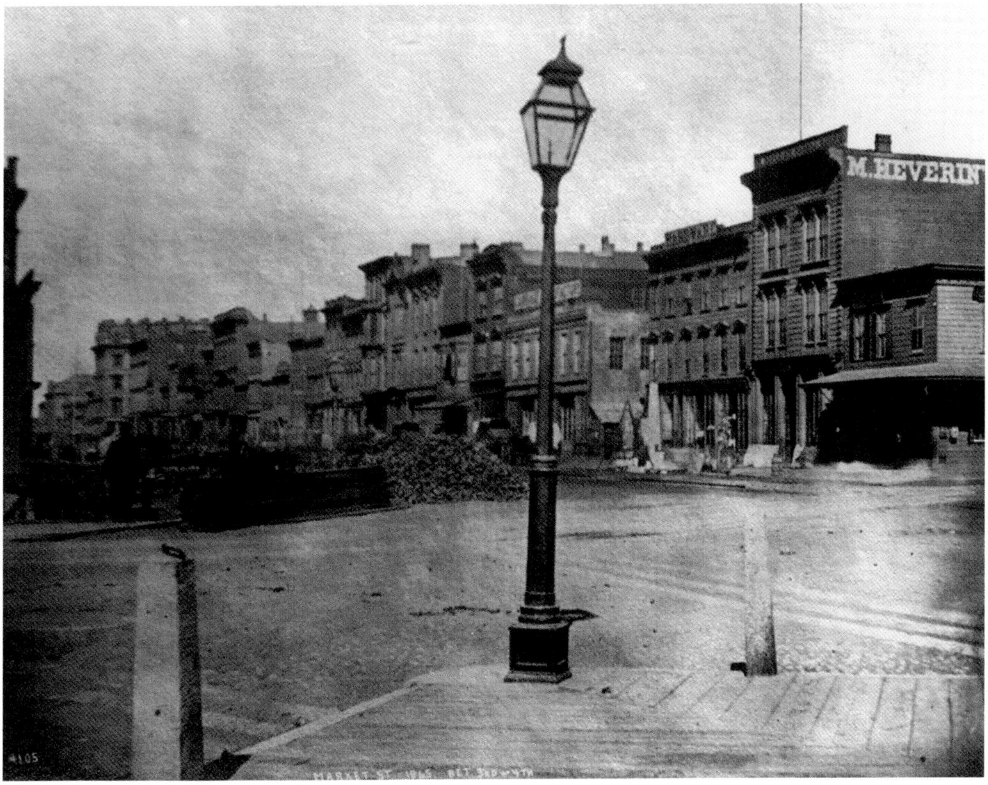
M.HEVERIN

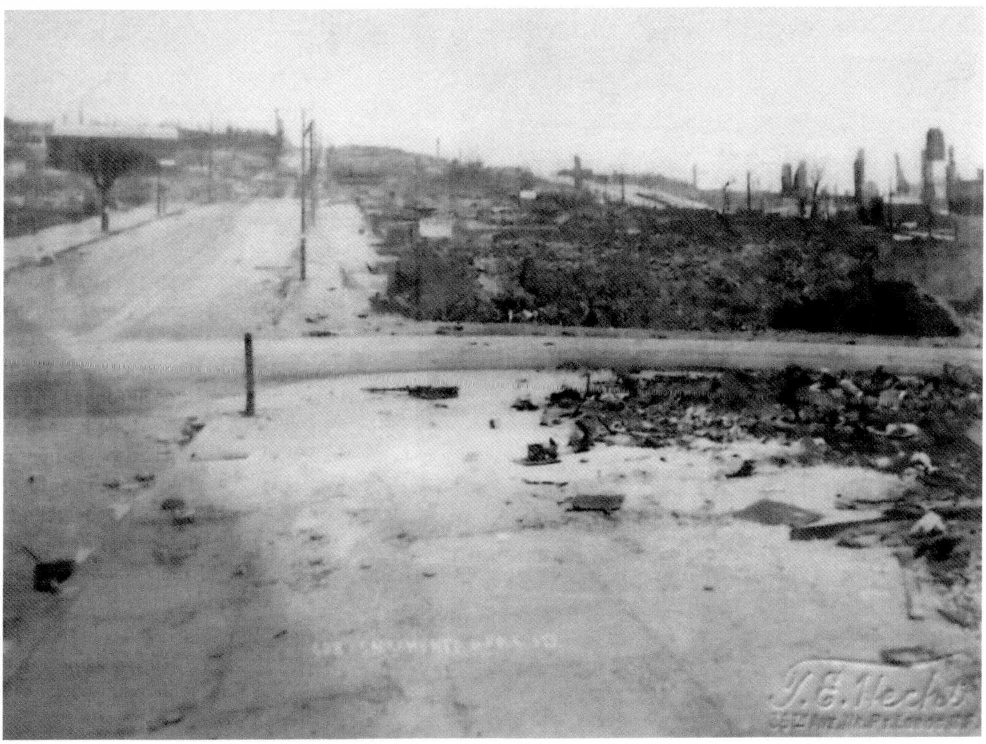

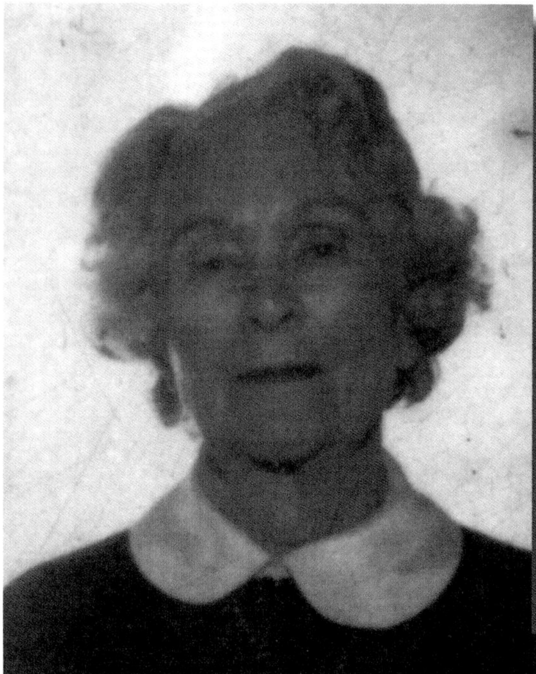

Author of the First Books on the Sunset
Mary "Ada" Williams was born in St. Louis on June 17, 1903. Her family moved to San Francisco in 1904. As a child, she loved to write stories and read them to her classmates. Until well into her 80s, she continued her storytelling in San Francisco parochial schools. Ada was the first person ever to write a book about the Sunset District. She published two books, *Parkside Pranks and Sunset Stunts: Growing Up with San Francisco* (1986) and *More Parkside Pranks and Sunset Stunts* (1990), both based on the recollections of her husband, Charles Williams (see page 8), who grew up in the Sunset District. Ada died in September 2000 at the age of 97. (Courtesy Ada and Charles Williams family.)

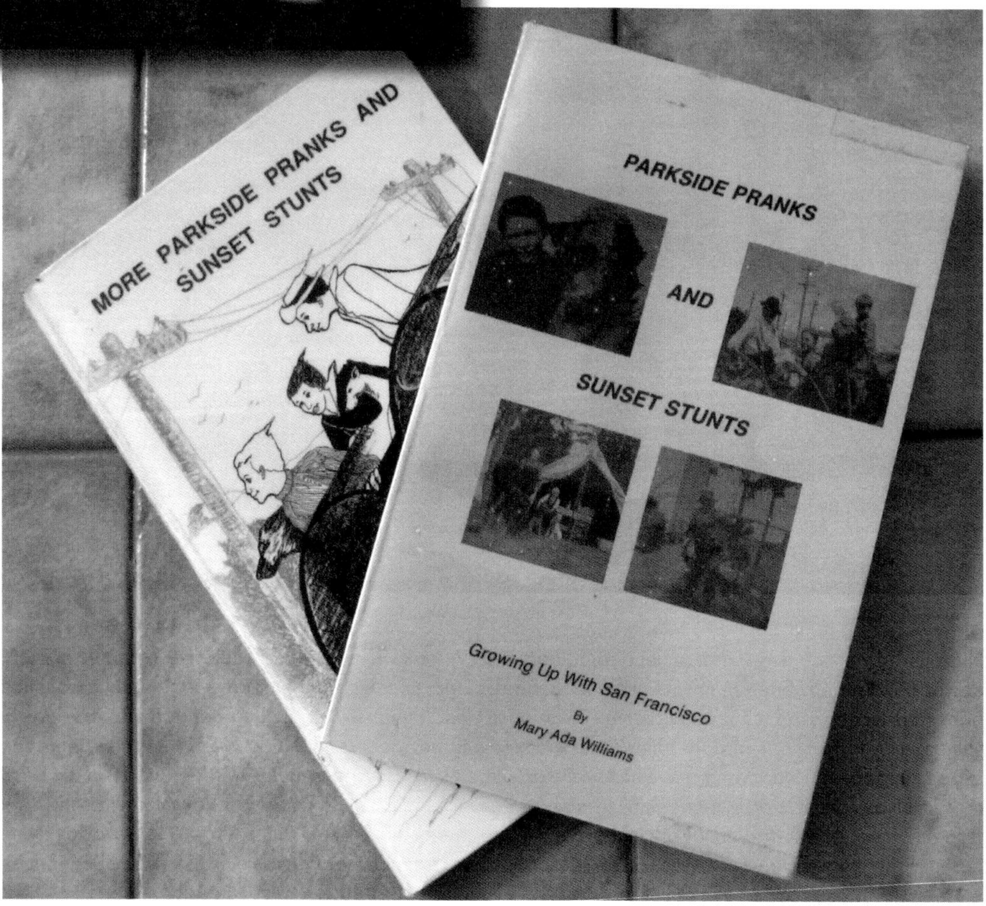

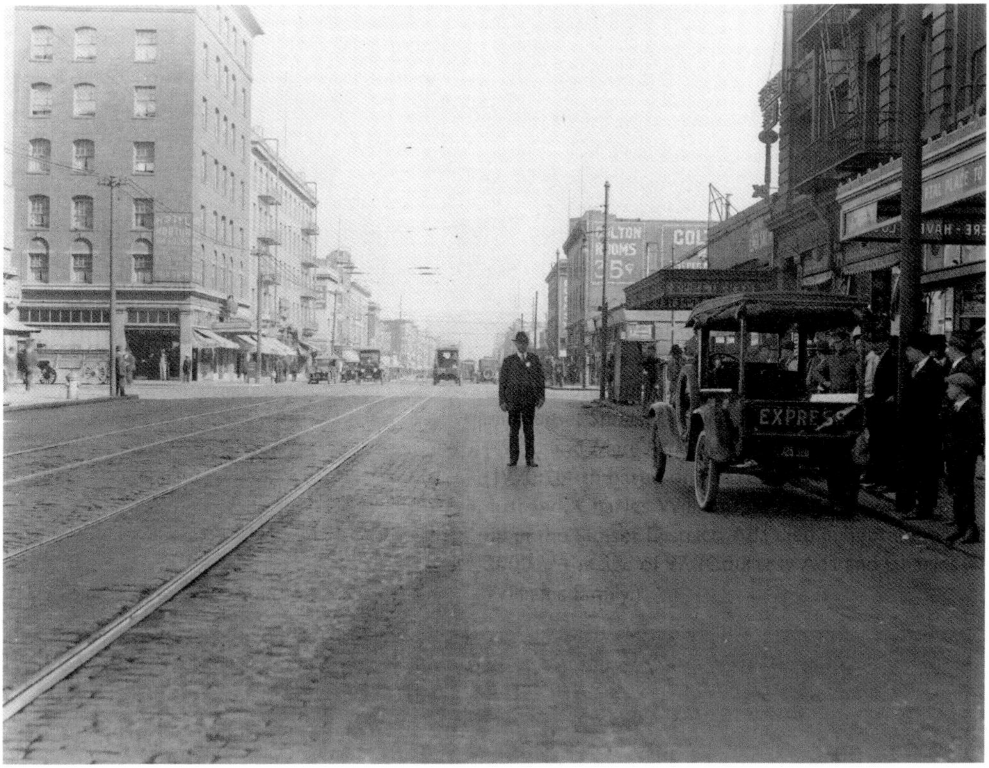

Police Chief and Photographer
Born in San Francisco in 1860, Jesse Brown Cook began his career as a police officer in San Antonio and San Diego. When he returned to San Francisco, he moved to the Richmond District and worked as a beat officer and, later, as sergeant of the "Chinatown Squad." He served as chief of police after the 1906 earthquake and was later appointed to the police commission. He took many photographs of accidents and crime scenes in San Francisco. He also collected photographs, clippings, and ephemera relating to the city. He died in 1938. Today, the Bancroft Library at the University of California, Berkeley, has an extensive collection of Jesse's photographs—ones he collected and ones that he took. (Above, courtesy Marilyn Blaisdell; right, courtesy San Francisco History Center, San Francisco Public Library.)

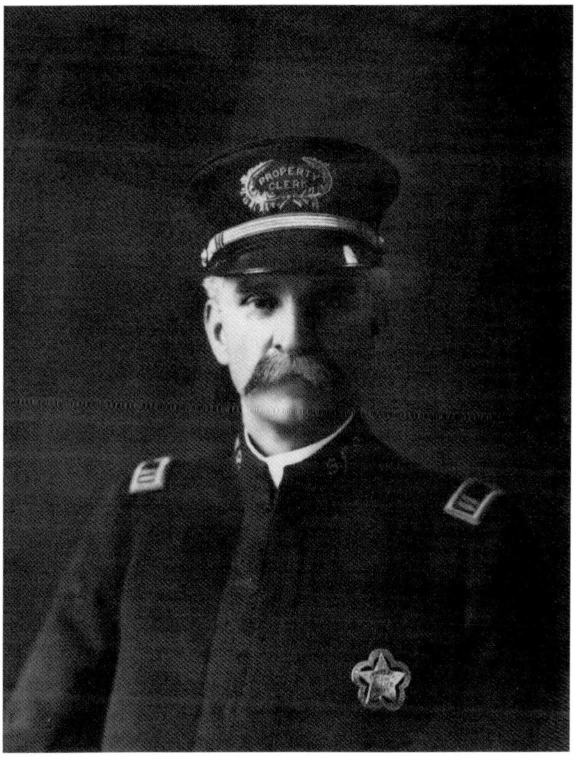

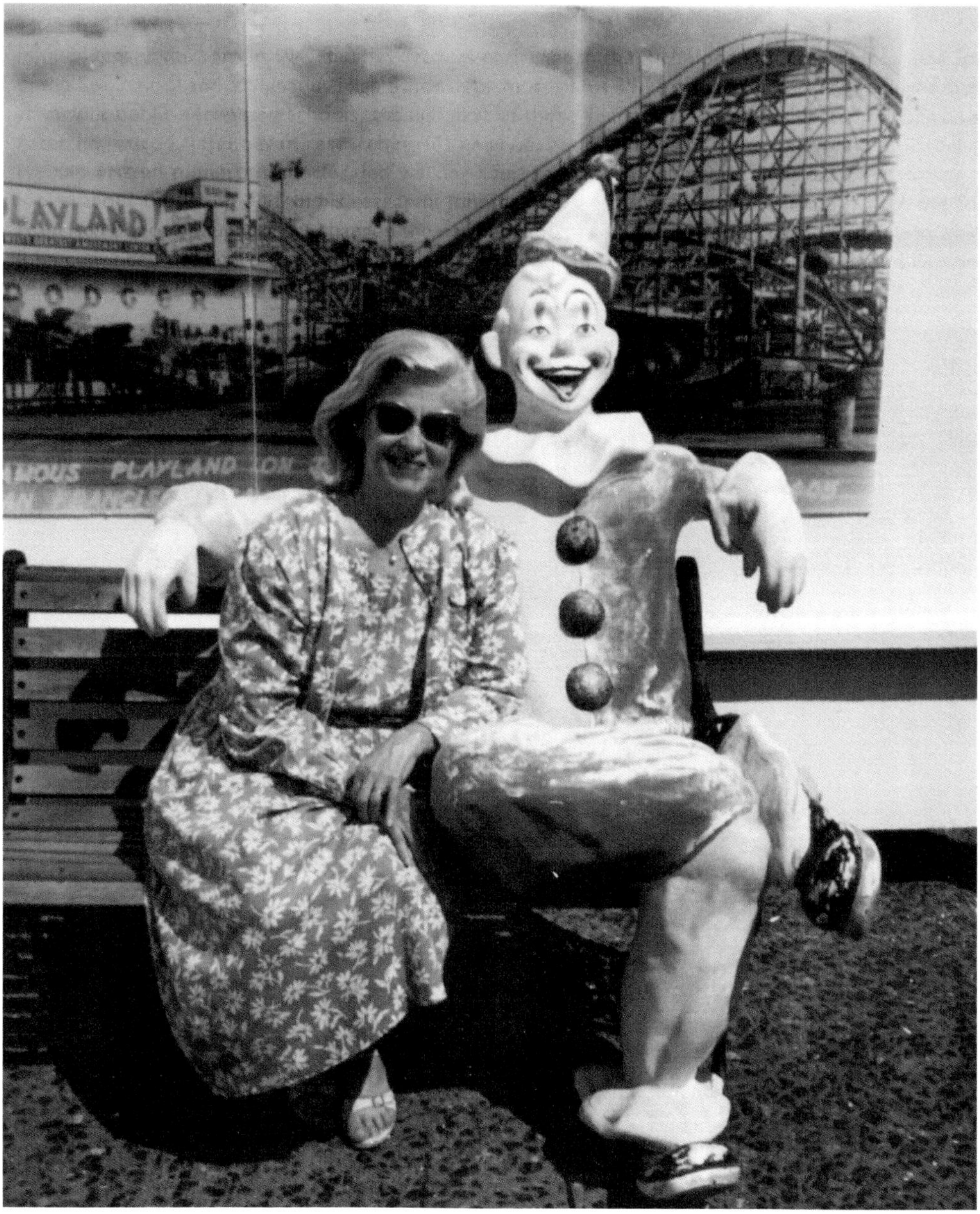

An Avid San Francisco Collector

Marilyn (Janeck) Blaisdell was born in 1928 in Washington State. Her paternal grandparents were avid collectors, and Marilyn soon caught the bug. She attended Stanford University and then moved to San Francisco. She started collecting anything "San Francisco"—maps, books, cards, photographs, and ephemera. From 1972 to 1984, she operated San Francisciana, a gift shop in the Cliff House, selling San Francisco memorabilia and photographs. She has published five San Francisco photograph books with rare historical photographs of the Cliff House, Sutro Baths, Playland-at-the-Beach, World's Fairs, and Woodward's Gardens. She and her husband, Bill, have lived in the Richmond District for the past decade. She says that her legacy is "six children and six books." (Courtesy Marilyn Blaisdell; photograph by Ron Ross.)

Historian of the Richmond

John Freeman was born in 1941 and has lived his entire life in the Richmond District. He attended Star of the Sea School and St. Ignatius High School. For most of his 35-year teaching career, he taught math at various public secondary schools, the last nine of those years at George Washington High School. After he retired, John began researching his neighborhood and has become its foremost historian. He has written numerous articles, led walking tours, and given public presentations on a variety of topics about the Richmond. In his research, John discovered the forgotten fact that, in 1917, the San Francisco Board of Supervisors changed the neighborhood name to the Park Presidio District. In 2009, John convinced the board to restore the neighborhood name officially back to the Richmond District. (Author's photograph.)

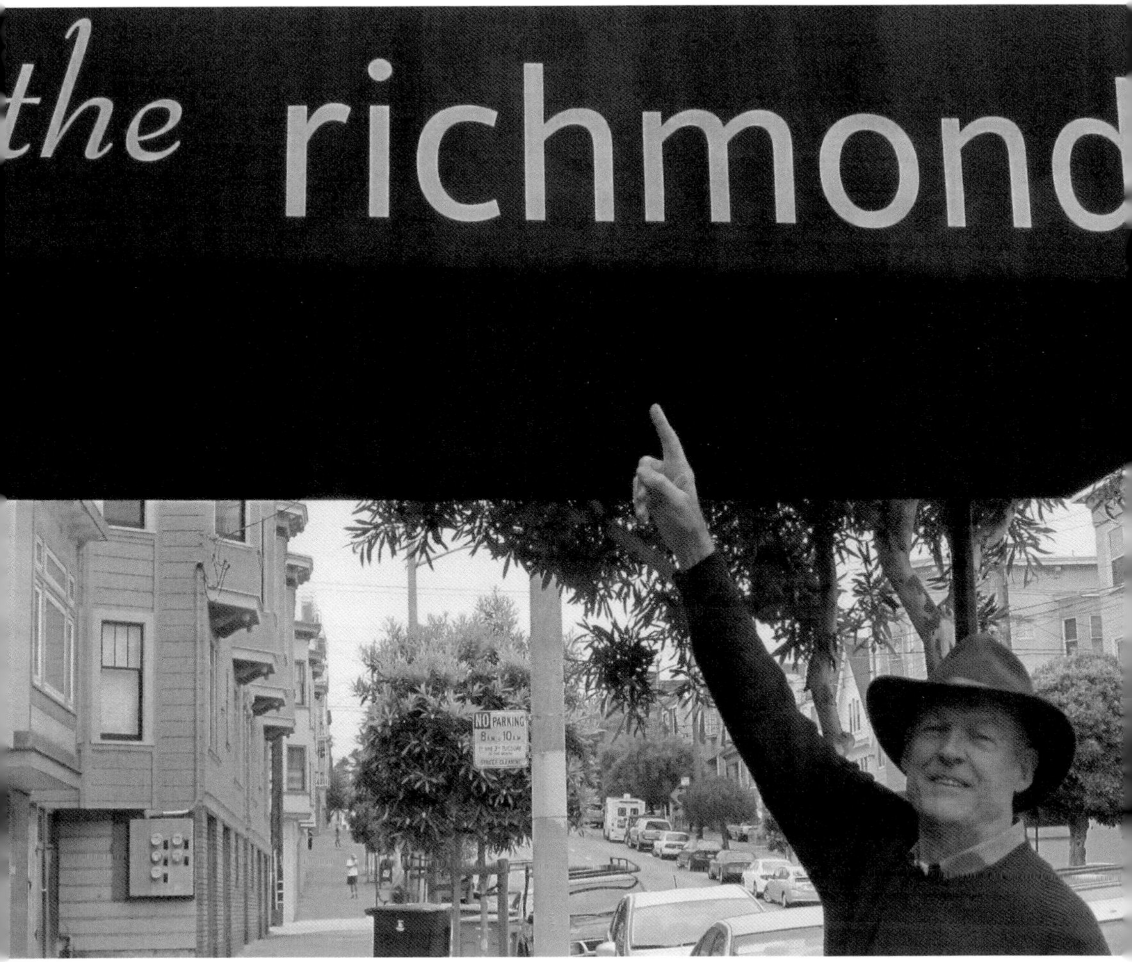

Sharing History

The Prelinger Archives, which can be found at www.archive.org, was founded in 1983 by Rick Prelinger in New York City. Now residents of the Richmond District, Rick and his wife, Megan, still run the archive, which collects, preserves, and makes available to the public films of historic significance that might not have been collected elsewhere. The archive holds more than 5,000 digitized and videotaped titles (all originally derived from film), as well as home movies and amateur and industrial films. Each year, at a large local theater, the Prelingers host "Lost Landscapes of San Francisco." The popular, sold-out program features films showing San Francisco scenes and encourages people in the audience to announce the locales they recognize. Rick and Megan also run the Prelinger Library, a public collection of books about US history. (Courtesy Rick and Megan Prelinger.)

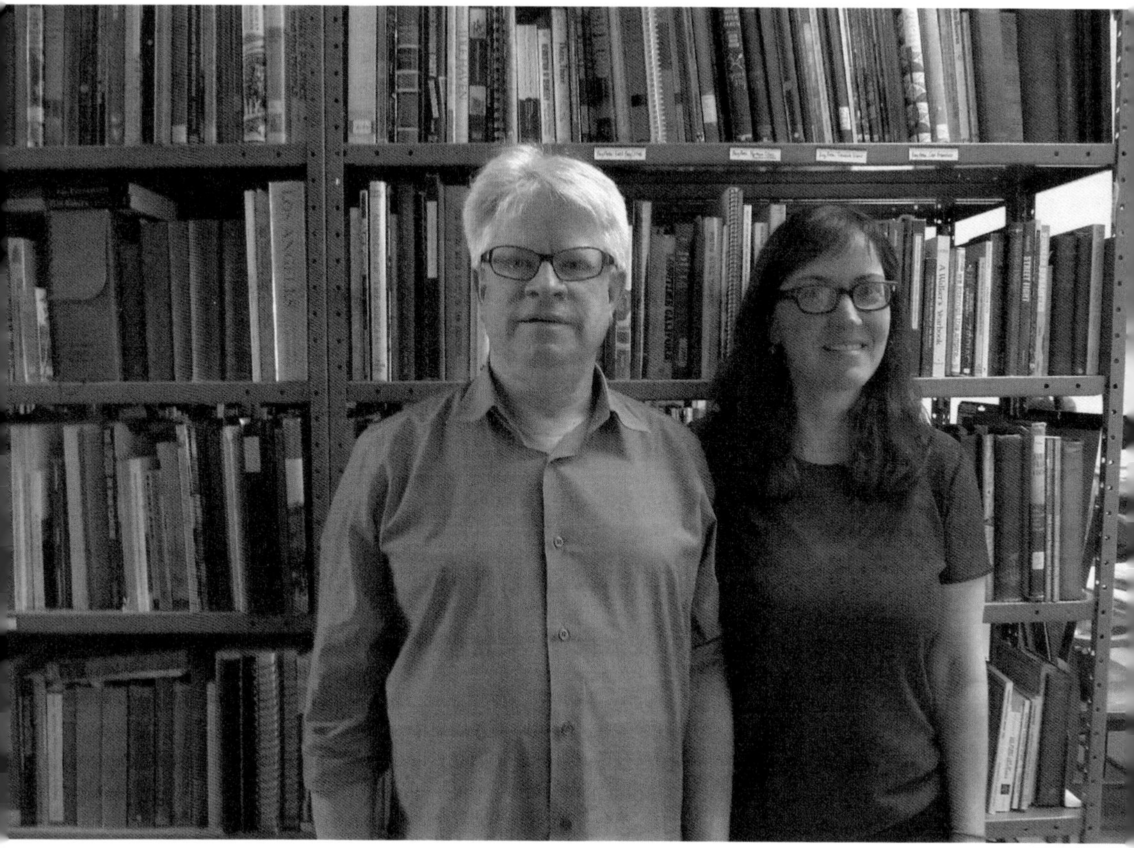

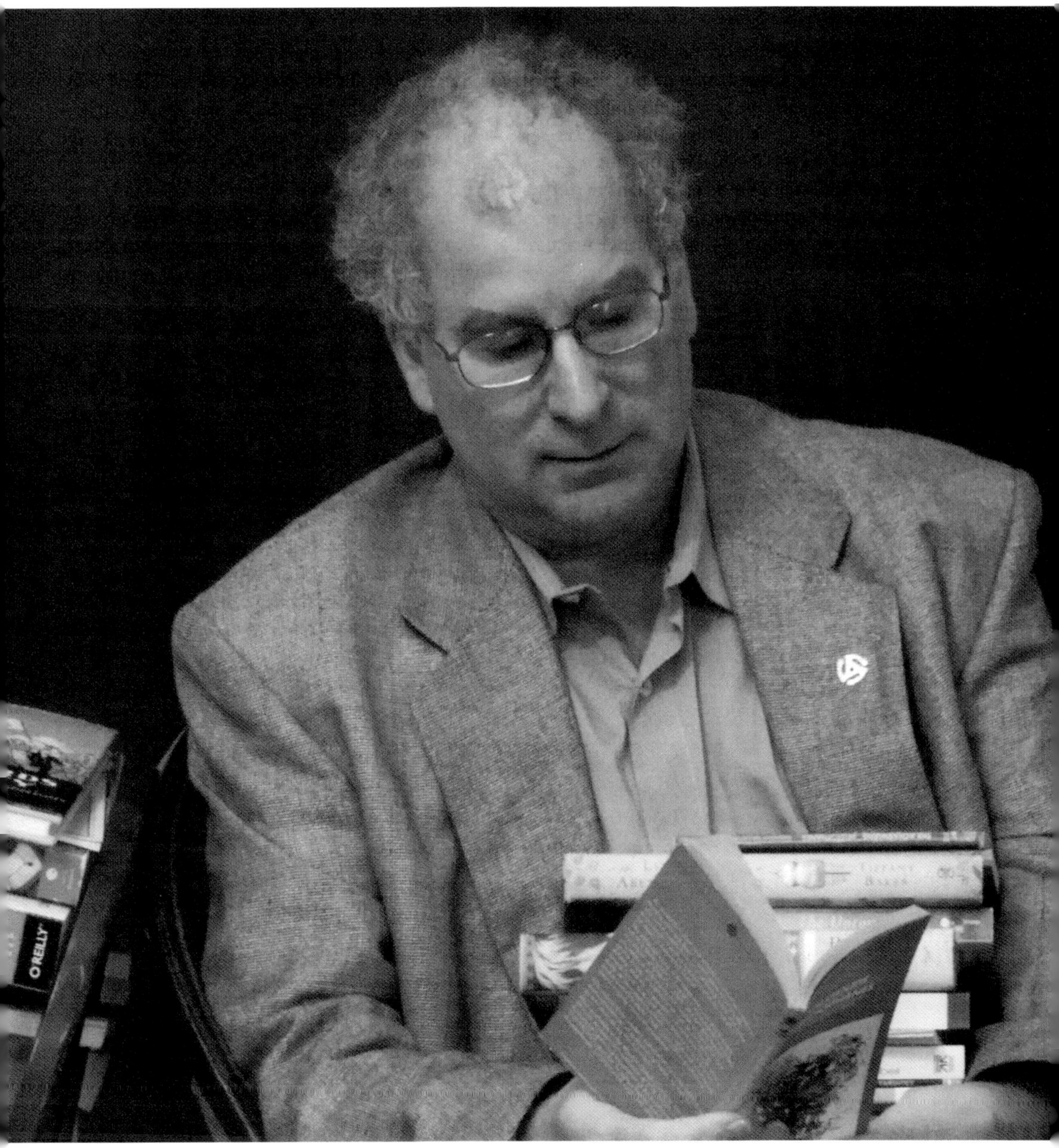

Sharing the Internet with All
Brewster Kahle was born in New York in 1960. He moved to San Francisco's Presidio in 1996 and founded the Internet Archive, a nonprofit agency that is building an Internet library offering access to historical collections in digital format for researchers, historians, scholars, people with disabilities, and the general public. The Internet Archive includes texts, audio, moving images, software, and archived web pages. It provides specialized services for people with disabilities. The archive website, www.archive.org, has the tagline "Universal access to all knowledge," which sums up Brewster's philosophy that all digital information should be available to all people. So far, the Internet Archive has approximately 10 million media items and 415 billion web captures. "This adds up to about 18 petabytes of unique data," Brewster explains. He and the archive moved to the Richmond District in 2009. (Photograph by June Goldsmith.)

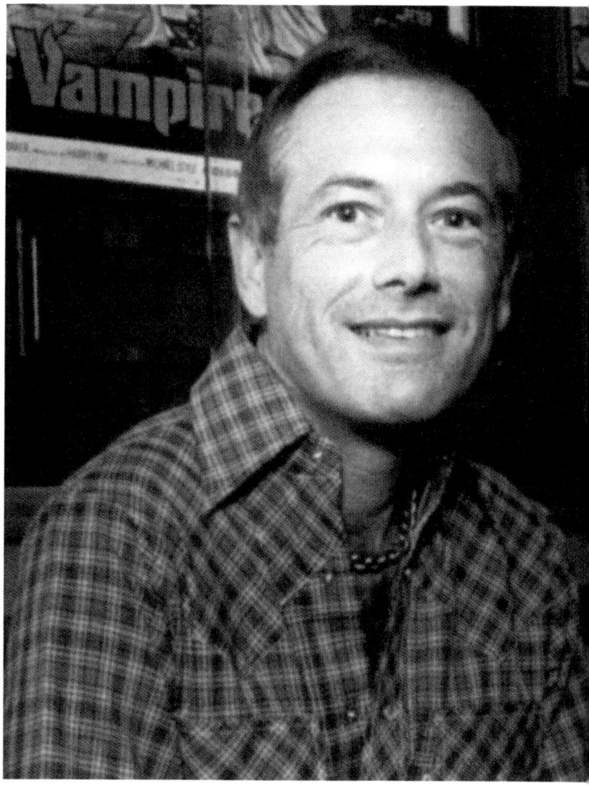

A Maven of Classic Movies

Before the digital age, people had to see a movie when it was first released or miss it forever. In San Francisco, all of this changed in 1970 when Jack Tillmany began managing film schedules at the Gateway Theatre, introducing a new generation of moviegoers to the glories of the cinematic past. Now retired and living in Walnut Creek, Jack has written three books on theaters in the Bay Area. One of the top contributors to the Internet Movie Database (www.imdb.com), Jack collects historical photographs and has a deep knowledge of classic movies. Jack is seen here as a toddler in the Richmond District (where he grew up) and as a movie-loving adult. (Courtesy Jack Tillmany.)

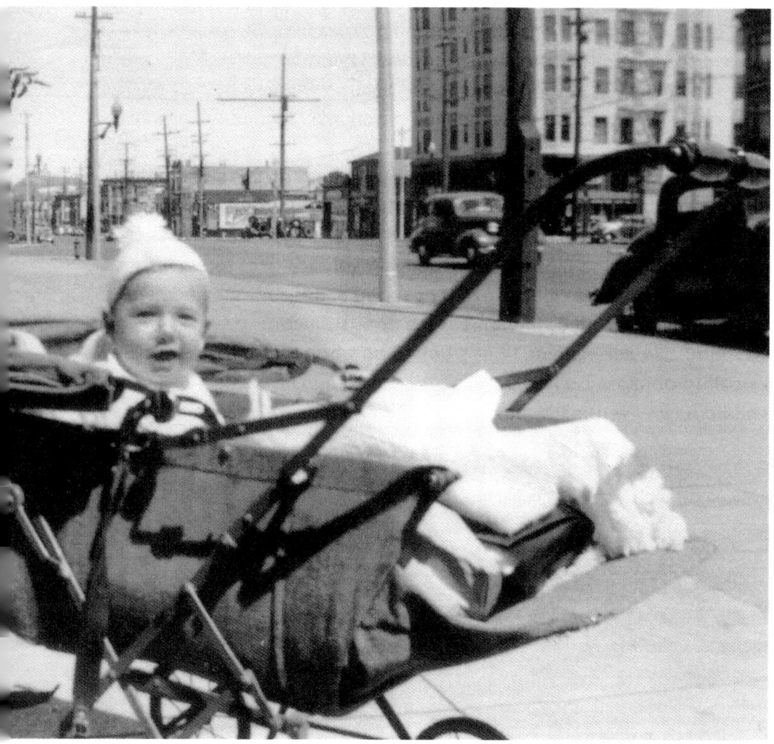

CHAPTER THREE

The Builders

The people who built houses in the Richmond and Sunset Districts can truly be considered visionary. Transforming two large sandy areas far from the central city into two neighborhoods with streets, housing, and businesses was a tremendous feat.

Mostly because of Adolph Sutro's work (see pages 100 and 101), public transportation and housing grew in the Richmond District earlier than in the Sunset. Housing is more varied in the Richmond, and many builders, such as Joseph Leonard and Gus Moeller, were responsible for constructing scattered houses, not entire blocks. By the early 20th century, much of the Richmond was developed. Life (or the lack of it) in the Sunset District was different. Until the 1920s, almost the entire area was still sand dunes. In the 1930s, Henry Doelger bought many blocks in the Sunset but could not sell "sandlots" to anyone until he started building houses. Suddenly, as houses and paved streets appeared, people were attracted to living in the Sunset. The house builders were heroes to people who wanted affordable homes of their own in a growing city.

Some of the Sunset builders, especially Henry Doelger and Ray Galli, bought entire blocks of sand and covered them with houses. In the 1930s, many streets ended in sand dunes, but, by the 1950s, almost all the land in the Sunset had been developed. This chapter talks about some of the builders who transformed the sand dunes into thriving neighborhoods within only about 30 years.

An important difference between these builders and the "developers" of today is that Henry Doelger and others were individual entrepreneurs who built in neighborhoods where they and their families would live. Creating good homes and good communities was important to these builders; the families of Henry Doelger, Ray Galli, Fred and Carl Gellert, Fernando Nelson, and Arthur and Oliver Rousseau all lived in houses these men had constructed while they were building houses nearby.

The Most Prolific Builder

Henry Doelger was the most prolific builder in the Sunset, covering the sand dunes with thousands of similar-looking houses. Henry was born in San Francisco in 1896. When he was eight years old, his father opened a grocery store at Seventh Avenue and Hugo Street in the Inner Sunset. The family lived upstairs. In the 1920s, Henry bought his first large piece of property: the block bounded by Thirty-ninth Avenue, Judah Street, Fortieth Avenue, and Kirkham Street. Henry built 25 homes on the Thirty-ninth Avenue side of this block. Henry once said that his Sunset houses were "the outgrowth of a boyhood dream that one day the desolate sand dunes of the Sunset might be replaced by trim modern homes, owned by 'Mr. and Mrs. Average San Franciscan.'"

Henry was a great marketer. He sponsored contests to bring customers to his model homes. For example, in a 1942 contest, Henry asked the public to complete the statement, "I am glad I am an American because . . . " To enter the contest, people had to visit a new Doelger model home, the Freedom House. Thousands of contest entries poured in, and the awards were eventually distributed at the Nantucket model home for another new development. (The winner was Richmond District resident Edward O'Brien, who had written, "I am glad I am an American because my life is my own to live and enjoy; my country a pleasure to defend.")

Henry was asked once where he got his money to build. He said he had saved his money from selling hot dogs in Golden Gate Park as a boy. His descendants have added to the story; he also sold bootleg liquor.

By the end of the 1940s, Henry had finished his work in the Sunset. In the early 1950s, he moved his office to Daly City and built houses in Westlake until 1962. He died of a heart attack in 1978 on his yacht in Italy, at age 82. (Below left and facing page above courtesy San Francisco History Center, San Francisco Public Library; facing page below, author's photograph.)

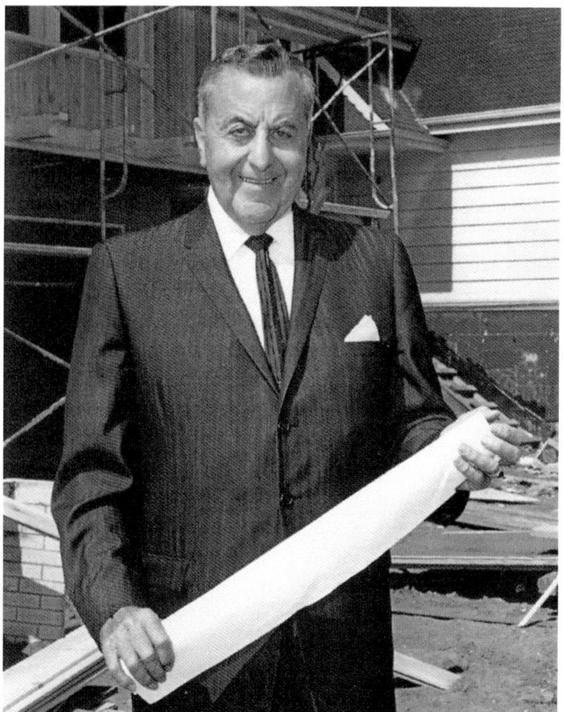

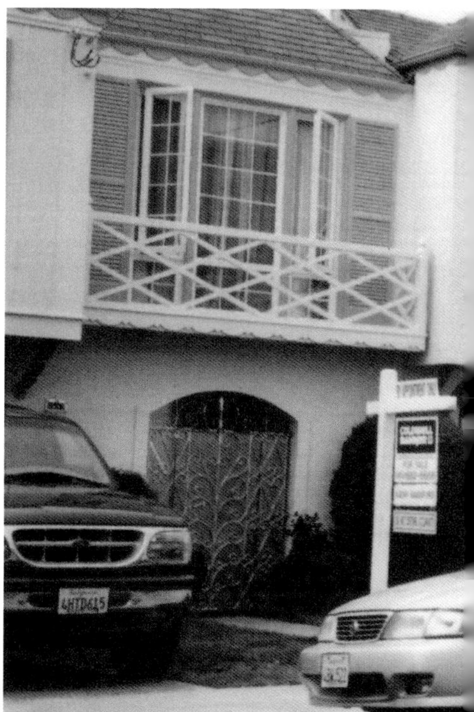

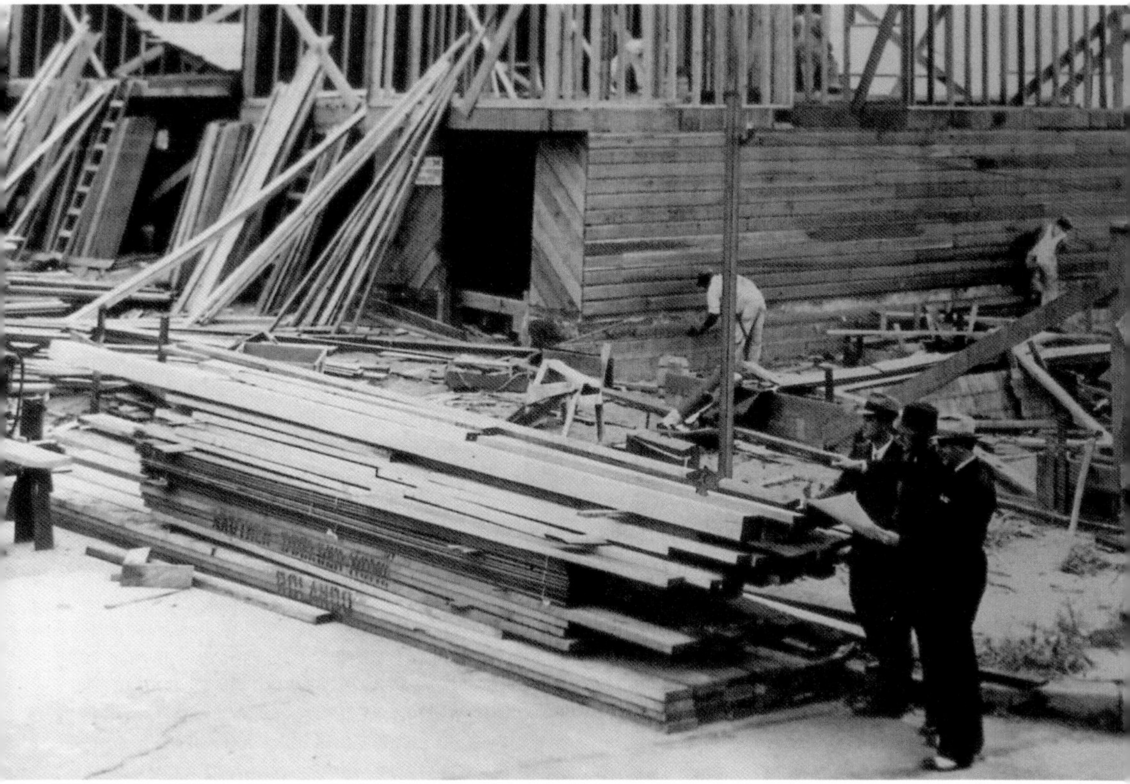

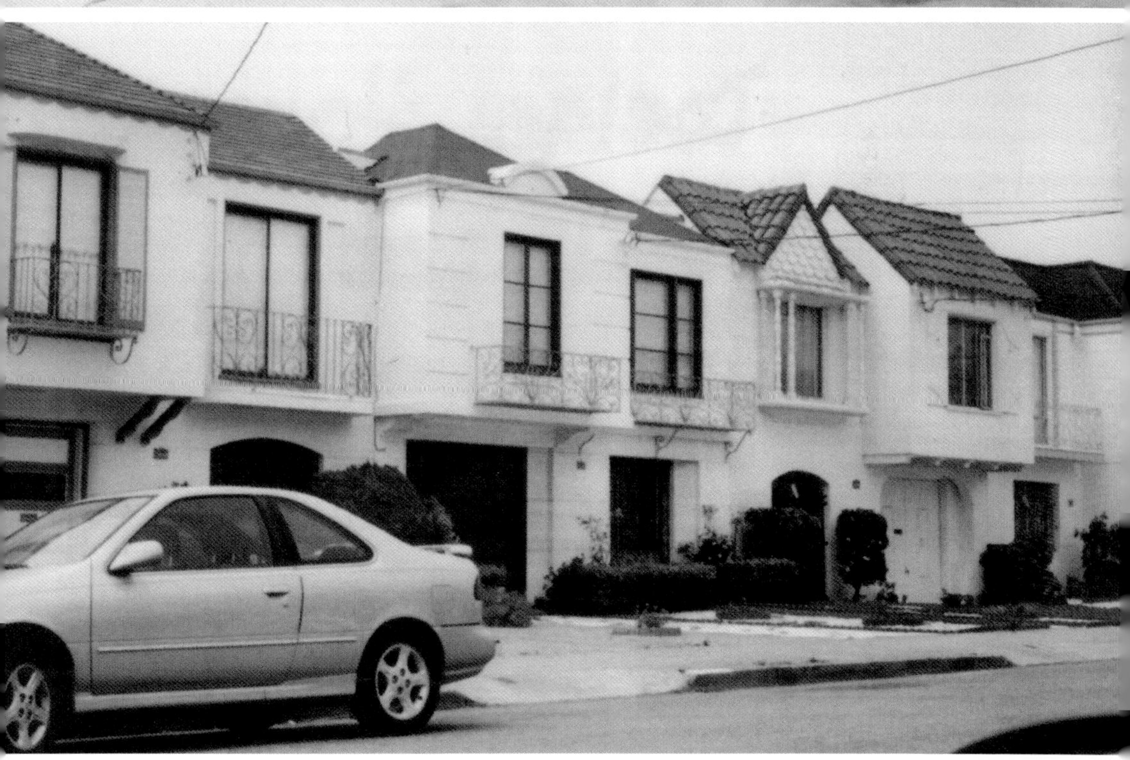

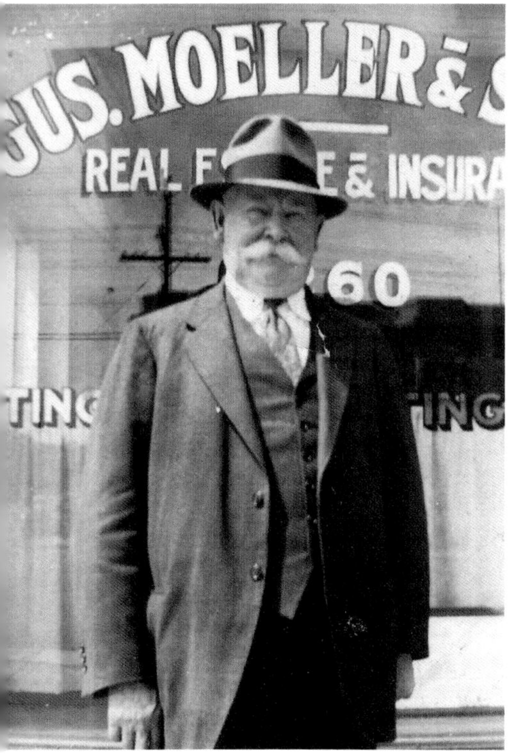

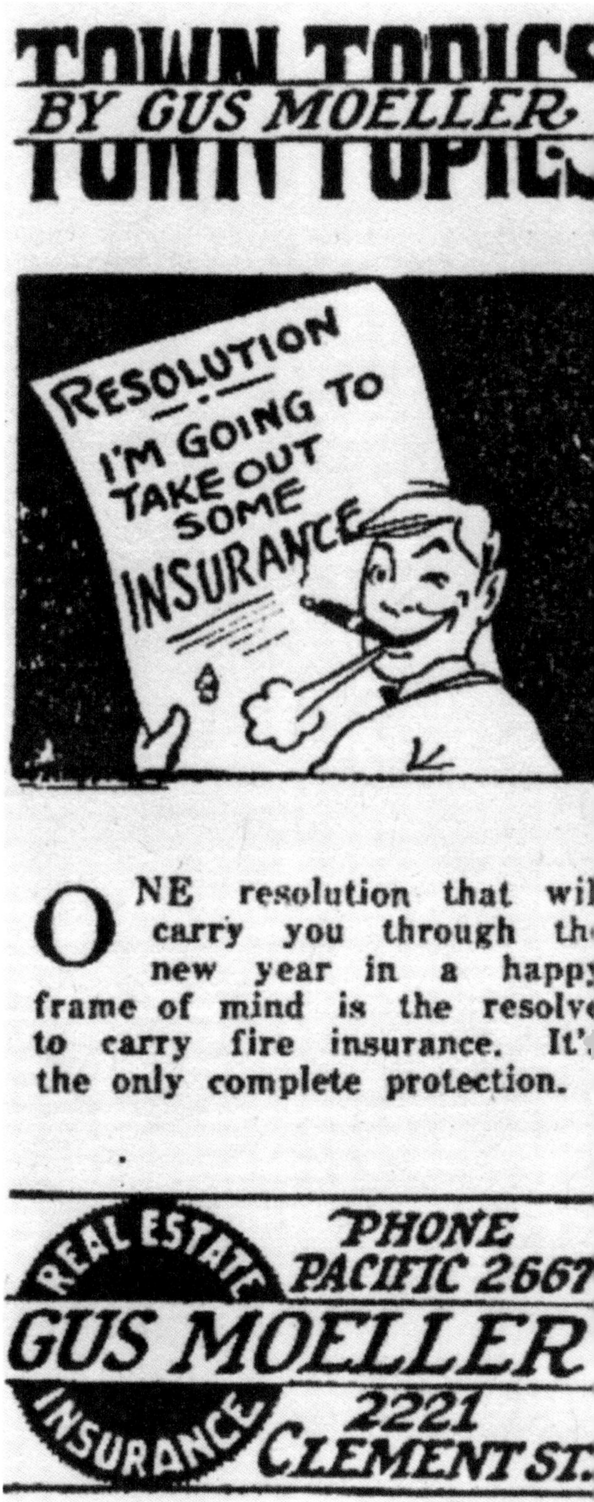

King of the Richmond

Gustave "Gus" Moeller was born in Germany in 1870 and came to the United States in 1894. He married in 1897, and he and his wife lived above a restaurant they operated on Geary Boulevard. In 1908, he started a real estate and insurance business on Geary Boulevard, and he later built an office on Clement Street (see newspaper ad). Unlike builders who worked independently, Gus worked with friends. They would pool their money, buy lots, build houses, and then sell the houses. Gus's houses are scattered throughout the mid-to-outer Richmond District. Many of his friends and business associates called him "the King of the Richmond" because he built his own home on the corner of Forty-eighth Avenue and Anza Street so he could keep an eye on the construction of other houses on the block. Gus died in January 1963. (Courtesy Henry Moeller.)

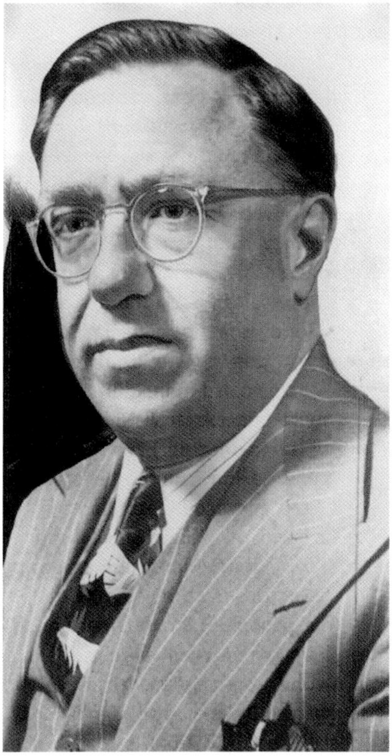

House Builder Galli

Galli Construction Company built a large number of houses in the Sunset, primarily in the late 1930s and early 1940s. The company slogan was "Galli-Built Means Better Built."

Always the innovator, Ray Galli is credited with inventing the "tunnel entrance" (see below). Introduced in the mid-1930s, the tunnel entrance soon became a popular Sunset house feature and was used by many builders.

Like many Sunset builders, Ray Galli built a home for his family in the neighborhood. When he built a row of houses on Twenty-eighth Avenue, he saved 1574 Twenty-eighth Avenue for his family.

Ray died in 1969, but his building legacy continues. His sons operate Galli Heritage in Burlingame, south of San Francisco. (Left, courtesy San Francisco History Center, San Francisco Public Library; below, author's photograph.)

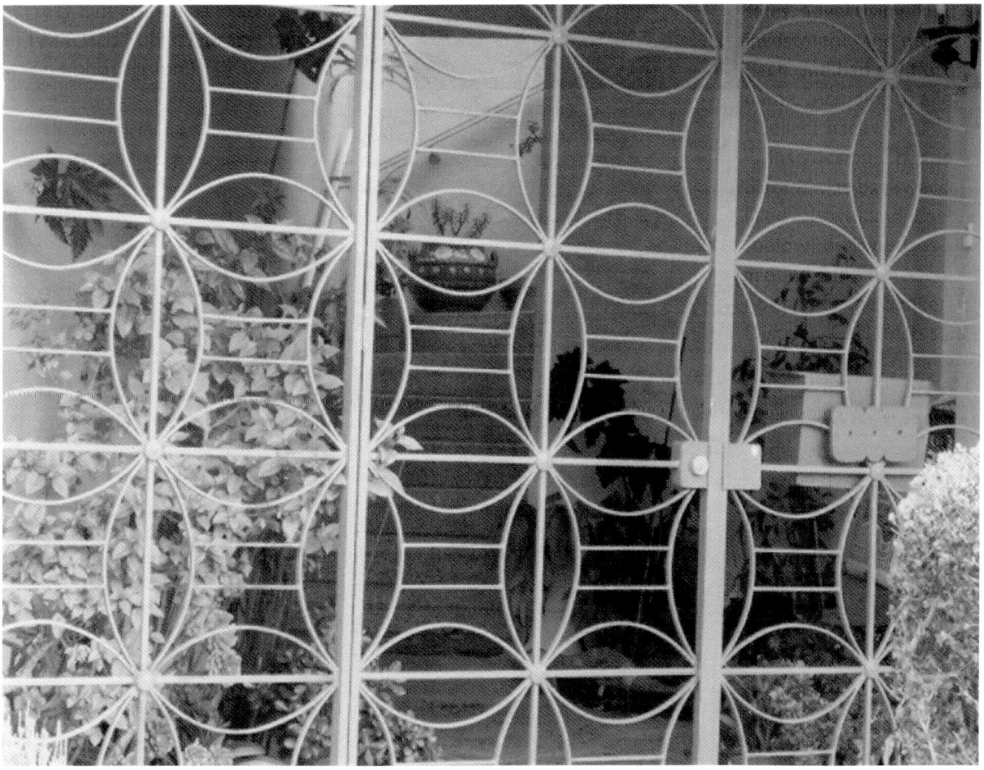

Storybook Houses
Oliver Rousseau (shown here) and his brother Arthur built almost 200 homes in the Sunset District from 1931 to 1933. Oliver and Arthur were trained architects who had worked with their architect father. Their houses, mostly between Thirty-third and Thirty-sixth Avenues, from Kirkham to Lawton, look like "fairytale" or "storybook" houses, with turrets, towers, dovecotes, full-length balconies, muscular chimney stacks, and other distinctive looks (see below). Inside, they featured optional sunken living rooms, small gates separating the dining and living rooms, and ornate bathrooms. Oliver and Arthur are credited with inventing the open-air patio in the middle of the house, a feature that other builders copied. The Rousseau brothers are better known for their larger houses in other parts of San Francisco and the Bay Area. (Right, courtesy San Francisco History Center, San Francisco Public Library; below, author's photograph.)

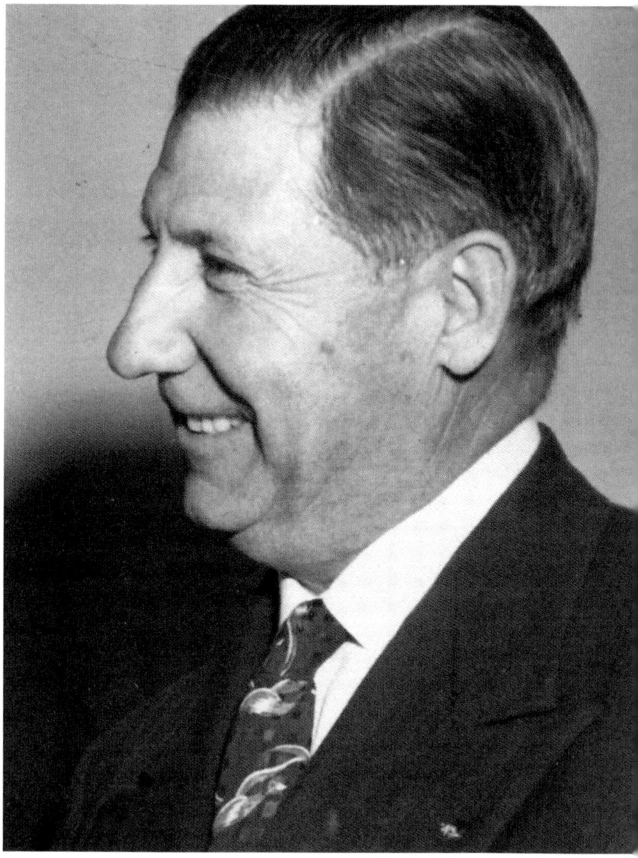

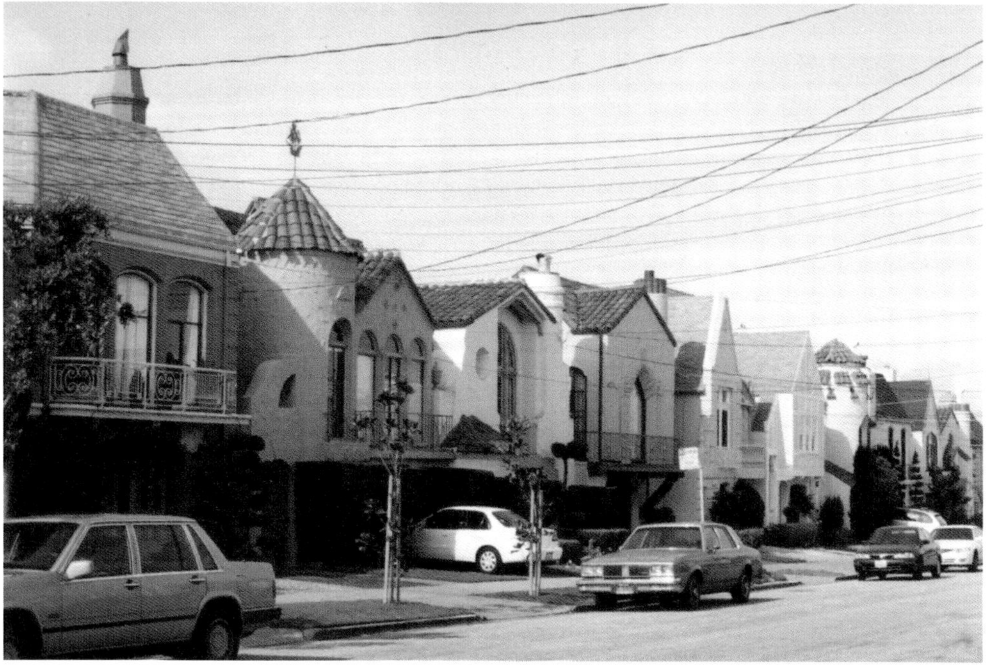

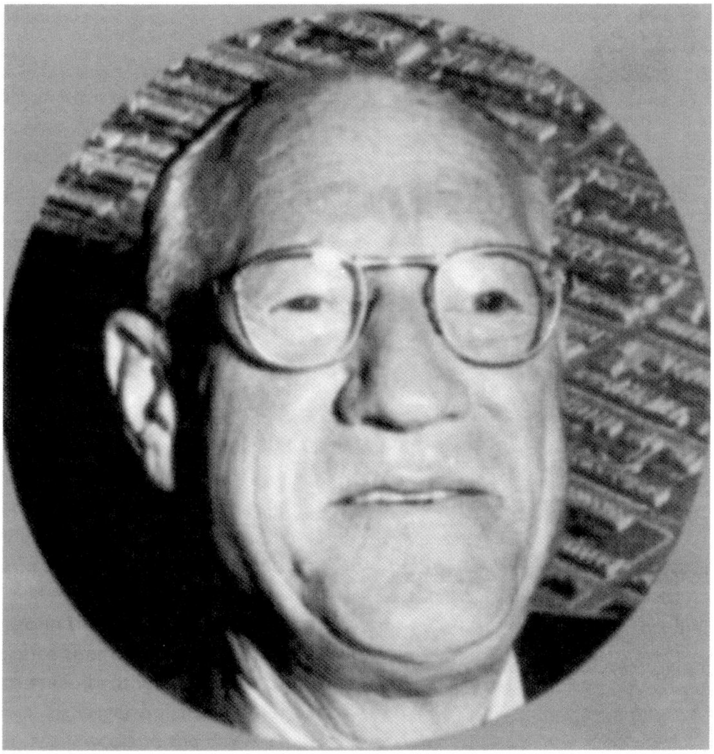

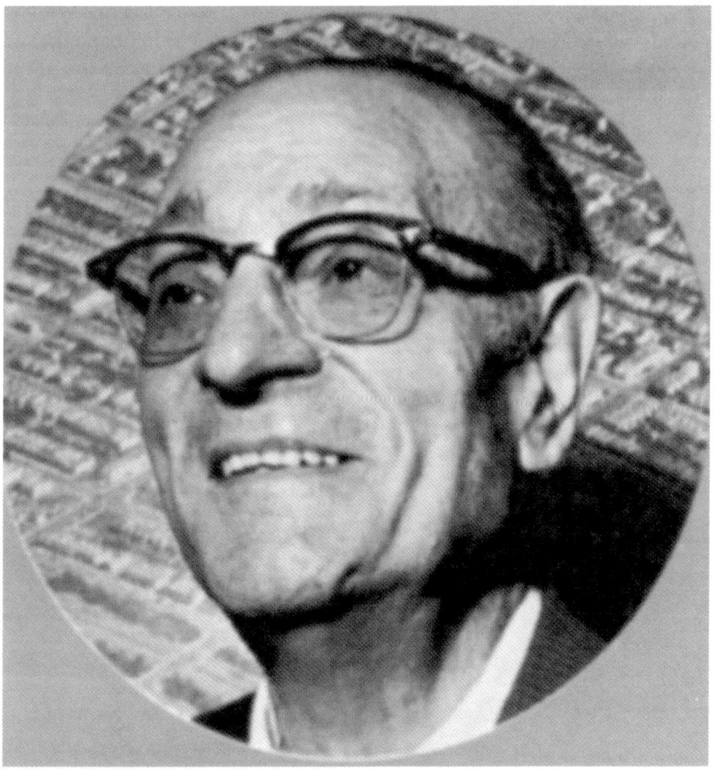

Builder Brothers, the Gellerts
Carl and Fred Gellert founded the Standard Building Company and began constructing houses in the central Sunset in 1922. Standard had buildings and warehouses scattered through the Sunset; the best-known office stood at 2222 Nineteenth Avenue. According to one former employee, "Carl and Fred created more than 40 companies for building, sales, advertising, land investment, and more. Each one had a different name, including Trelleg (Gellert backward) Construction Co. and Salta (Atlas backward)." Fred (above) and Carl (below) built houses all around San Francisco, not just in the Sunset District. Carl once said, "We can stand on any hill in San Francisco and look down on some home or apartment we have built." (Courtesy Peter Brusati.)

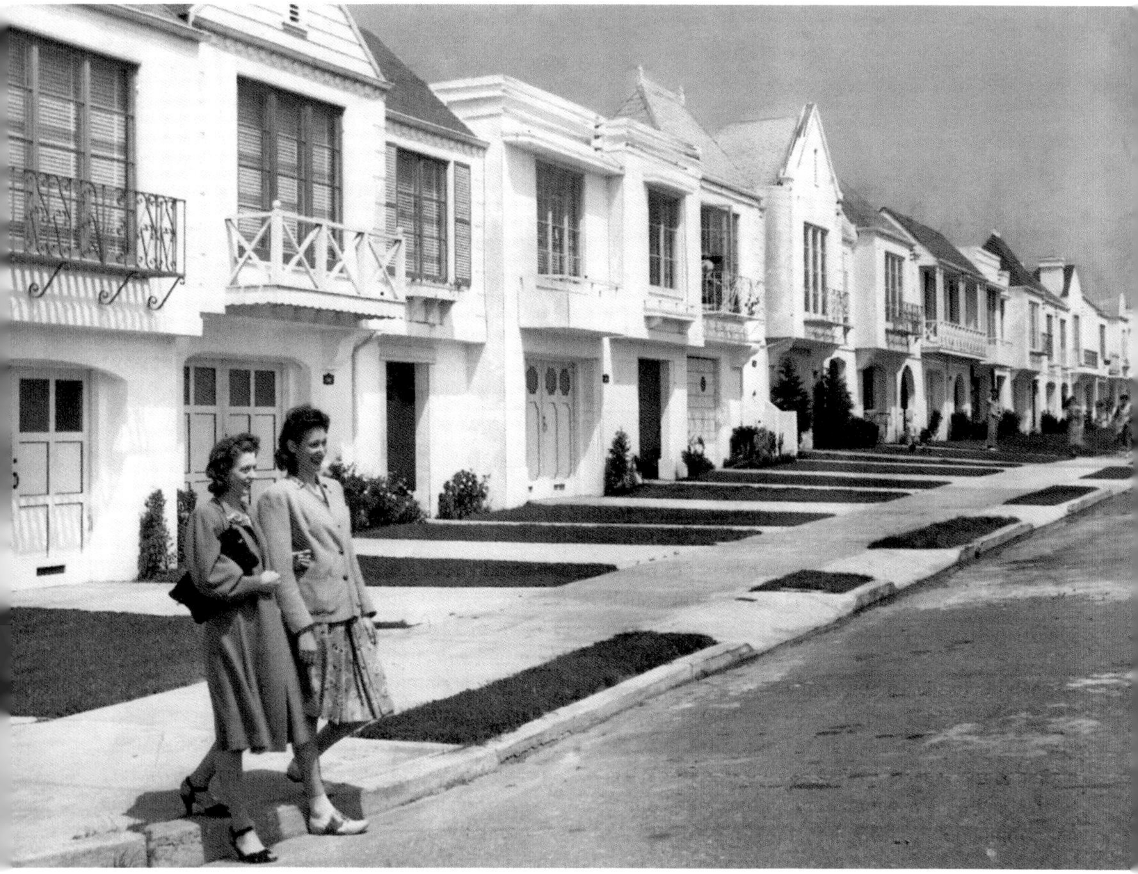

House Builder McKeon

Chris McKeon was born in San Francisco and raised in the Mission District. As a young man, he worked for his family's meatpacking firm. He entered construction in 1927. When he began building in the Sunset, his sales office, Happy Homes Building Company, stood at 948 Taraval Street, and he lived at 345 Santiago Street. Chris built houses on various Sunset lots, including those on Thirty-fifth Avenue between Moraga and Noriega Streets, on Noriega between Thirty-seventh and Thirty-eighth Avenues, and on Twenty-ninth and Thirtieth Avenues between Ortega and Rivera Streets. The image here shows a row of houses Chris built in the Parkside District. He was active in San Francisco political and social causes, and, in 1959, the local Eagles group gave him an award for his "unselfish devotion to the City of San Francisco." He died on August 29, 1967. (Courtesy Parkside Tavern, Larry Doyle collection.)

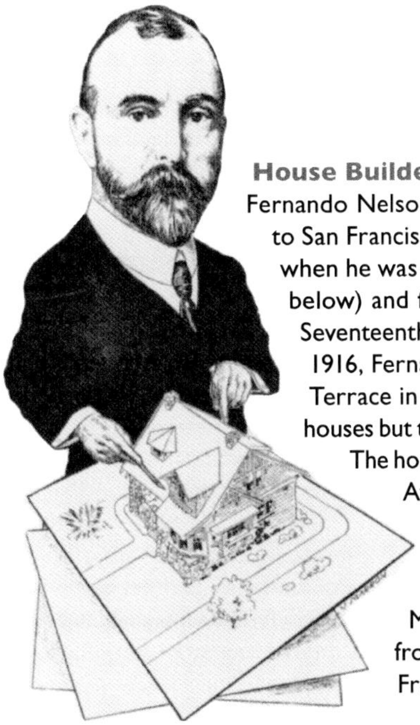

House Builder Nelson

Fernando Nelson was born in New York in 1860. He moved to San Francisco when he was 15 and began building houses when he was 22. In the Richmond District, his houses (see below) and flats occupy sections of blocks from First to Seventeenth Avenues, between Lake and Fulton Streets. In 1916, Fernando Nelson & Sons started building Parkway Terrace in the Sunset District. They built two blocks of houses but then sold the remaining blocks to other builders. The houses built on Twenty-seventh and Twenty-eighth Avenues from Lincoln Way to Irving Street are among the largest and grandest houses built in the Sunset District. Fernando went on to build houses in West Portal and Merced Manor. He died in 1953 at the age of 93. (Left, from *Men Who Made San Francisco*, courtesy John Freeman; below, courtesy Peter Field.)

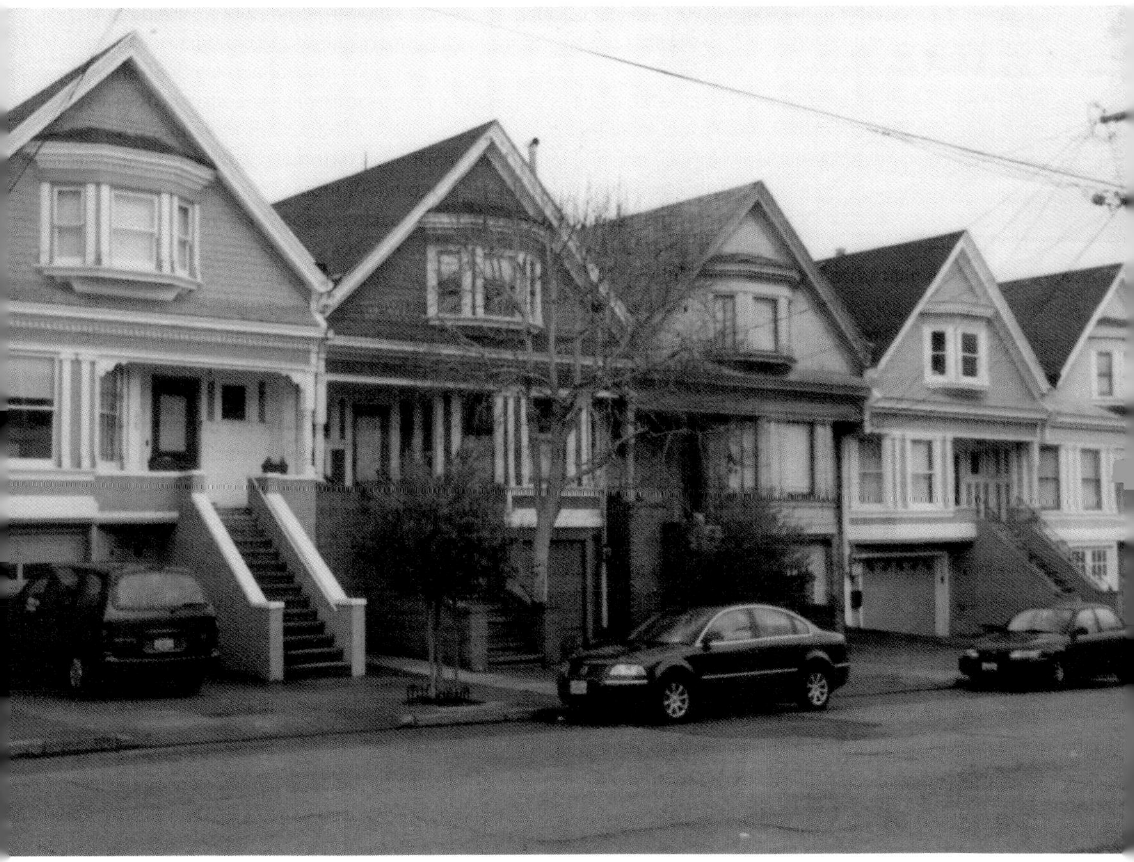

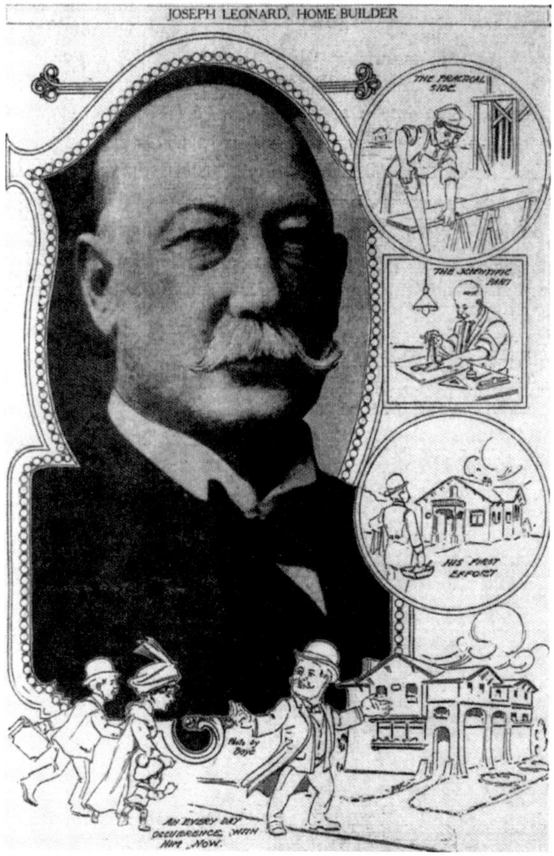

A Quality Builder

Joseph Leonard was a pioneer residential developer in the Richmond District who left a legacy of homes of quality craftsmanship that are the pride of the neighborhood today. Born in 1849, he came to California in 1875. He designed Victorian homes in Alameda and Craftsmen bungalows in Berkeley, and his first development project in San Francisco was Jordan Park. When the 1906 earthquake interrupted that project, Joseph developed assembly-line methods to rapidly provide cottages for the quake homeless. By 1909, he had moved his family into the Richmond, where he built houses south of California Street, between Eighth and Ninth Avenues, and two full blocks between Ninth and Eleventh Avenues, from Anza Street to Balboa Street, which he called Richmond Heights. By 1913, Joseph had moved to another part of the city and begun to build Ingleside Terraces. He died in 1929. The illustration at right originally appeared in *San Francisco Call* on February 23, 1913. (Both, courtesy John Freeman.)

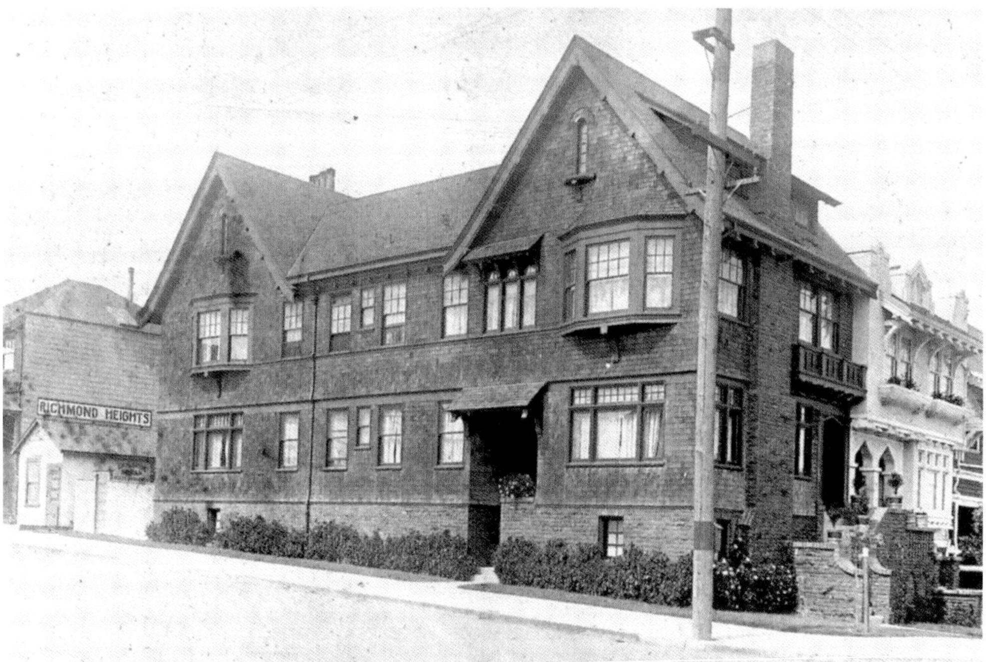

CHAPTER FOUR

Making a Difference

People make a difference in their local communities and in the world by the choices they make in their lives. Some are educators, some work with troubled youth, some advocate for the environment, some open their wallets to donate to good causes, and some are trailblazers in their community, while others contribute to their neighborhoods in other ways.

As dean at A.P. Giannini Middle School, Judy Huey worked to motivate middle-school children at risk. Gwen Chan made lasting changes as assistant principal at George Washington High School in the Richmond District and as principal at Abraham Lincoln High School in the Sunset. Janet Pomeroy and Dewey Rosetti founded institutions for children who learn differently from others. Michael Funk helped create a center in the Outer Sunset for youth who needed support and assistance. When Linda Fries learned that a closed school in the Richmond was to be razed and replaced with condominiums, she worked to help establish the Richmond District Neighborhood Center.

Some people's advocacy relates directly to their local communities. Ray Schiller was a friendly neighborhood activist who advocated for many improvements to the Sunset-Parkside area in the early years of its development. Ray fought for the building of Lincoln High School, a streetcar extension to the beach, park and business activities, and more. Today, we can thank people like Inge Horton, who volunteered for years for the Sunset Parkside Education and Action Committee; and Sarah Bacon, Woody LaBounty, David Gallagher, and Paul Kozakiewicz, who publish and share information about the past and ongoing history of their neighborhoods.

San Francisco has a tradition of wealthy people who have given back to their communities. In the early 1900s, French-born Edouard Le Breton donated enough money to help the Little Sisters of the Poor build a retirement home for people who could not afford to pay for housing. Rosalie Stern purchased 12 acres of land in the southern Sunset to create a city park named in honor of her deceased husband, Sigmund. Her gift to the Sunset draws thousands of visitors each year.

Other people who make a difference—writers, politicians, environmentalists, and philosophers—are those we look up to and admire for their choices and actions.

A Trailblazing Man

Audley Cole broke the color barrier by becoming the first black motorman hired by the San Francisco Municipal Railway (Muni). In 1940, he passed the motorman's examination, and Muni assigned other motormen to train him. At first, 17 motormen agreed to train Audley, but one by one they refused. When the story was reported in local newspapers, people wrote letters to the editors. One reader wrote, "It seems ironical that we are all engaged in a war for freedom and democracy and such a case as this exists in San Francisco."

Eventually, Audley was trained, and, in 1942, he joined the ranks of Muni as the first black motorman. He had married Josephine Foreman (see facing page) in 1941, and they bought a house in the primarily Caucasian Sunset District in 1957. Audley died in 2008. (Courtesy the Labor Archives and Research Center, San Francisco State University.)

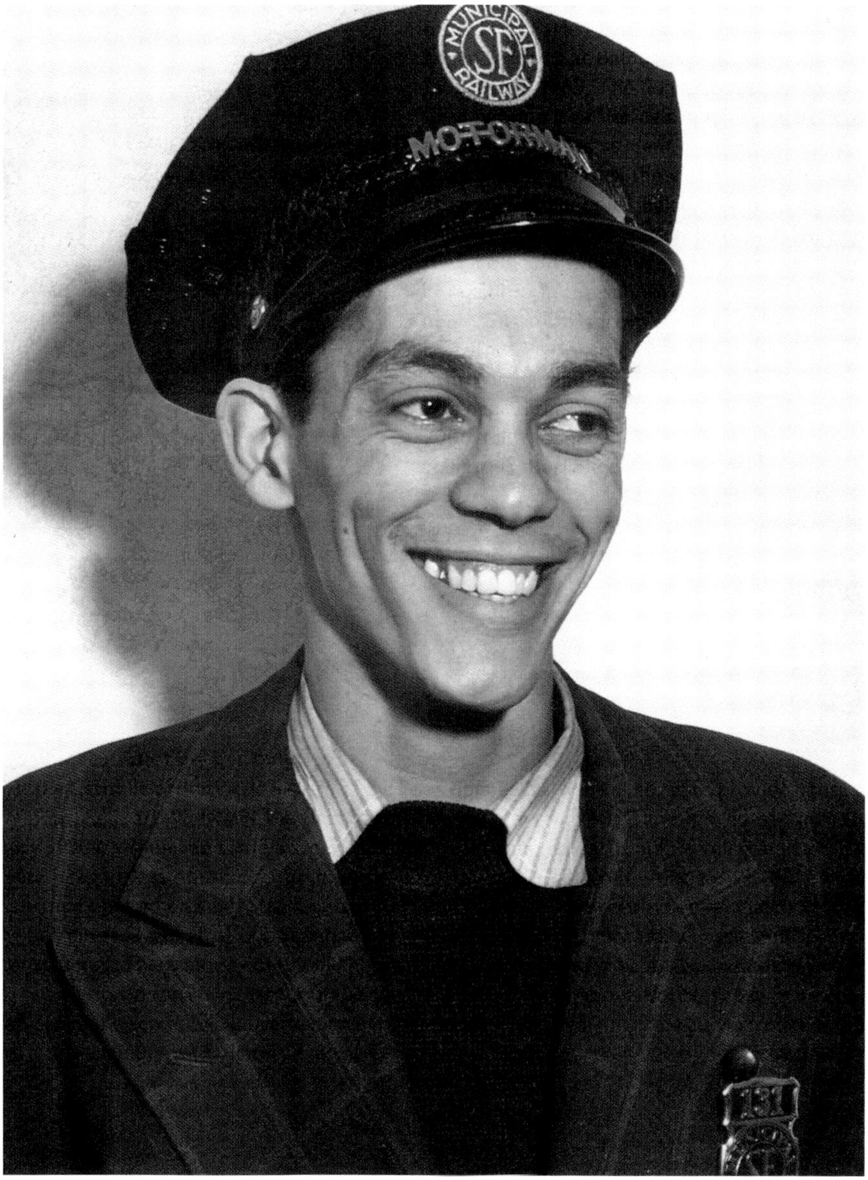

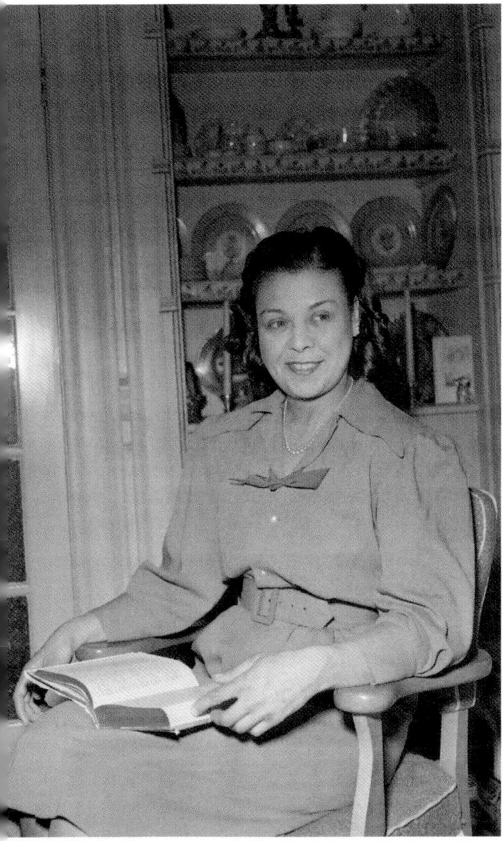

A Trailblazing Woman

Josephine Elizabeth Foreman was born in San Francisco in 1913. In 1935, African American teachers were not welcome in San Francisco schools, so she began teaching at a girls' Catholic elementary school. She met Audley Cole (see facing page) in 1940. They married in 1941 and, in 1957, moved into a Rousseau-designed home (below) on Thirty-sixth Avenue in the Sunset, where they lived for the rest of their lives.

Josephine "Jo" Cole became the first African American teacher hired by the San Francisco Unified School District in 1944. She taught at Raphael Weill (now Rosa Parks) Elementary School. In 1948, she began teaching at Balboa High School, where she taught until 1963. The Sunset house where the Coles lived became a gathering place for Jo's students. She frequently hosted student meetings and classes. For one series of classes, the Coles invited a variety of accomplished people, including actor Vincent Price and entertainer and actress Josephine Baker, to their home. In subsequent years, Jo held a variety of positions in the school district and received numerous awards from the City of San Francisco and other organizations. In 1992, the library at the southeast campus of City College of San Francisco was named the Josephine Cole Library. Cole died in 2006. (Left, courtesy Bancroft Library, University of California, Berkeley; below, author's photograph.)

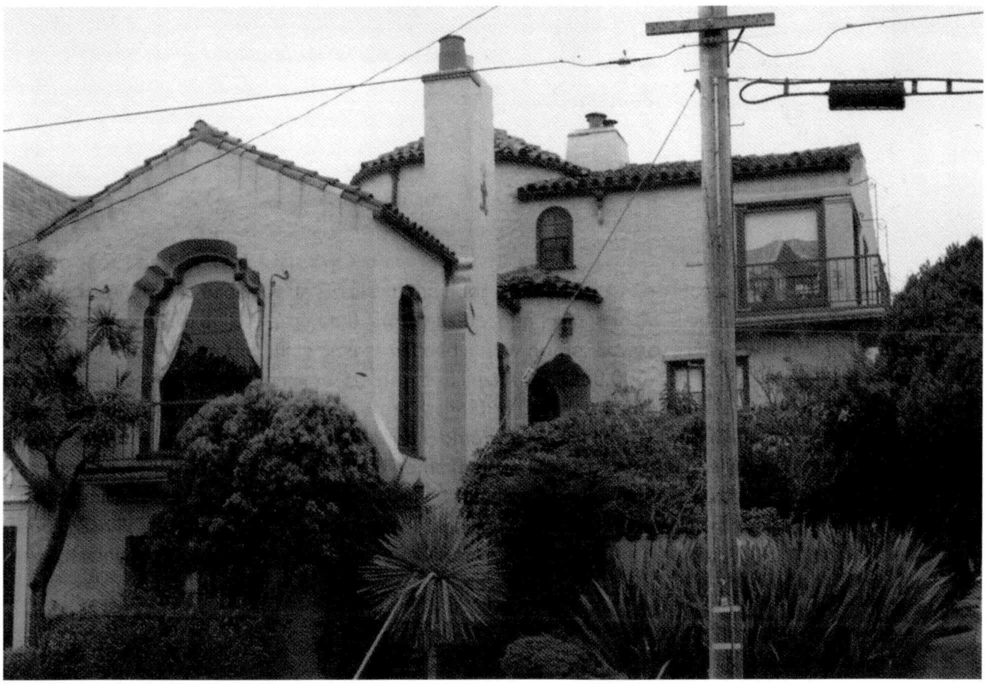

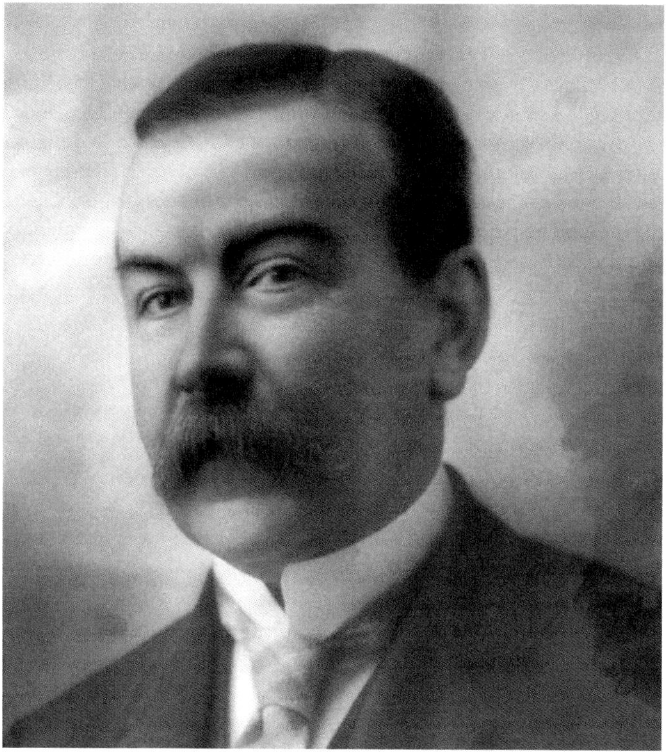

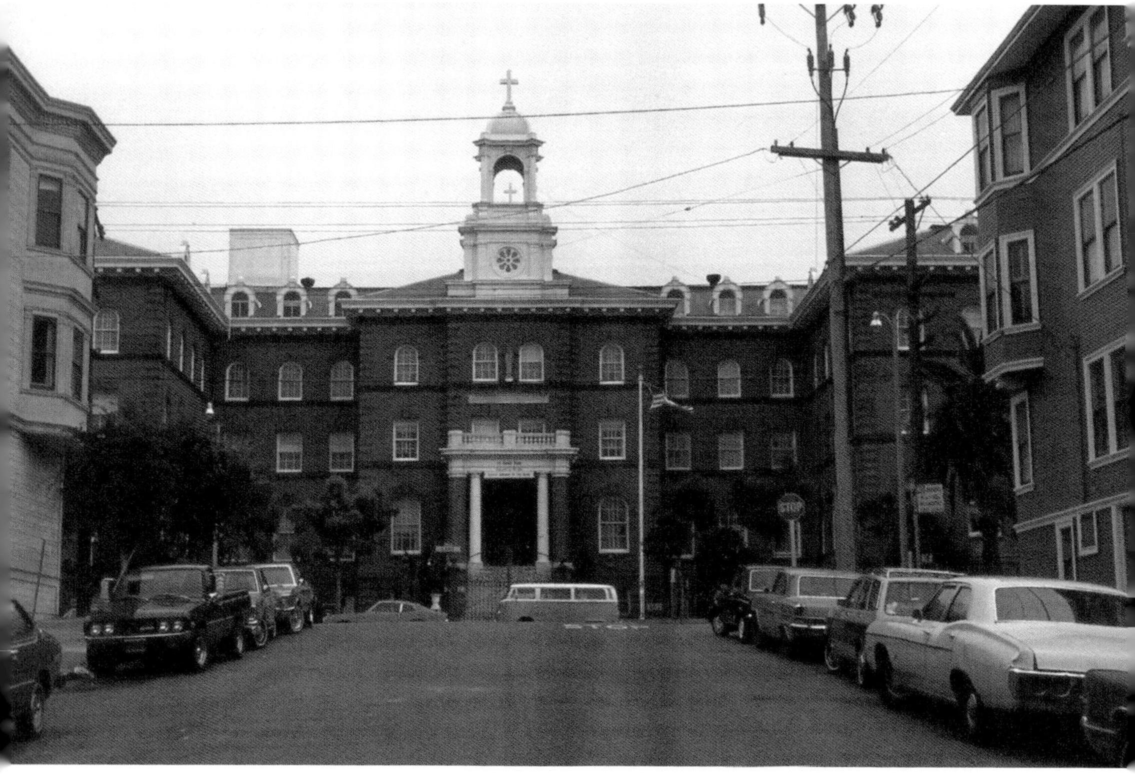

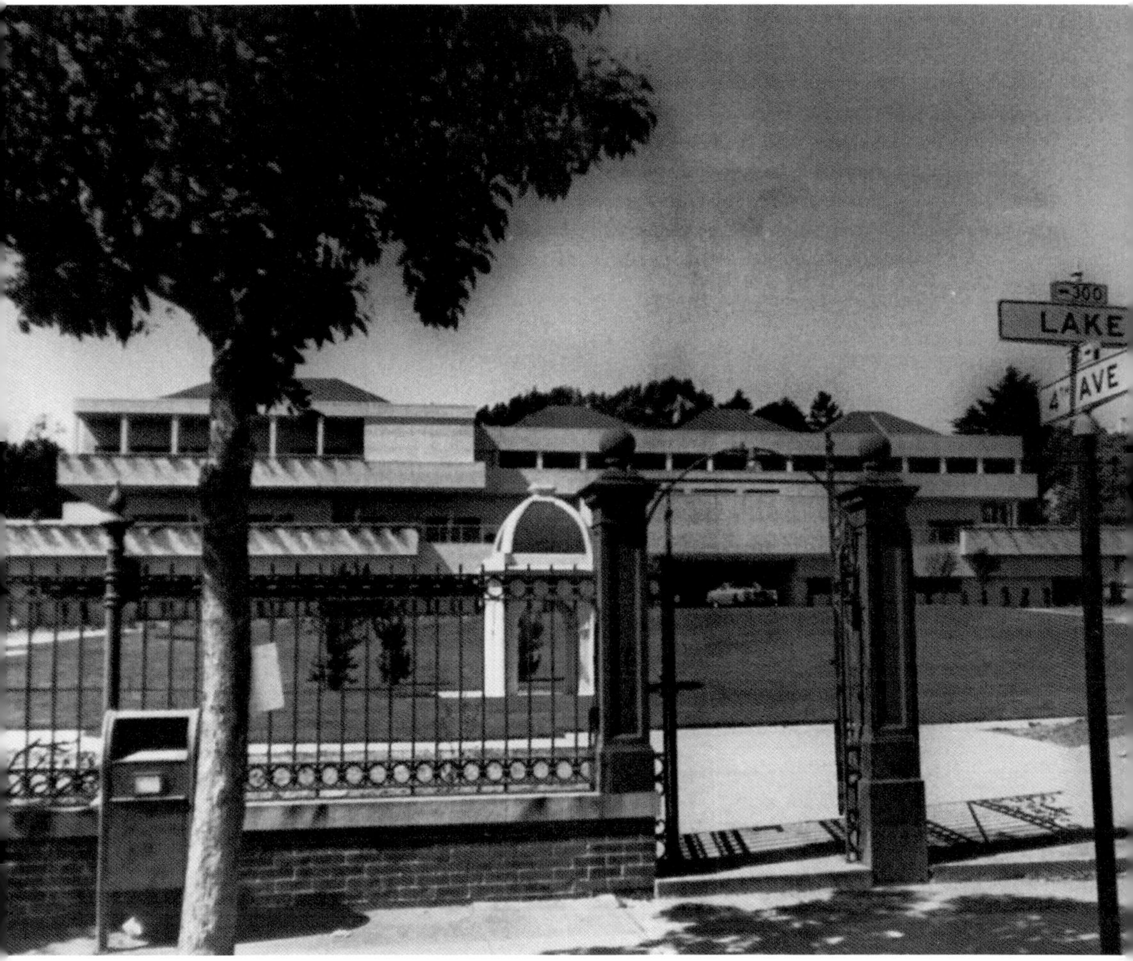

A Benefactor for the Elderly Poor

In 1901, the Catholic order Little Sisters of the Poor opened St. Anne's Home to provide housing for the elderly poor. Eduoard "Edward" Le Breton was born in France in 1852 and moved to San Francisco in the early 1900s. When the Little Sisters needed a new home, Edward said, "I will give you the home—complete—regardless of the cost." He donated a total of $250,000. On May 15, 1904, the doors at St. Anne's Home opened on Lake Street in the Richmond District. Le Breton died on March 19, 1910, while visiting St. Anne's Home. In 1977, St. Anne's Home was declared structurally unsafe, and a new building was constructed. The memory of the old home (below, facing page) is kept alive by the original building's cupola, which sits on the lawn in front of the new building (above). (Above, courtesy San Francisco History Center, San Francisco Public Library; photograph by Larry Moon; facing page above, courtesy St. Anne's Home; facing page below, courtesy Dennis O'Rorke.)

A New National Park

Phillip Burton was born in 1926 in Cincinnati, and, in 1941, his family moved to Kirkham Street in San Francisco's Sunset District. He graduated from George Washington High School in the Richmond and served in the US House of Representatives from 1964 to 1983. In 1972, he helped to create the Golden Gate National Recreation Area (GGNRA), the largest urban national park in the world extending 80,000 acres around the San Francisco Bay Area. When the GGNRA was established, Burton said it would "save for the people of the United States and the world a magnificent open space immediately adjacent to one of the major metropolitan regions of the United States." Phillip Burton died on April 10, 1983. The statue of him on this page stands in Fort Mason, which is part of the GGNRA. (Author's photograph.)

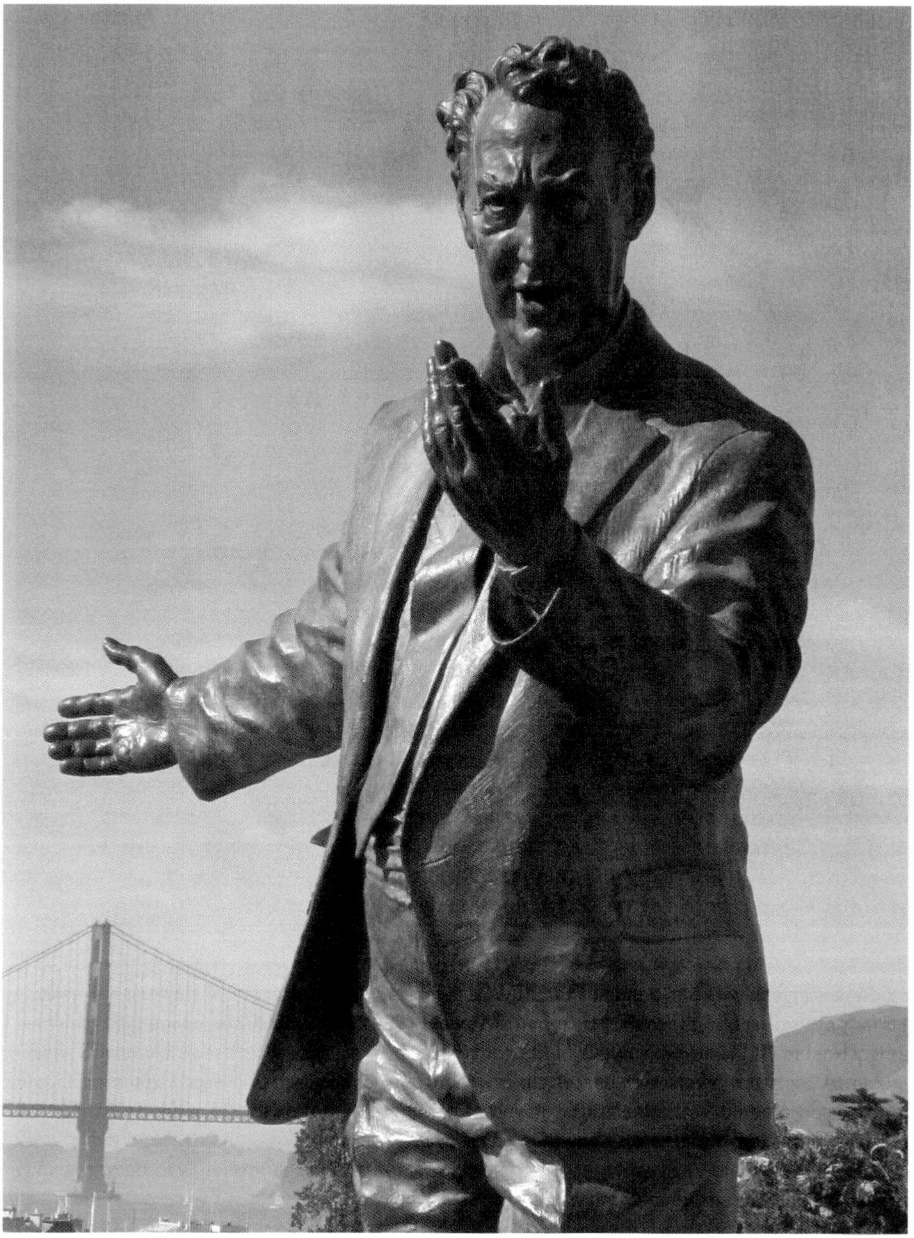

A Politician Who Made a Difference

John Burton, the brother of Phillip (see facing page) was born in Cincinnati in 1932. In 1941, his family moved to Kirkham Street in San Francisco. John graduated from Lincoln High School. He later served in the California State Assembly from 1965 to 1974, as a US congressman from 1975 to 1982, and then as a state assemblyman from 1988 to 1996. He was a state senator from 1996 to 2004, serving as president pro tem. Known for using blunt and "colorful" language, he has won numerous awards, both as a politician and as a child advocate. In 2004, after retiring from politics, he founded the John Burton Foundation for Children without Homes, a nonprofit group in San Francisco focusing on foster and homeless children. (Courtesy John Burton.)

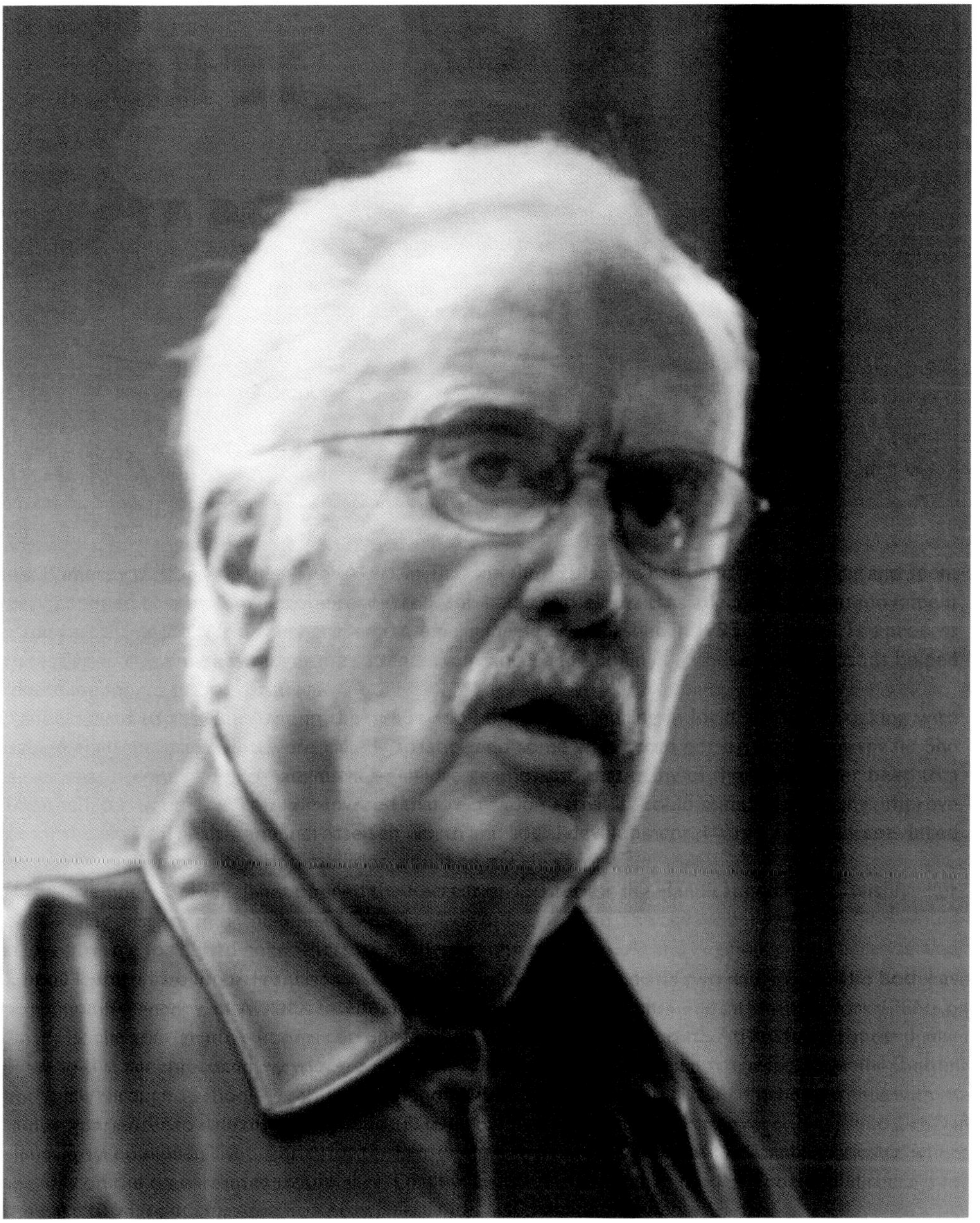

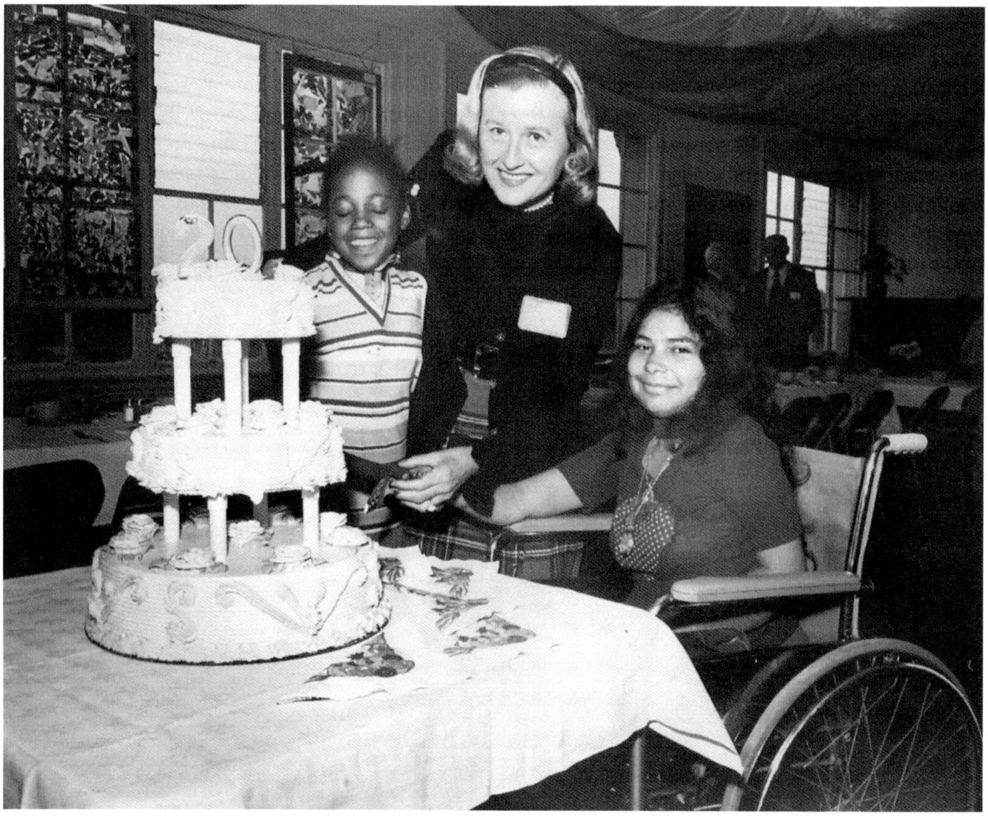

Pioneering Programs for the Disabled

Janet Pomeroy was born Esther Janet Akers in Texas in the 1910s. She had polio as a teenager and spent a year confined to a bed. When she recovered, she had a stiff elbow that affected her arm movement for the rest of her life. Writing in her memoir, *Among the Roses*, published in 1993, she said, "The process of adapting to this disability taught me patience, tolerance, and humility . . . these painful lessons helped prepare me for my future vocation."

Janet moved to the Bay Area in the 1950s and began volunteering in local schools, working with disabled children, many who were called "spastic" and some who could not or would not speak. She learned that no one had ever taught these children games and that many of them had never been to a park. She later wrote, "When I discovered that recreation activities could stimulate learning, improve mental and physical health, and increase self worth and social development, I was thoroughly convinced that recreation for people with disabilities would be my life's work."

On November 18, 1952, Janet opened the Recreation Center for the Handicapped in the Fleishhacker Pool building, just south of the Sunset District. A devout Christian, she always believed that God would make it possible for her to help others, regardless of any obstacles. At the beginning, the center served six people and was open three days a week. By the mid-1960s, the center served 600 people and was open six days a week. Today, the center serves 2,000 people per week.

In 1973, the center moved to its current facility at 207 Skyline Boulevard. At the time, the land was owned by the San Francisco Recreation and Park Department, which leased it to the Recreational Center for the Handicapped for $1 a year. In 2003, the center was renamed the Janet Pomeroy Center (now called Pomeroy Recreation & Rehabilitation Center) in honor of its founder.

Janet worked at and raised money for the center for 40 years, until her retirement. She never accepted any money for her work, insisting that it was part of God's plan for her. She died on November 26, 2005, at the age of 93. (Courtesy the Pomeroy Recreation & Rehabilitation Center.)

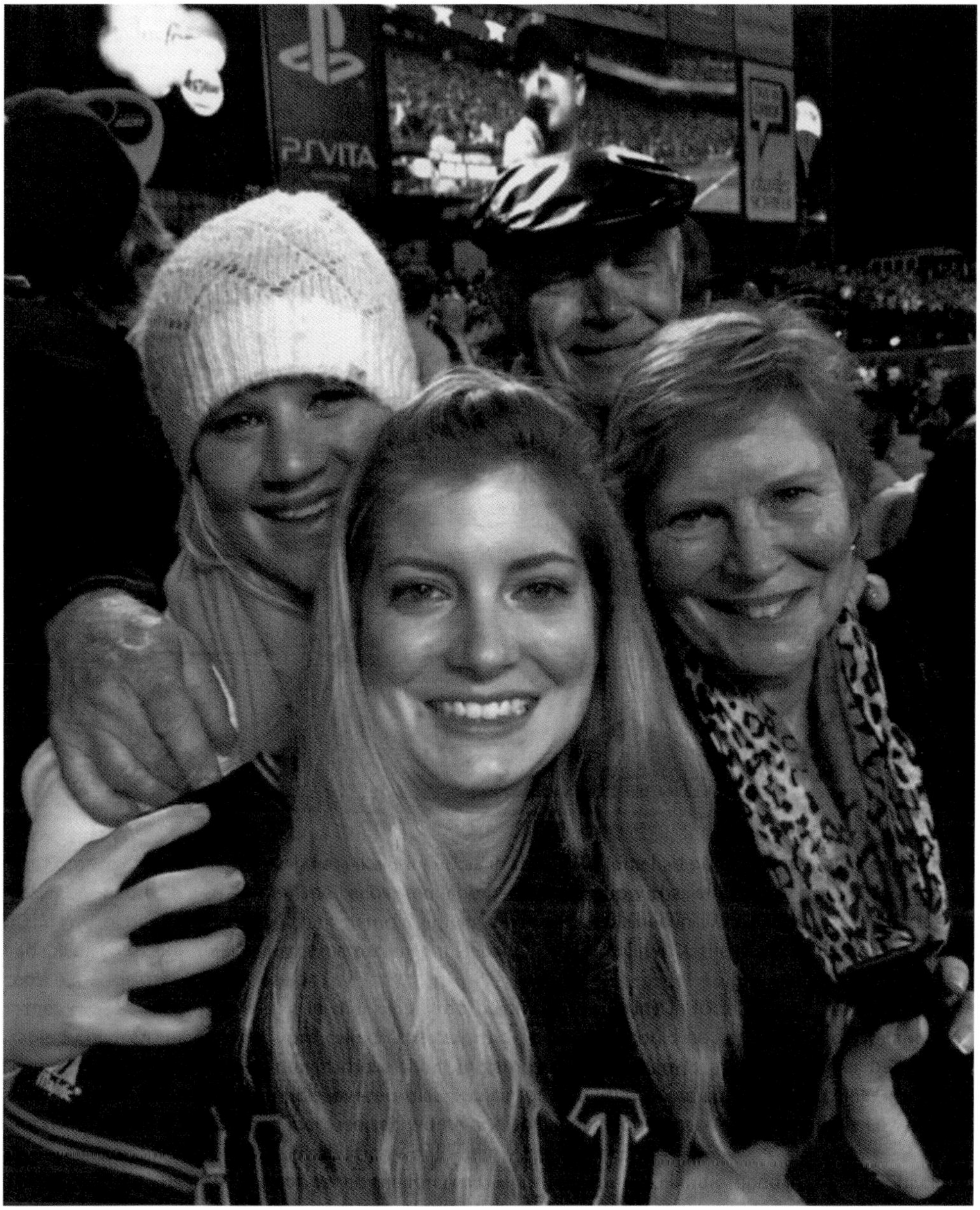

Advocating for Students with Learning Differences
Dewey Rosetti lives in San Francisco's Seacliff area with her husband and two daughters, who both have learning differences and ADHD. In 2003, Dewey founded the Parents Education Network (PEN) on Geary Boulevard. "I had a personal reason for starting PEN," Dewey explains. "My older daughter flunked preschool at age three, and my younger daughter was diagnosed as dyslexic at age six. After shepherding both girls through a school system ill-equipped to develop their talents, I joined other parents with the same experiences to help others with the LD journey." Dewey's older daughter recently earned a PhD in clinical psychology; her younger daughter just graduated from University of California, Berkeley, where she was on the crew team for four years. Dewey has been a member of the PEN board of directors for the past 10 years. (Courtesy the Rosetti family.)

Serving Sunset Youth

Michael Funk cofounded what is now Sunset Youth Services in 1993. "Many of the Outer Sunset youth we served had been in and out of juvenile hall but had great potential and needed support," Michael recollects. Sunset Youth Services enlisted police, faith-based groups, libraries, and schools to help strengthen neighborhood families. When San Francisco established citywide "Beacon Centers" in 1996, Michael and the other cofounders were asked to head up the Sunset Neighborhood Beacon Center, which offered after-school programs, including field trips to museums, mountains, and other places. "Some of these kids had never been to the beach, even though they lived only eight blocks away from it," Michael said. In 2012, state superintendent of public schools Tom Torlakson appointed Michael director of a new after-school division that oversees 4,400 youth programs statewide. Michael now lives in Sacramento. (Courtesy Michael Funk; photograph by Matt Beardsley.)

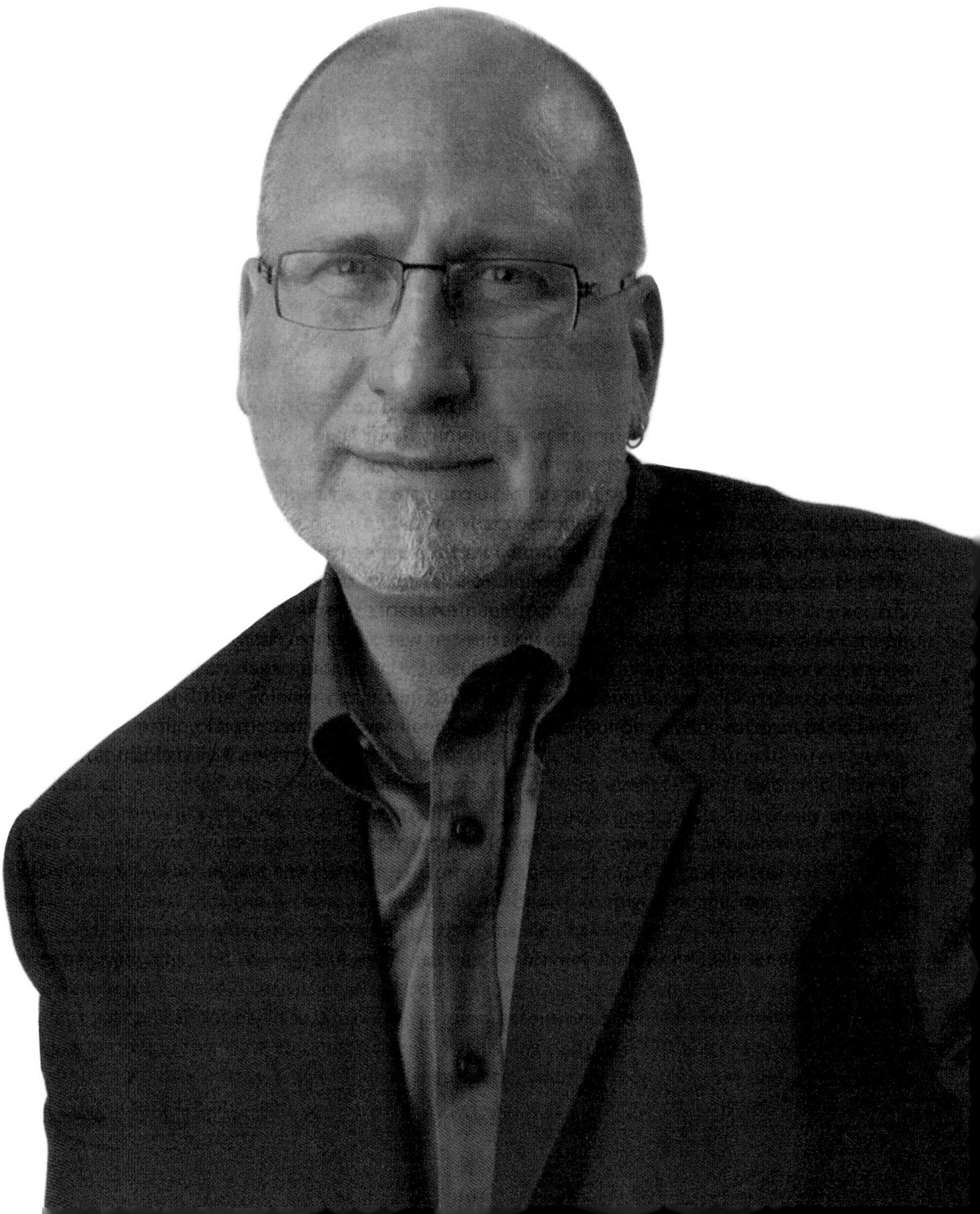

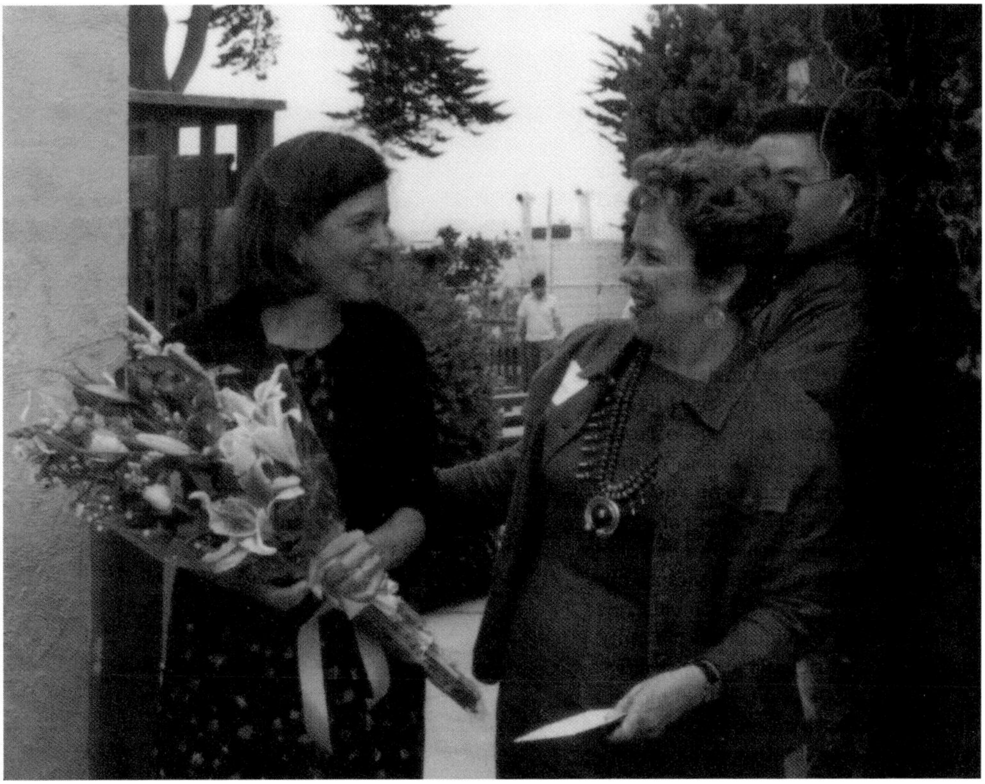

The Richmond District Neighborhood Center

In the 1960s, the Lucinda Weeks School, in the Richmond District, closed. The land on which Lucinda Weeks School stood, at 741 Thirtieth Avenue, is owned by the San Francisco Unified School District, which in 1980 planned to raze the unique, Spanish-style, stucco buildings and replace them with condominiums. Local resident Linda Fries (left) spent more than two years working with neighborhood residents and the City of San Francisco, insisting that the buildings be saved and turned into a multicultural arts and social-service community center. In 1983, the Richmond District Neighborhood Center (RDNC) opened in the old Lucinda Weeks School. Patricia Kaussen (right) joined RDNC in 1990 as executive director, a position she held for 23 years. She saw her mission as "serving 2 to 102-year-olds." RDNC has grown into a thriving community center with programs that serve all ages. Linda remained a major force in the center until 2004; Patricia retired in 2013. Both have been honored for their dedication and hard work. According to the center's website, "The center flourishes with children hard at play at the Cross Cultural Family Center, jazz music piping through the Community Music Center, families seeking an after school program, or teeming with people at our many events. Our mission is to nurture a diverse urban community by developing and providing high quality youth, adult, and family programs that address critical community needs and foster respect for all people and our environment." Sue Lee, one of RDNC's early leaders and the current executive director of the Chinese Historical Society in San Francisco, once said that the Richmond District is filled with immigrants and that, thanks to the RDNC, "our kids know the difference between pirozhki, cha sieu bow, sushi, bagels, and burritos. They know about bar mitzvahs, and red egg and ginger parties." A former Richmond District resident wrote the following on Yelp!: "I have directly benefited from their fantastic after-school program, RDASC, for more than four years. I cannot begin to convey the passion, attention, and creativity employed to sustain this amazing program. In this time of funding cuts and vanishing budgets RDASC continues to provide a superior opportunity for so many. And it doesn't stop there. Their Beacon program runs all the way to high school." (Courtesy Linda Fries.)

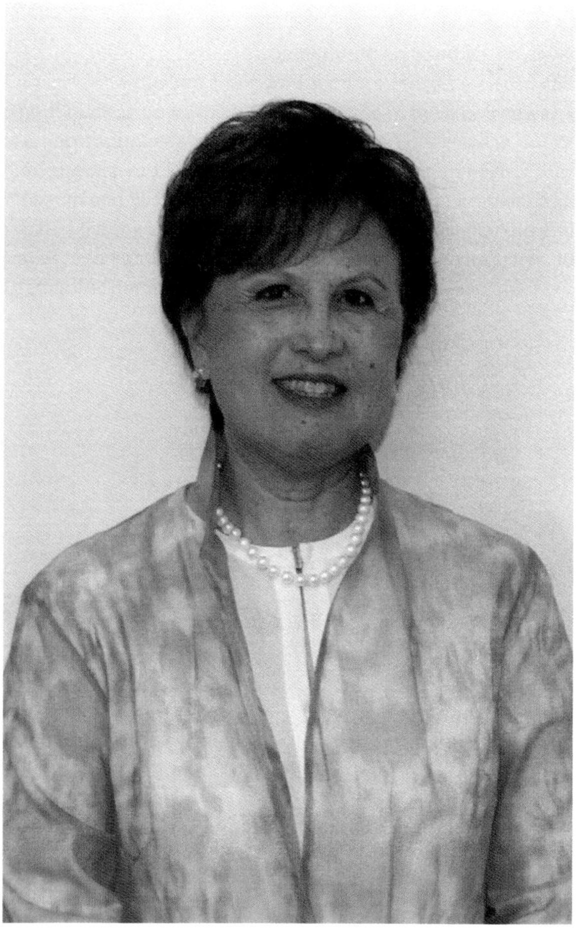

Creating Schools Where Learning Thrives

Gwen Chan's life is a true success story. Born in 1945 and raised in San Francisco's Chinatown by immigrant parents, she attended Commodore Stockton Elementary School, where she was tossed into an "Americanization" class because of poor English skills. At Francisco Junior High School, a teacher screamed at her in class and called her "Stupid." Not deterred, she proved that teacher wrong by becoming the class valedictorian. Gwen attended Lowell High School and San Francisco State College, which named her Alumna of the Year in 2007.

Gwen's first teaching assignment was at Marina Junior High School in 1967, followed by Galileo High School. Later, she was appointed assistant principal of curriculum at George Washington High School in the Richmond.

But it was her tenure as principal at Lincoln High School, starting in 1992, that remains Gwen's most challenging and valued educational leadership experience. Assigned by superintendent Bill Rojas, Gwen was not welcomed by some Lincoln students, teachers, and staff. (She still has the posters demanding her ouster.) With the support of the superintendent and a team of dedicated teachers and staff, over time, Gwen helped transform the struggling school into a California Distinguished School. At Gwen's suggestion, the alumni association gave mini-grants to teachers and college scholarships to students. Lincoln remains a popular high school choice today, with many students on the waiting list.

Gwen was brought up in a nurturing home environment with strong family values, and she carried these beliefs into her career in education. She says, "My mother modeled work ethics and perseverance through hard times, compassion, and taking responsibility for one's actions." Gwen's early educational experiences also made her determined to promote a nurturing school culture where students feel safe and excited to learn. "I was dedicated to seeking a high quality of teaching for all students, providing structure, direction, and opportunities for students to become self-confident individuals who rely on both scholarly achievements and character development through community leadership and service."

Gwen received various awards through the years, including the California School Master of the Year (1996). After 40 years of distinguished service, she retired in 2007, as the first Asian American superintendent of the San Francisco School District. "Each stage in my career prepared me for the next stage," Gwen says. "I'm grateful to the school district for all the opportunities I've had—even the most challenging and difficult ones—and to all the people who were part of my educational journey." (Courtesy Gwen Chan.)

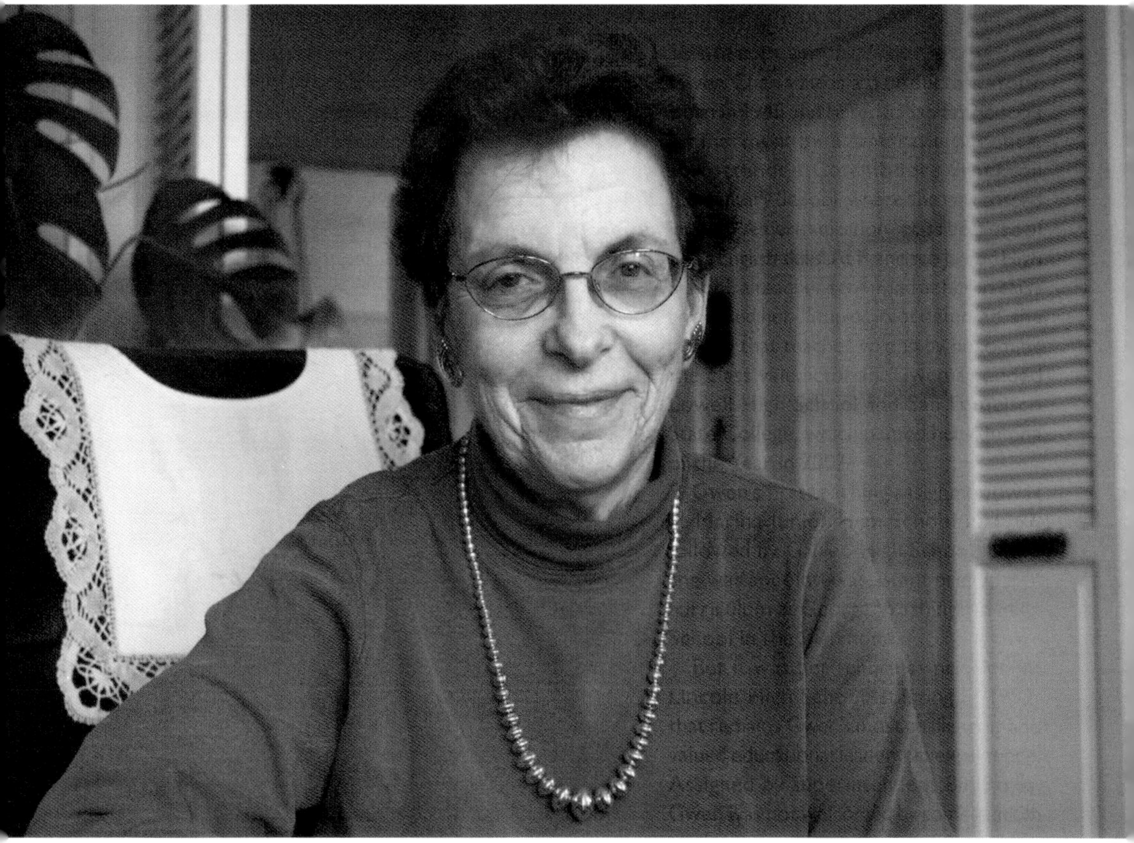

Golden Gate National Recreation Area
Amy Meyer has lived in the Richmond District for more than 50 years. She is a conservationist known for her advocacy to create the Golden Gate National Recreation Area (GGNRA). The park includes 80,000 acres from northern Marin County to the middle of San Mateo County and is one of the world's largest national parks in an urban area. Amy's book *New Guardians for the Golden Gate* describes how, between 1970 and 1996, she helped organize local residents to advocate for GGNRA legislation. Amy has served on the boards of the Presidio Trust, the Sierra Club Bay Chapter, and the San Francisco Planning and Urban Research Association (SPUR). She has also been on the San Francisco Recreation and Park Commission and the Golden Gate-Point Reyes Advisory Commission. For the past 11 years, she has convened a group of park advocates who continue the work of protecting national parklands at the Golden Gate. (Courtesy Amy Meyer.)

An Activist Writer

Harold Gilliam, a highly respected writer, used to be an environmental columnist at the *San Francisco Chronicle* and the *San Francisco Examiner*. He has written about the San Francisco Bay, national and state parks, nuclear power, the "obsolescence of the city freeway," and much more. Harold's 13 books describe the natural beauty of San Francisco and other areas. In 1999, the Bay Institute named an award after him: the Harold Gilliam Award for Excellence in Environmental Reporting. In 2011, the San Francisco Museum and Historical Society gave Harold the Francisco Palou Award for Extraordinary Contributions to the History of San Francisco. Now in his 90s, Harold Gilliam still writes on environmental and social issues. He has lived in the Inner Sunset since the early 1990s. (Courtesy Phil Gangi; photograph by Patrick Mckinnie.)

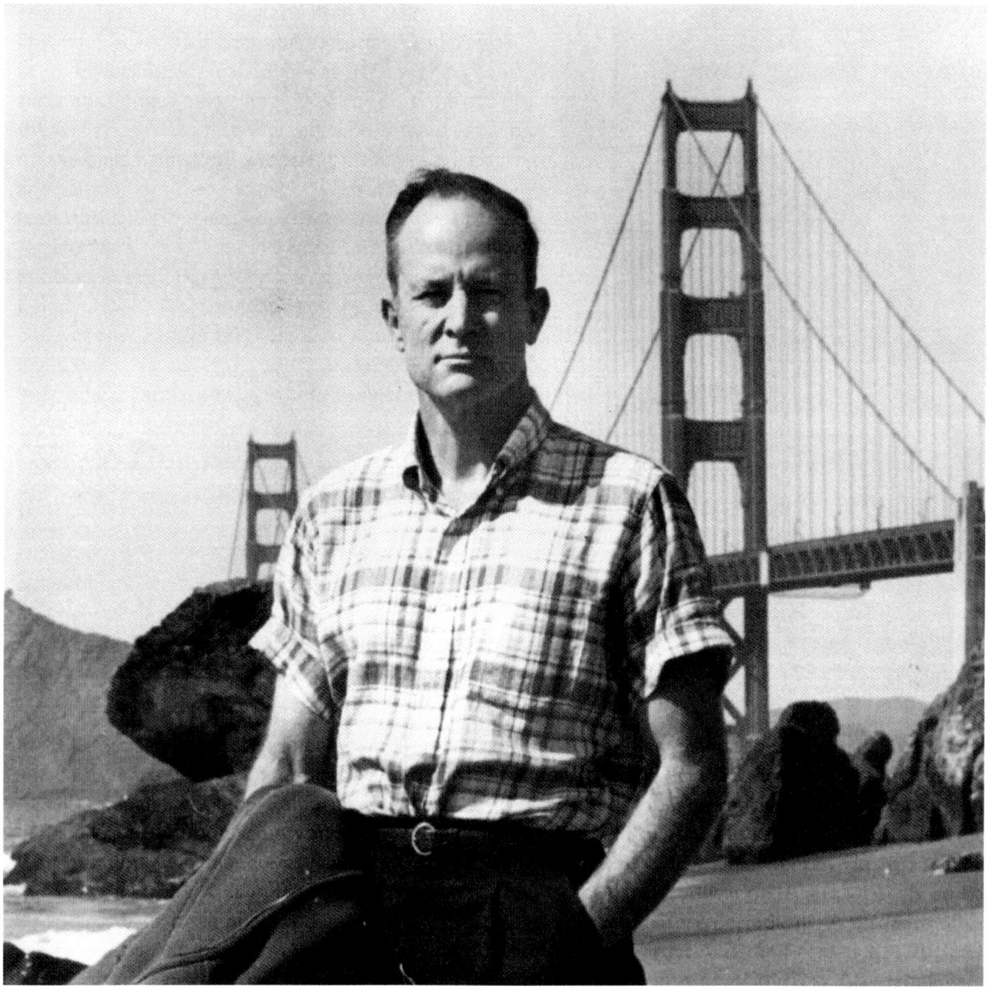

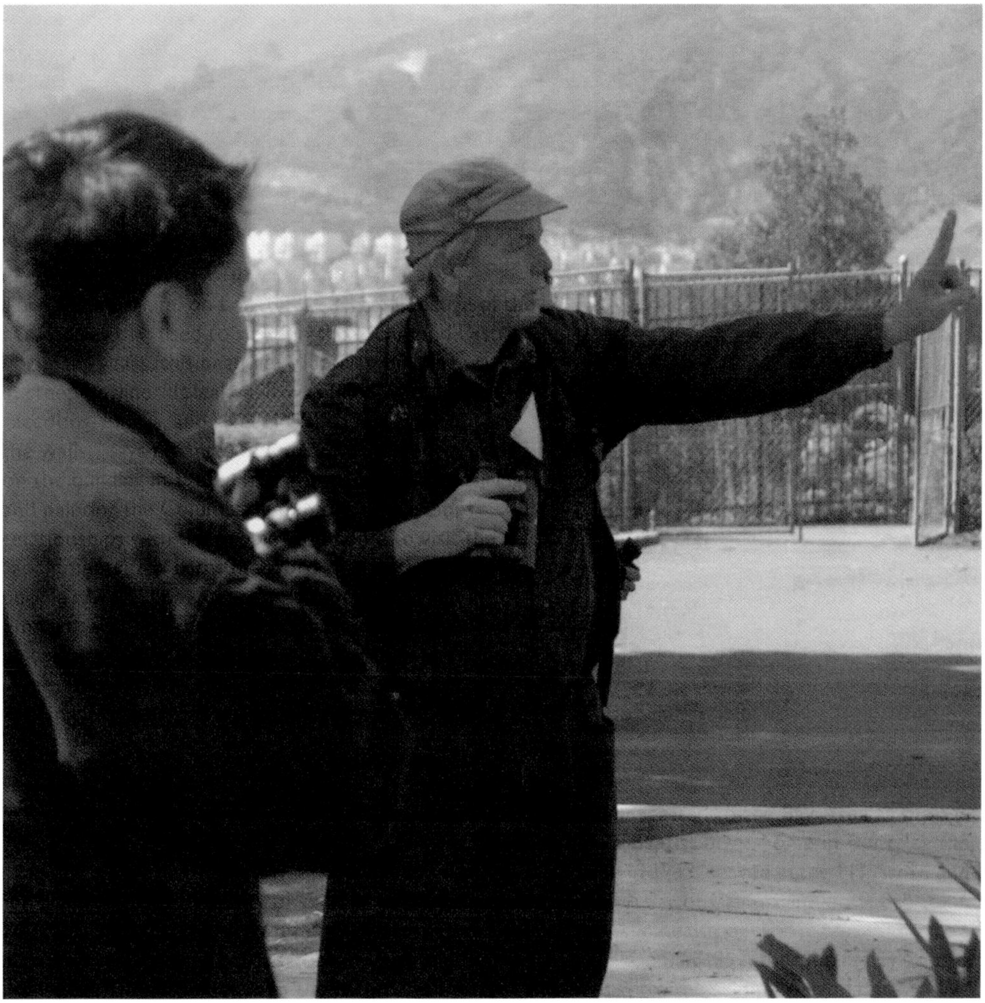

Nature and Bird Advocate

In 1978, Sunset District resident Alan Hopkins cofounded the San Francisco Christmas Bird Count, whose data are used by naturalists and biologists around the world. In 1998, he founded the "Save the Quail" campaign to keep California quail alive on the west side of San Francisco. He works with the Golden Gate Audubon Society and was president from 1998 to 2000. Alan has received the Elsie Roemer Conservation Award and was named a Community Hero by the Crissy Field Center. He also teaches for San Francisco's Kids In Parks program and San Francisco Nature Education. Alan's writings on Bay Area birds have been published in many bird-watching books and nature periodicals. A graduate of the San Francisco Art Institute, Alan was the San Francisco Shipyard Trust Artist in Residence in 2010. He is now creating new art informed by his work with birds and conservation. (Courtesy Alan Hopkins.)

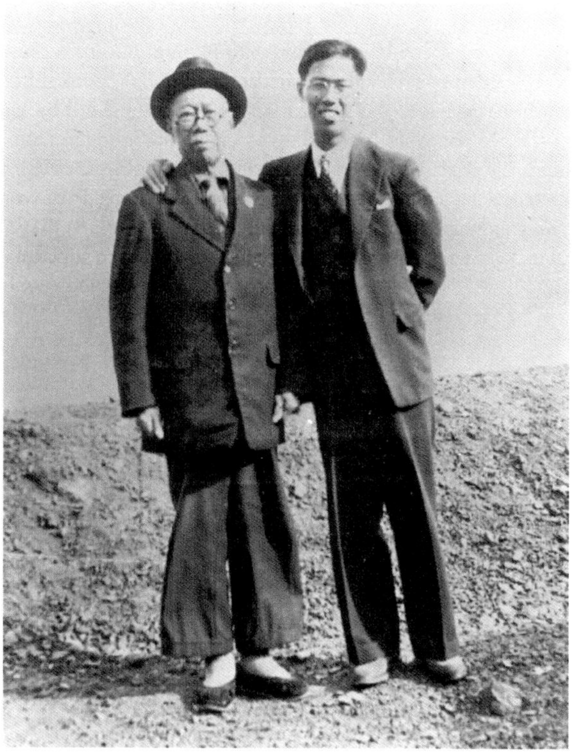

Helping the Elderly

Dr. William Gee was born in 1914 near Guangzhou, China, and immigrated to the Bay Area at the age of six. His father traveled often, so Gee grew up in Chung Mei, a Baptist boys' home in Berkeley (he never saw his mother after leaving China). He became a US citizen in 1943, served in the US Army, and then attended the University of California, Berkeley, and the University of California Dental School in San Francisco. Dr. Gee, shown here with his father, became a public health dentist in San Francisco's Chinatown. He married Marian Tong in 1936, and they had four children. In 1954, the Gee family bought a house on Fifteenth Avenue in the Richmond District; the Gees were the second Asian family to live on the block.

As a public health dentist, Dr. Gee became aware of the lack of services for the Chinatown community's elderly people. In 1971, along with Harding Leong, Marie-Louise Ansak, and Maylian Lee, he started the organization On Lok. The four founders were so dedicated to this cause that they put their homes up as collateral to help start it. (Happily, the collateral was not needed.) Gee used many connections he had to help get funding from various sources, including Congress and the Department of Health, Education, and Welfare. On Lok was the first organization in the United States to provide adult day health care and ensure long-term health care for the frail elderly. The organization served as a prototype for senior programs nationwide; instead of being forced to live in nursing homes, participants were able to stay with their families in their own communities.

Dr. Gee died in January 1993, while planning for a second center. Today, On Lok is one of the largest organizations serving seniors in the San Francisco Bay Area, providing health plans, senior centers, meals, housing, and more. The Dr. William L. Gee House opened in 1994 at 1333 Bush Street, with 42 units specially designed for the elderly.

Dr. Gee volunteered his services to many organizations, including On Lok, North East Medical Services (NEMS), the San Francisco Dental Society, the United Way, the San Francisco Cancer Society, and the American Red Cross. "I can ask for anything," he used to say, "because it's not for me." (Courtesy the Gee family.)

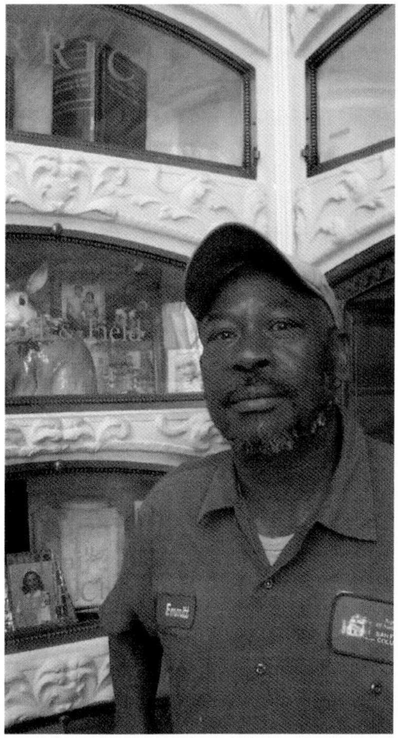

Overseeing the Columbarium

The Columbarium, on Loraine Court, is a vestige of the cemeteries that used to stand in the Richmond District. For many years, this beautiful Victorian building was in steep decline. "It leaked. It was filled with pigeons, raccoons, fungus, and slime. Mushrooms grew out of the walls," says Emmitt Watson, who started working on the building in 1988. He spent many years repairing and painting the Columbarium. Now, he develops relationships with the people who come to visit the "apartments" (he hates the word "niches") that show people's lives. "I pay attention to everyone I run into," Emmitt says. "Words mean nothing; it's what you do." He believes that part of this role is to watch over people's loved ones. He also gives tours of the Columbarium, keeping its history alive. (Author's photographs.)

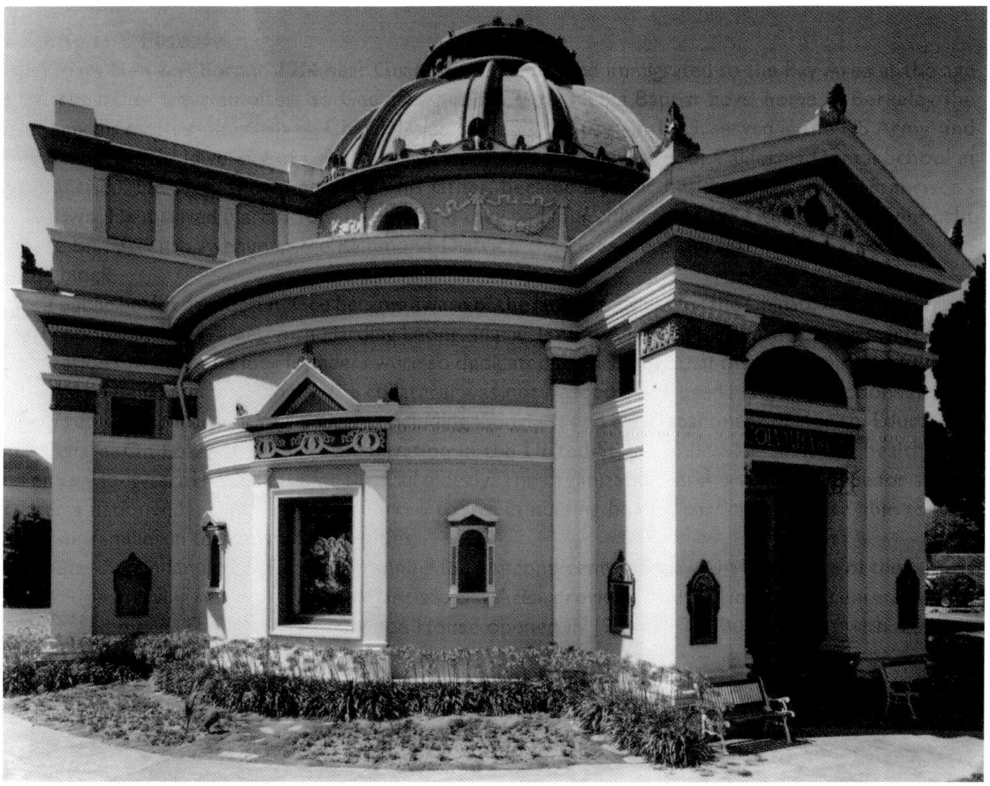

The Jewel of the Sunset

Rosalie Stern never lived in the Outside Lands, but her generosity gave the Sunset one of its most glorious and valued destinations. When her husband, Sigmund, died in 1931, Rosalie bought 12 heavily wooded acres and donated the land to San Francisco as a park for recreation, "music, dramatics, and pageantry." The city later bought adjoining acreage. Bernard Maybeck oversaw the restoration of the Trocadero Inn, built in 1872. Developers had hoped to cover this area with housing. Instead, the west side of San Francisco now has Sigmund Stern Grove, a 60-acre public park that has hosted free summer music concerts since 1938. (Below, courtesy the San Francisco Performing Arts Library, Museum of Performance and Design; facing page above, courtesy San Francisco History Center, San Francisco Public Library; facing page below, courtesy private collection.)

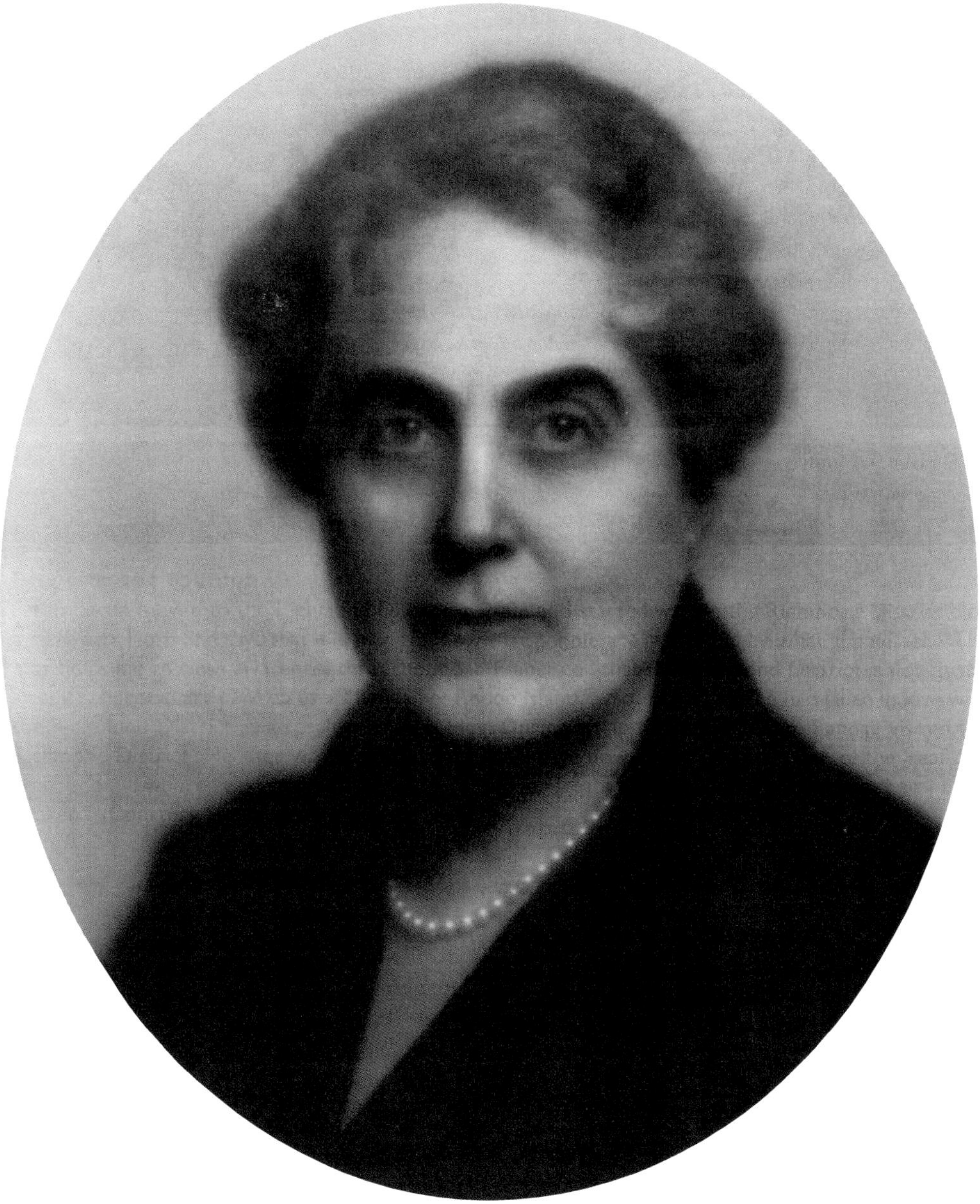

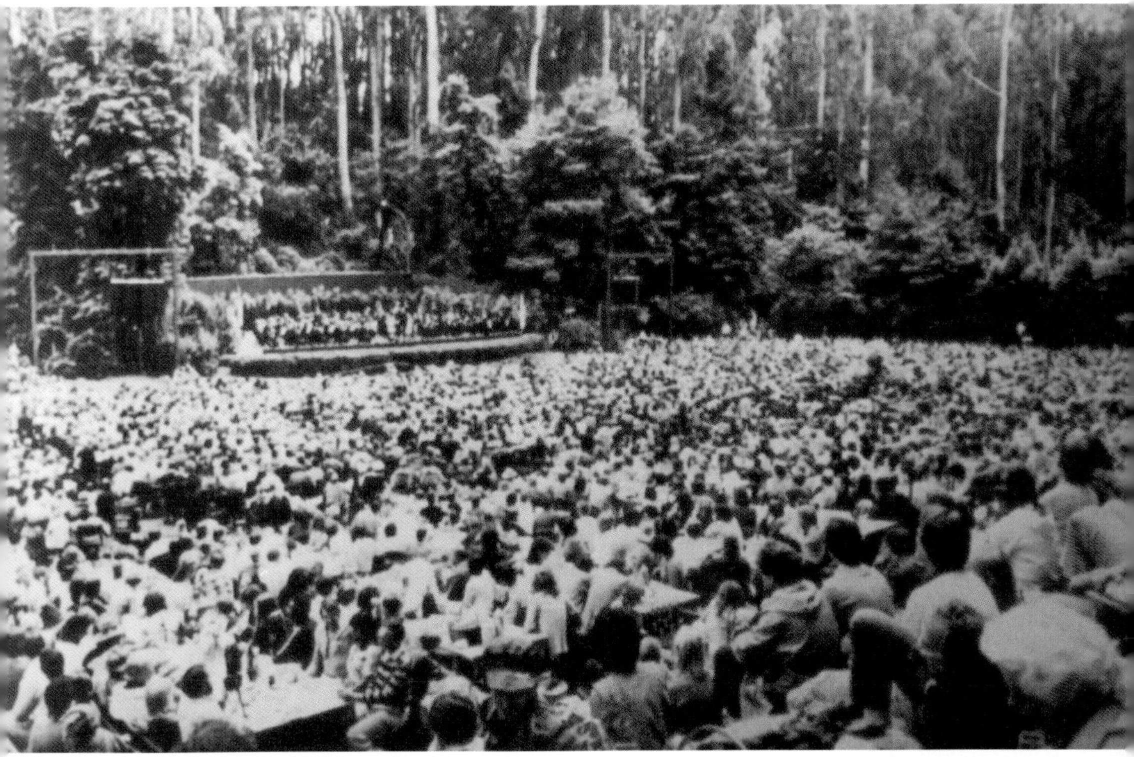

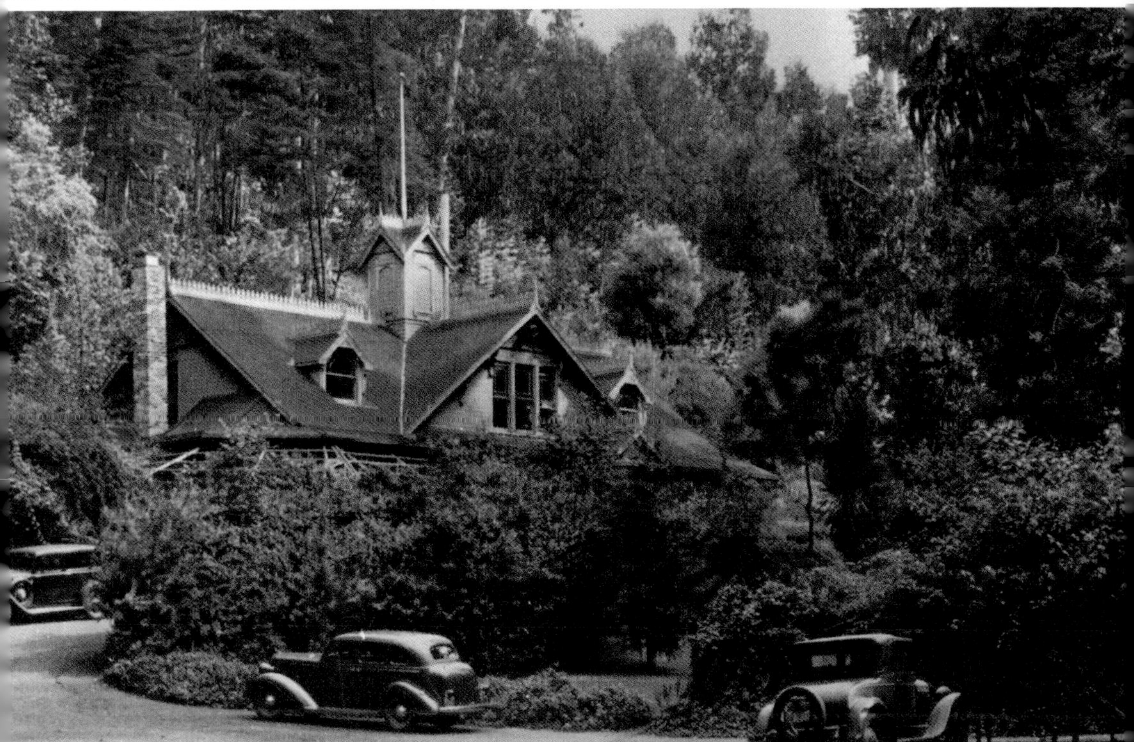

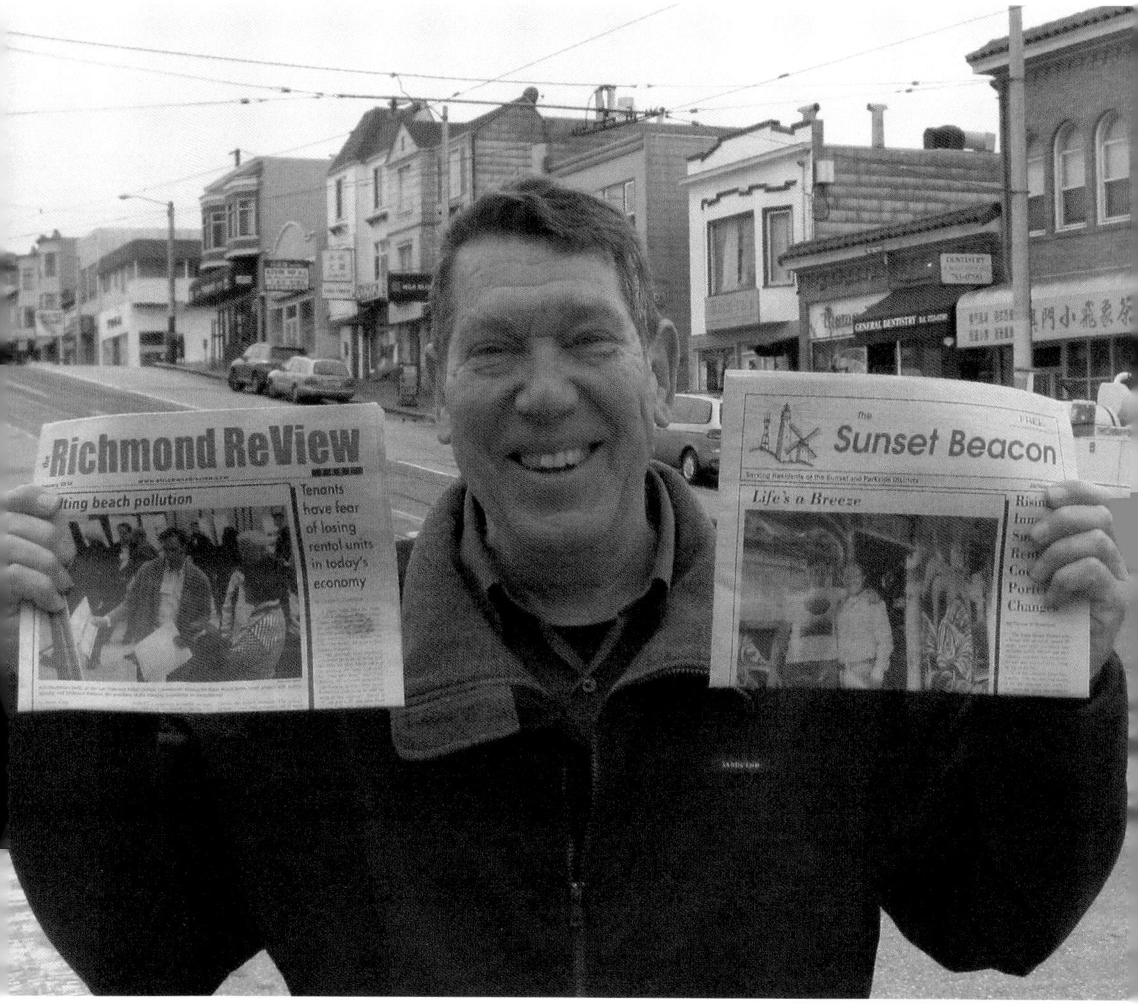

Publications that Serve the Community
"Community service. That's what it's all about," says Paul Kozakiewicz. He moved to San Francisco in 1981, and to the Richmond District in 1988, when he started publishing the *Richmond Review* to serve the diverse communities in the neighborhood. In 1991, Paul cofounded the *Sunset Beacon* to serve the needs of Sunset District residents. Both monthly publications have provided local news and information, published profiles of local residents doing good works, and provided low-cost advertising to help the local business community. Paul believes that with cutbacks in the editorial departments of large newspapers across the country, smaller community newspapers fill an important need. He adds, "I welcome the challenge of doing my part, keeping an eye on the politicians and bureaucrats managing our government, and telling my neighbors about the good things going on in our community." (Author's photograph.)

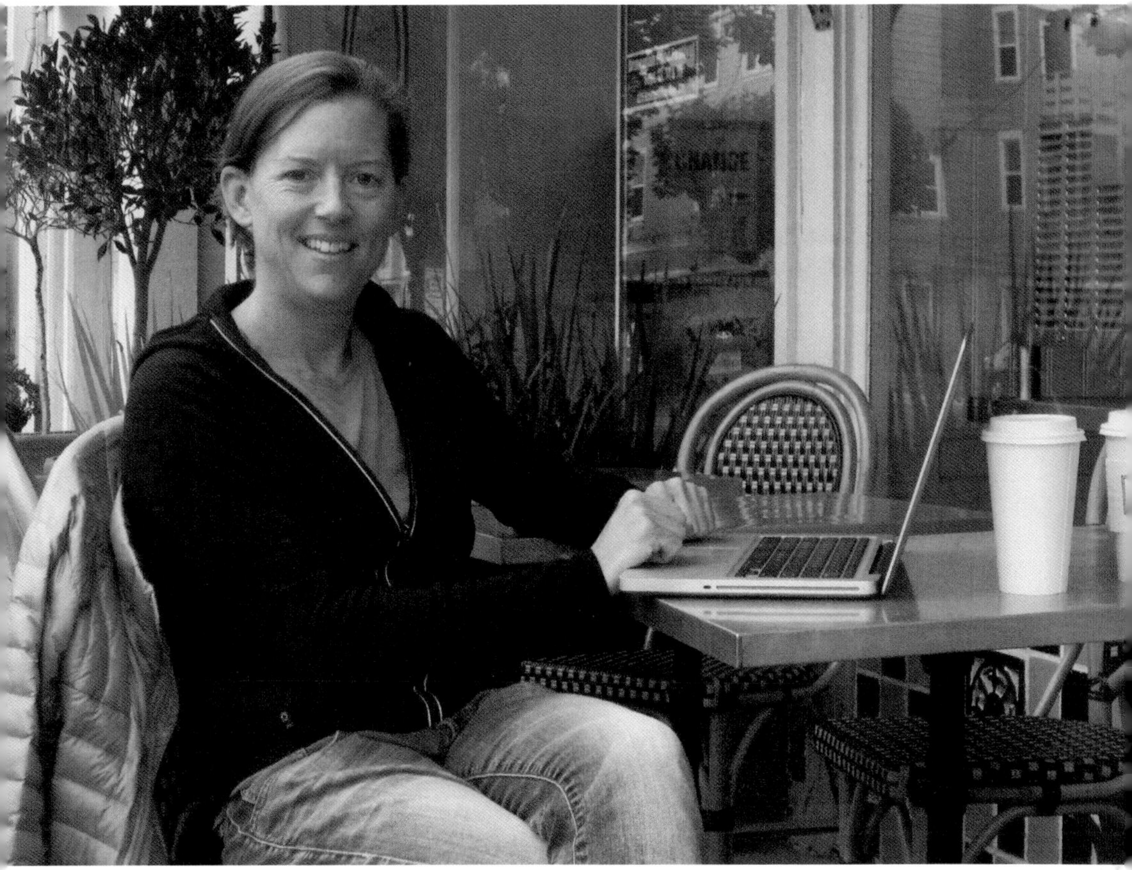

Blogging the Richmond

Sarah Bacon moved to the Richmond District in 2006 and started writing the Richmond District blog a few years later. She says that it is nice to know that people are influenced by what she writes. "The blog helps me to raise awareness throughout San Francisco" that the Richmond District is not "just a sleepy residential area." Web user "Randall of Rhode Island" wrote once that he had fallen in love with the Richmond District as a result of Sarah's blog. During a trip to San Francisco, Randall visited the Richmond District. He later wrote, "I truly feel that I have now seen a small portion of the 'real' San Francisco . . . where real San Franciscans live, toil, love, dream, fight, fall in love, and have their hearts broken." (Courtesy Sarah Bacon.)

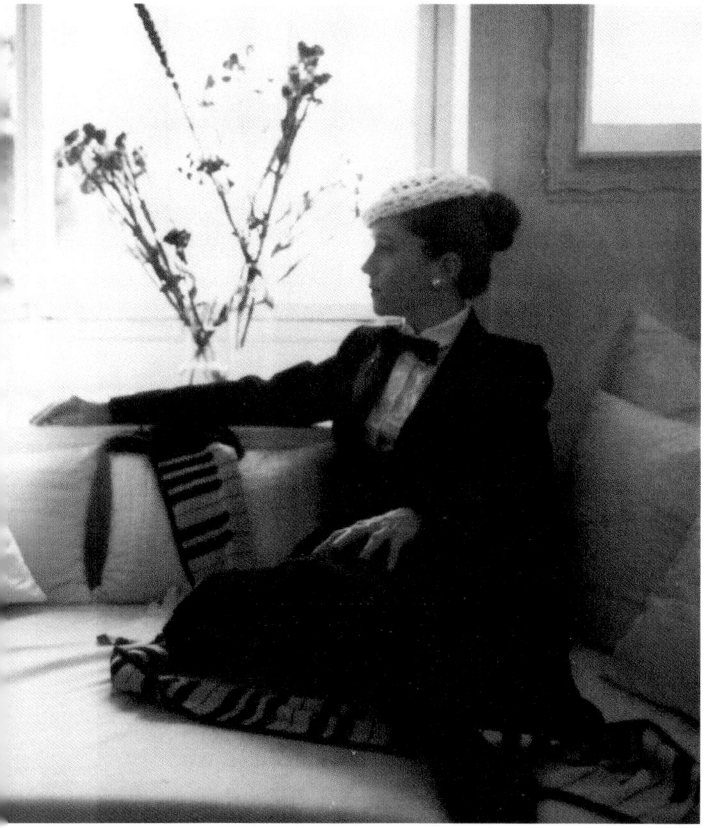

San Francisco's Shack Lady
In 1982, Jane Cryan leased a ramshackle cottage on Twenty-fourth Avenue in the Sunset District, and she soon discovered the property was an amalgamation of four tiny cabins, rare survivors of 5,610 refugee shacks constructed in 1906 to house survivors of the earthquake and fire. By 1983, Jane had restored the property, amassed the first research on the subject since 1915, and founded the Society for the Preservation and Appreciation of San Francisco's 1906 Earthquake Refugee Shacks, which she directed until 2000. In 1984, she won over the San Francisco Planning Department, who declared the cottage San Francisco Landmark No. 171. (Left, courtesy Jane Cryan; below, author's photograph.)

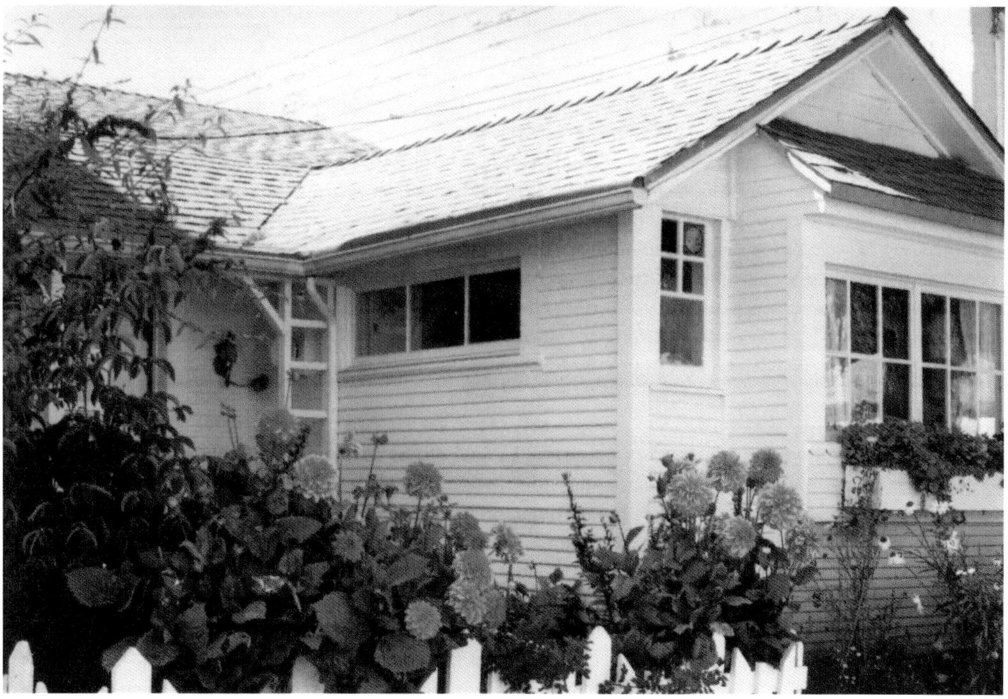

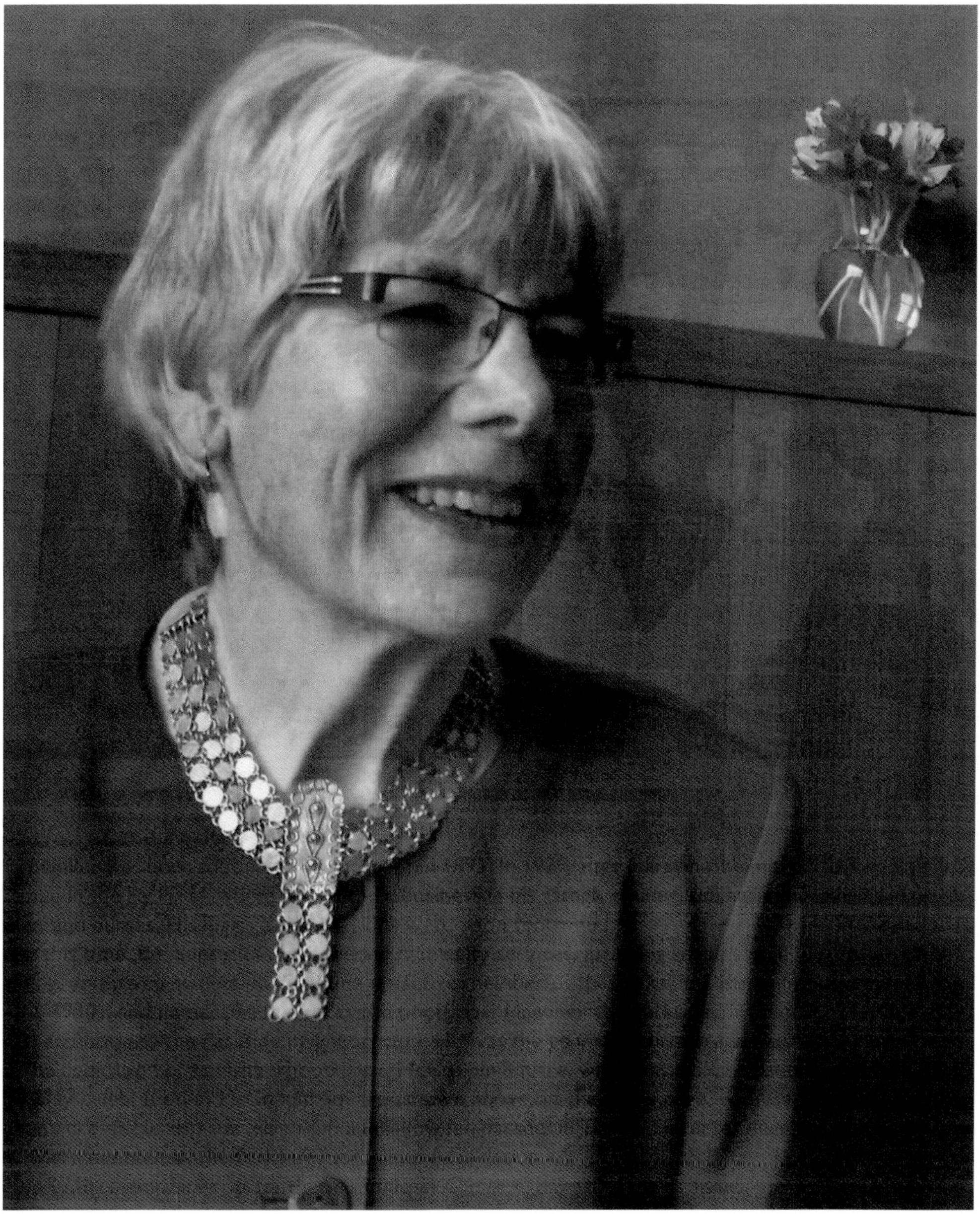

Planning Professional to Community Activist
German-born Inge Horton immigrated to the United States in 1969, settling in Montana and California. Since 1972, she has lived with her family in a modest home near the beach in the Sunset District. After working as a city planner from 1980 to 1998, she focused on improving the quality of life in the Sunset. In 2004, the Sunset Parkside Education and Action Committee (SPEAK) established a subcommittee under her leadership with the goal of furthering the city's appreciation of the historic resources in the Sunset. For these efforts, which are documented in a series of reports, and for her book *Early Women Architects of the San Francisco Bay Area* (2010), Inge was awarded the Unsung Hero Award by San Francisco Tomorrow. Now retired from the planning department, Inge keeps abreast of preservation issues and enjoys her daily walks on Ocean Beach. (Courtesy Inge Horton.)

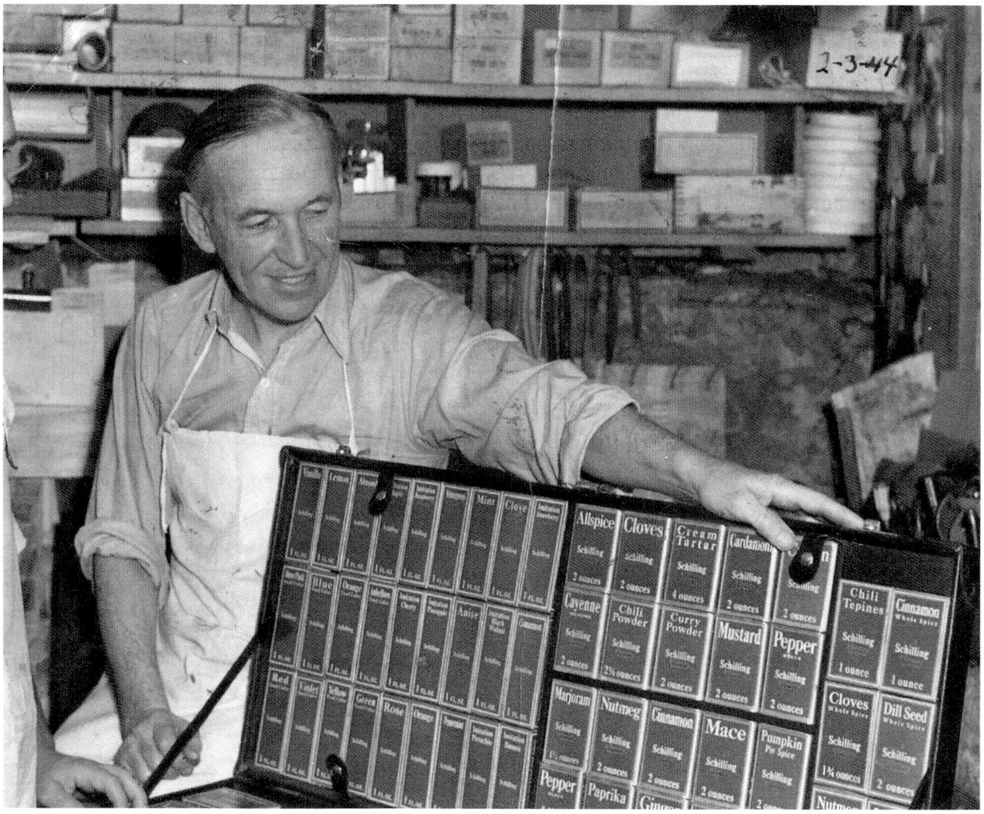

"Mayor of the Parkside"

Ray Schiller was born south of Market Street in 1895. In 1929, after marrying, he moved to Twenty-fifth Avenue in the Parkside, where he started a business in his garage, making, selling, and repairing luggage, cases, and purses. His luggage-making skills were soon renowned.

At this time, the Sunset District needed many city services, including schools, public transportation, lighting, and paved streets. Ray became an active member of the Parkside District Improvement Club in the 1930s, and he became known as the unofficial "Mayor of the Parkside." Whenever possible, Ray drew attention to the Parkside neighborhood. He was the general chairman and master of ceremonies for the dedication of a neighborhood park, McCoppin Square, where, in 1939, he established the annual May Day celebration in McCoppin Square (shown above on the facing page, with Ray holding the May queen's dress). He also started an annual Halloween parade on Taraval Street for neighborhood children and was a member of the Parkside Merchants Association.

In a 1940 column he wrote for the *San Francisco Chronicle*, Ray called the Parkside "the district that knows how." He wrote, "That's Parkside, the fastest growing part of town. Those hardy pioneers who came from the downtown section just after the turn of the century started the growth. Today Parkside is in the second largest voting district of San Francisco and boasts leaders in every phase of civic activity."

One reporter wrote that Ray "is not a conniver, not a string puller nor a cheap politician. He expresses the honest wants of his community and the powers that be listen to him." Ray always seemed to be smiling—and whistling. He could silence a crowd with his distinctive whistles, which sounded like fire engine and police sirens.

Ray was attending a New Year's Eve party when he collapsed shortly after midnight, just as 1949 was beginning. A heart attack had taken his life. He was 53 years old. Obituaries ran in publications throughout the city. One said, "We have lost a fine pal, true friend, and loyal worker and will long miss Ray's genial personality." (Courtesy the Schiller family.)

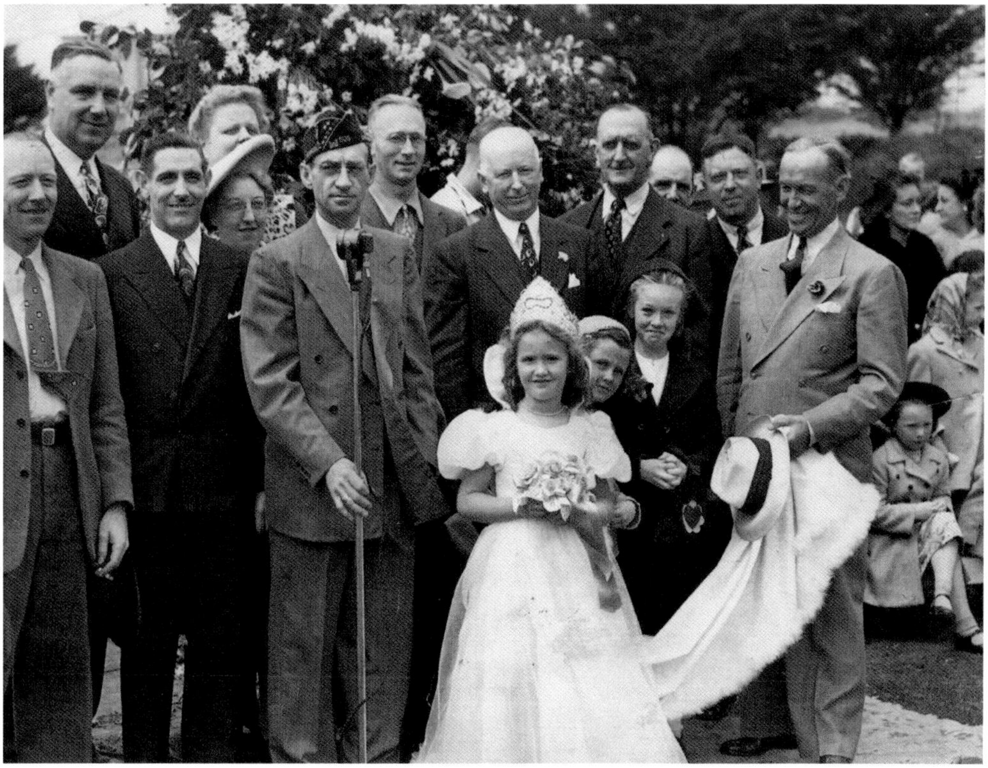

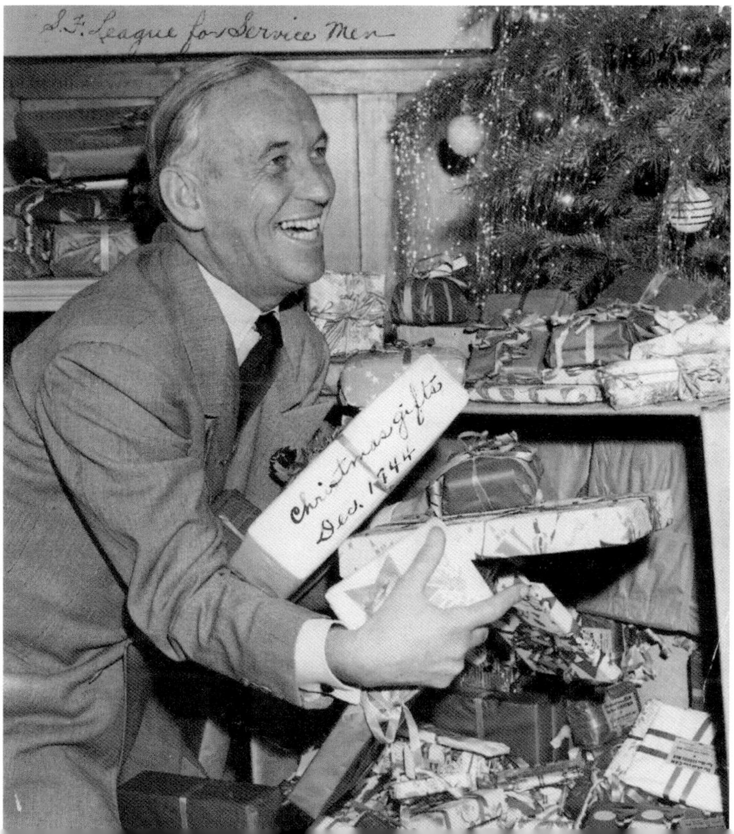
S.F. League for Service Men
Christmas gifts
Dec. 1944

Advocating for Her Neighborhood

Susan Suval began her community volunteering at Sunset Cooperative Preschool and continued volunteering in the schools her three children attended in the Sunset. She worked in various school programs and classrooms, but it was while serving on the PTA boards at each school and at the district level that the advocacy bug took hold. She began volunteering with Sunset Youth Services, the Sunset Neighborhood Beacon Center, the Sunset District Neighborhood Coalition, and other groups responsive to the needs of the community, especially to children. In 1994, she helped found the Sunset Community Festival. Why does she do this work for the Sunset District? "I like to give back to the community," she smiles. (Author's photograph.)

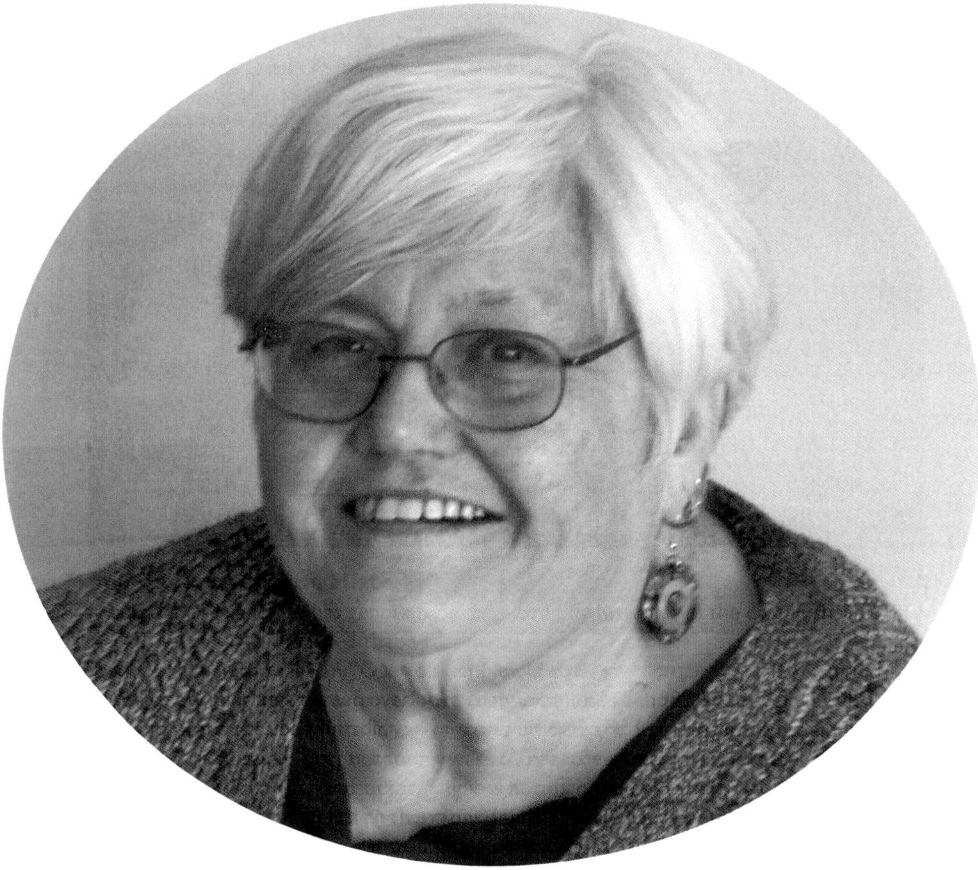

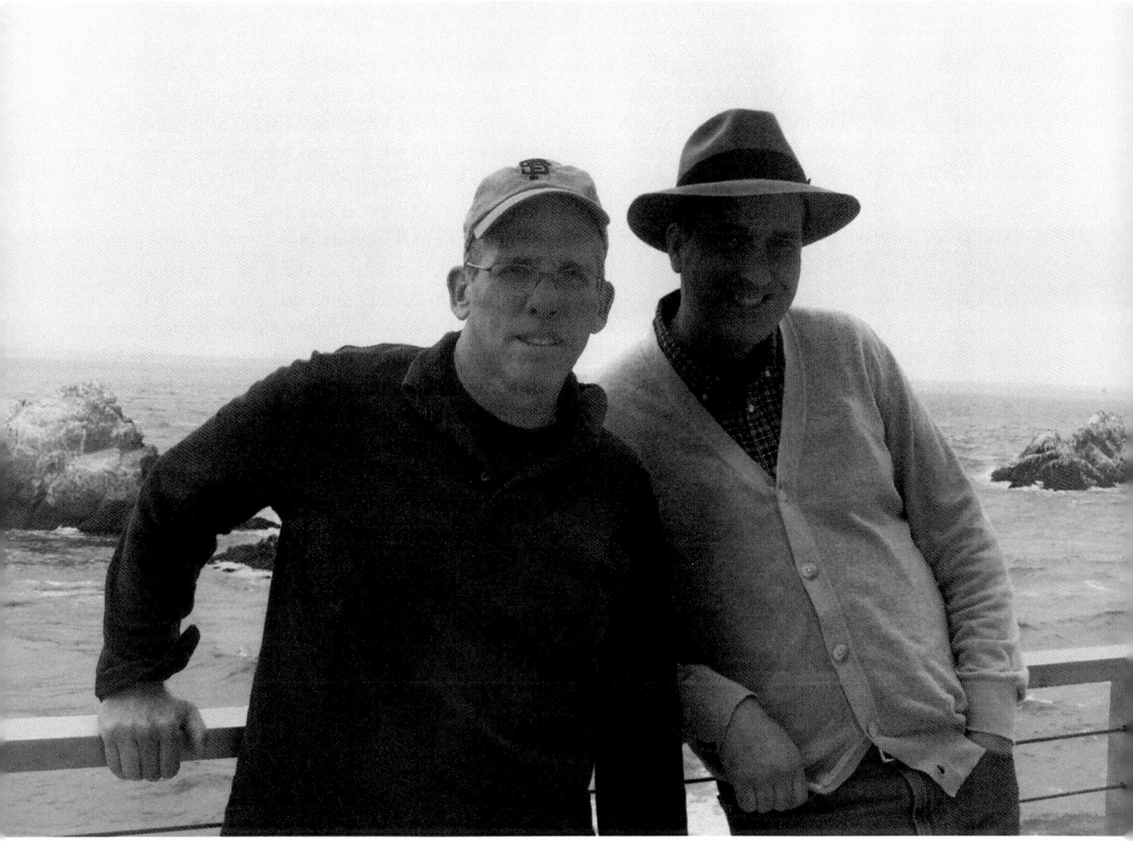

San Francisco's West Side History
The west side of San Francisco has generally been ignored by histories of the city. In the 1990s, Stephen "Woody" LaBounty (right) believed that a Richmond District historical society should be created. His friend David Gallagher thought an "Overlooked Neighborhood Historical Society" should be formed, embracing and celebrating other great, overlooked neighborhoods. In 1999, Woody and David compromised and split the city in two, taking jurisdiction of the west side and forming the Western Neighborhoods Project (WNP). This nonprofit organization works to preserve and share the history and culture of the Richmond and Sunset Districts and other neighborhoods on the west side of the city. WNP records people's memories, copies historical photographs, leads walking tours, and unearths interesting stories. The WNP website, at www.outsidelands.org, features images, historical articles, and message boards related to these neighborhoods. (Author's photograph.)

Richmond Restaurant Owners' Vision
Lara and Gar Truppelli revitalized the historic Willis Polk building, where Golden Gate Park meets Ocean Beach, when they opened the Beach Chalet (below) in 1996. They expanded with the Park Chalet in 2004. "We are passionate about offering thriving eateries that celebrate Bay Area treasured landmarks," says Gar. They expanded their vision again in 2009, opening the Lake Chalet in Oakland. Lara and Gar also work with the Ocean Beach Master Plan, a 17-year effort to ensure the future of the beach. "It's been an incredible experience to translate our community commitment into significant achievements for Ocean Beach's future," says Lara. Along with service on several industry boards, Lara is an advisory board member of International Rivers and the Namaste Foundation, founder of Sustainable Alliance of Nature & Design at Ocean Beach (SAND@OB), and chair of the Community Advisory and Steering Committee for the Ocean Beach Master Plan. (Courtesy Lara and Gar Truppelli.)

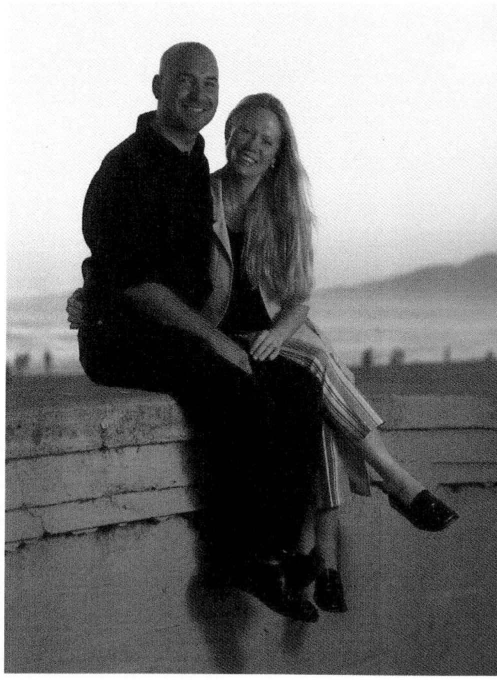

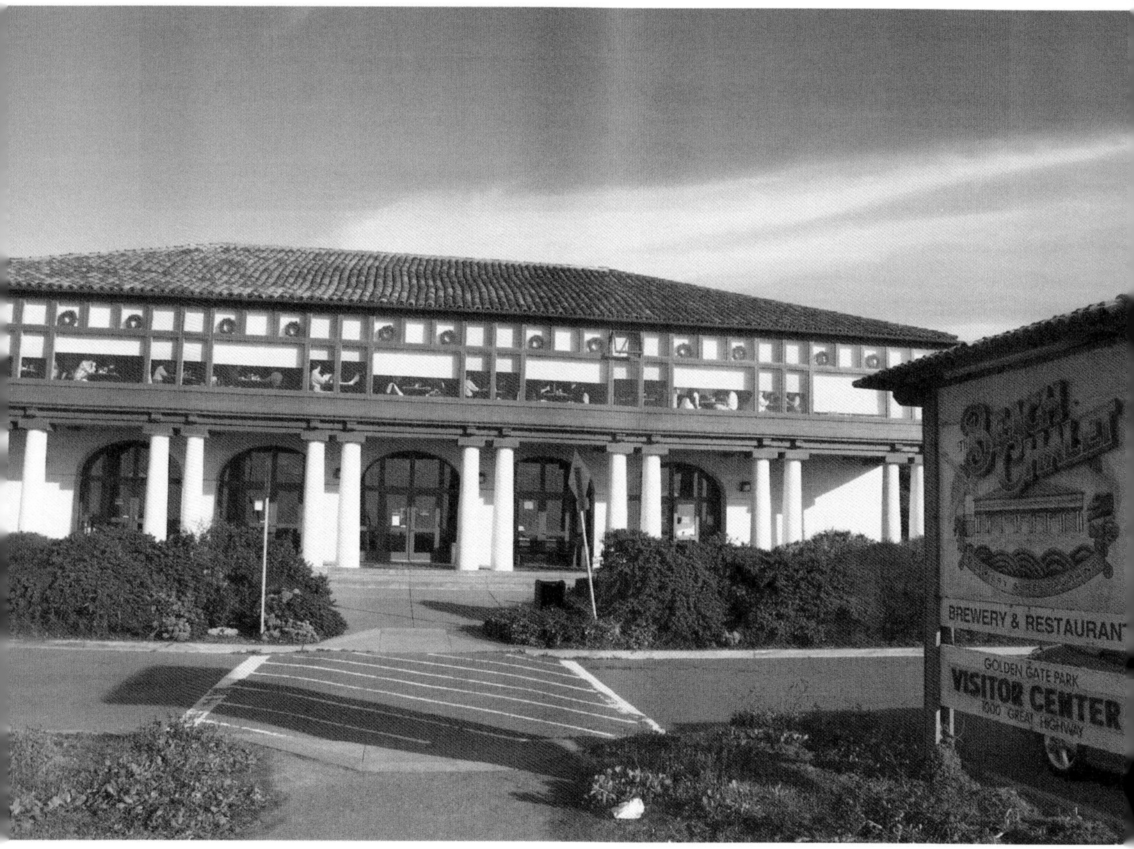

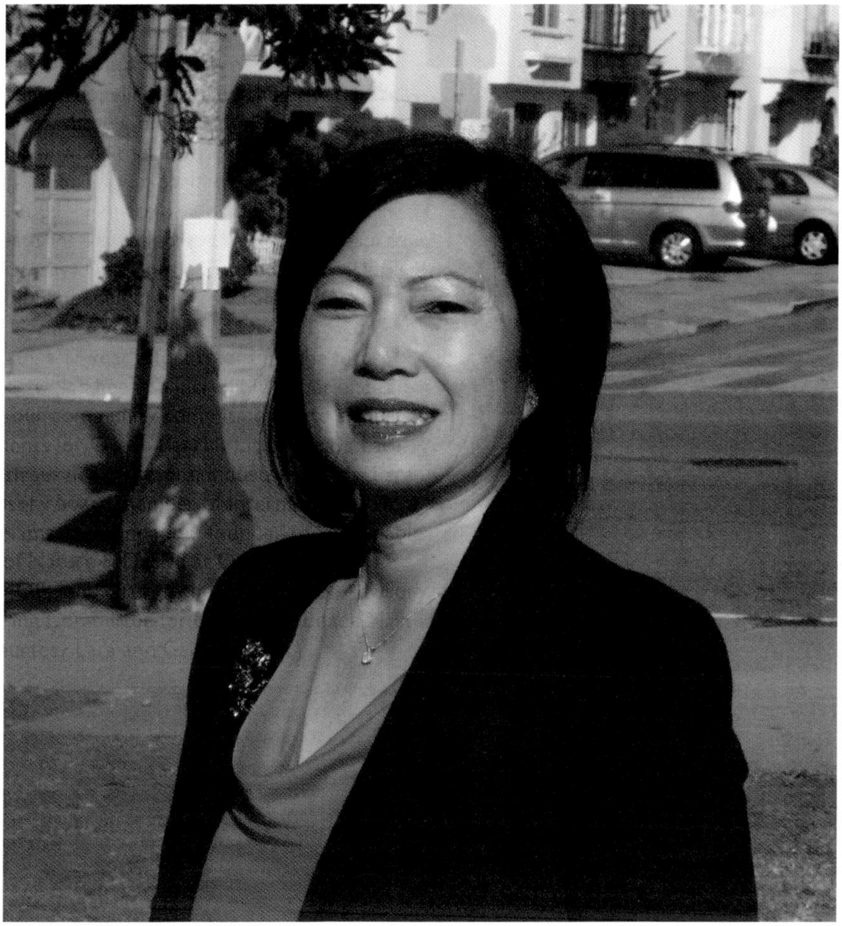

Versatile Educator
Judy Huey is best known for her work at A.P. Giannini Middle School, in the Sunset District. "This is a very challenging age group, where in one second students are crying and the next acting like they know everything," Judy says. "My philosophy was to treat the students with respect and give them the opportunity to learn from their mistakes." Judy was tough, had a no-nonsense attitude, and treated students fairly. To address the needs of the many different students at Giannini, Judy started groups for girls and for boys, as well as groups for students who had a hard time socializing, including Dim Sum for Chinese girls and the Pho Girls for girls whose families had escaped the Vietnam War. Discussions with new students helped them make the transition from elementary school to middle school. Judy took rival gangs on ropes courses and started kickball games and basketball tournaments. After-school cooking classes taught students how to make easy, healthful dishes. Judy and a colleague offered to the African American girls the social event of each week, "Afternoon Tea at the Dean's Office." The girls came dressed up, drank tea from a silver service, and had cookies or tea sandwiches.

After 17 years at A.P. Giannini Middle School, Judy retired in 2008. "I loved my job," she says. "It was hard, demanding and thankless — one that could only be done if you really had the passion to work with young people. Many of the students that I worked with at A.P. Giannini, who have since graduated from college and are working, have come up to me and given me a hug and said 'Thanks!' All the hard work, the sacrifice of personal time, and the effort must have paid off. I miss the students, and I'm glad I was there in their time of need, when growing up as an adolescent was very trying and scary!" (Author's photograph.)

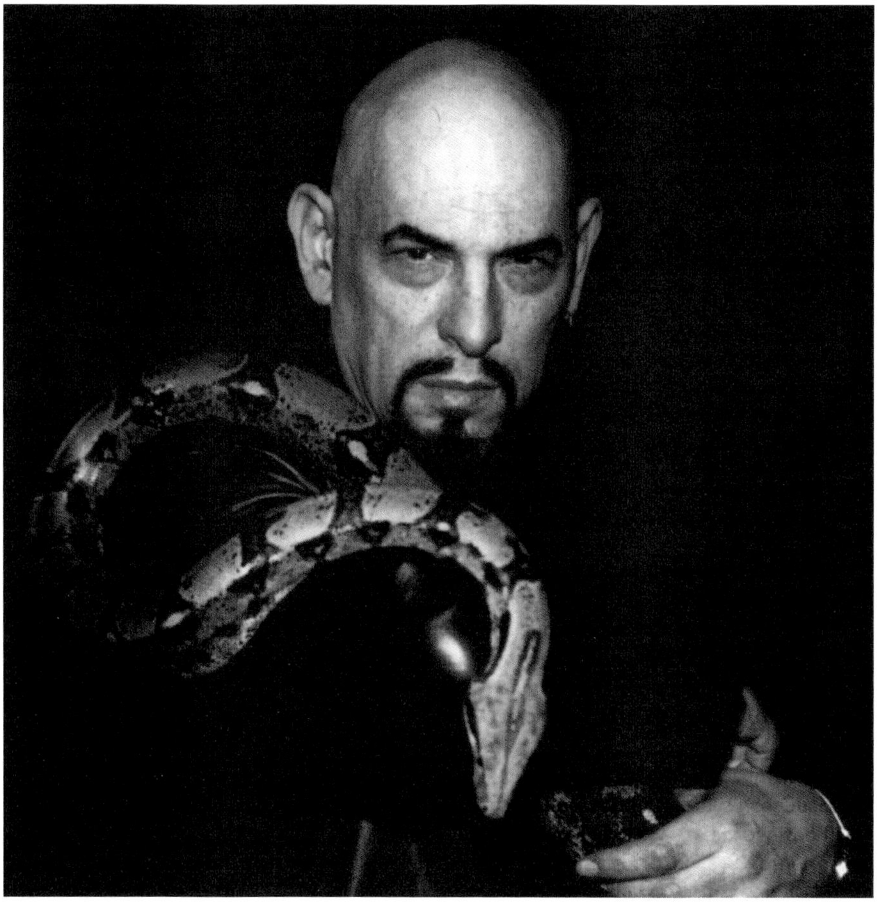

Church of Satan

Anton Szandor LaVey was born in Chicago in 1930 as Howard Stanton Levey. His family moved to San Francisco when he was a young child. In 1966, he founded the Church of Satan, an atheism-based religion using Satan as a symbol of pride, liberty, and individualism. During its early years, members attended rituals held in his mysterious black house at 6114 California Street in the Richmond District. Interviewed in the 1969 documentary, *Satanis: The Devil's Mass*, LaVey said that until he founded the Church of Satan, no religion existed that was "based on man's carnal needs or fleshly pursuits." He explained that most religions were based on abstinence, rather than indulgence, so the rational pursuit of pleasure is the hallmark of the Church of Satan. He acknowledged that his philosophy was "very selfish," one that accepted greed, selfishness, and lustful thoughts. "If you're going to be a sinner," he said, "be the best sinner on the block . . . If you're going to do something naughty, realize that it's naughty and enjoy it." The church's rituals were influenced by those in secret societies, West Indian voodoo, Norse rituals, the Catholic Church, and various exotic groups.

In 1969, LaVey published *The Satanic Bible*, featuring essays, observations, and rituals related to his Church of Satan. Four more books followed. He also released two record albums, *The Satanic Mass* and *Satan Takes a Holiday*. A second documentary, *Speak of the Devil*, was made in 1993. LaVey loved San Francisco and his Victorian house, which was demolished in 2001, and he had fond memories of Playland amusement park, Fort Point, and the ruins of the Sutro Baths. He died on October 29, 1997, although his death certificate listed the date of death as October 31 (Halloween). His body was cremated after a Satanic funeral rite attended by a few family members. (Courtesy the Church of Satan; photograph by Nick Bougas.)

CHAPTER FIVE

The Arts

Many people who live in or have lived in the Richmond and Sunset Districts work in the arts, a category that covers many different creative venues, including painting, writing, photography, sculpture, music, and acting. Internationally known photographer Ansel Adams lived in the Richmond District for much of his life. Herman Schmidt was a picture framer who was one of the first people to create frames for art sold by the now internationally known store Gump's.

Some people pursued an artistic career after they left their childhood homes in the Richmond or Sunset District. Actress Barbara Eden, comedienne Gracie Allen, and musician Vince Guaraldi became famous after they left San Francisco. Others, like singer Johnny Mathis, were recognized first in their home communities and later became well known outside San Francisco. And, as in other categories in this book, some people in the arts never lived in the Richmond or Sunset Districts but contributed in a large way to the growth of the neighborhoods. Dominican nun Sister Justina was living at Mission San Jose in Fremont, California, when the San Francisco Archdiocese invited her to sculpt the frieze at St. Anne's Church in the Sunset. Muralist Victor Arnautoff, who created some of the murals at Coit Tower, never lived in the Richmond District, but he painted striking murals at Washington High School that students and faculty have seen for more than seven decades.

Pioneer surfer Fred Van Dyke is also in this chapter. It was hard to categorize what he has done as a surfer, but, to many people, surfing is an art—and Fred's early life in the Sunset helped develop his surfing talent.

All of these people have contributed in various ways to the community or have been influenced by the community as they grew into their arts.

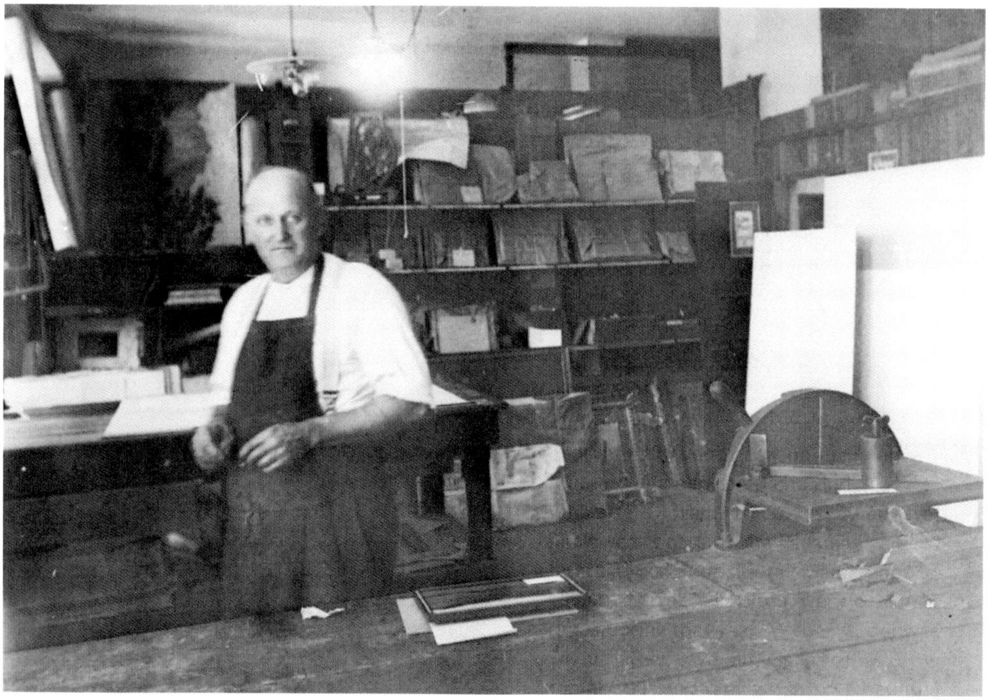

A Woodcarver for Gump's

John Herman "Herman" Schmidt was born in San Francisco's French Hospital in 1876. In 1909, he and his wife purchased a house on Twenty-third Avenue in the Richmond District. He worked in the framing department for the leading San Francisco fine-art dealer Courvoisier Galleries. He is shown here in his workroom. In the 1940s, Herman worked as a woodcarver in the framing department at Gump's, which originally began as a mirror and frame shop. Many early California artists exchanged their art for frames created by Herman (see below). By the 1950s, more than 50 pieces created by these artists between 1912 and 1929 hung on the walls of his home. Herman died in November 1956, and his son Albert lived in the house until his death in 1991. Sadly, more than 25 pieces of art were stolen from the home while Albert was hospitalized in 1989. (Courtesy Nancy Gold.)

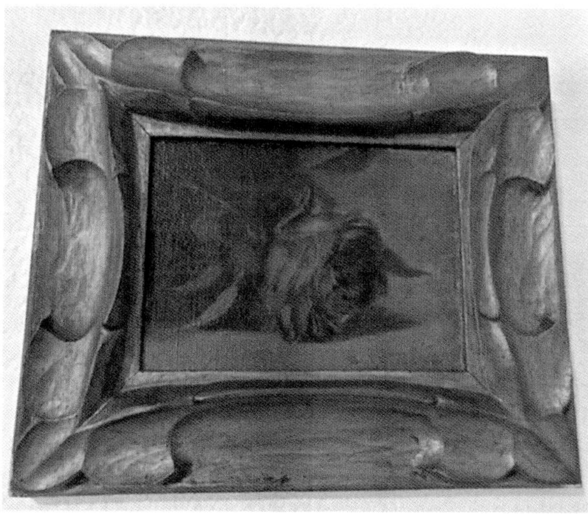

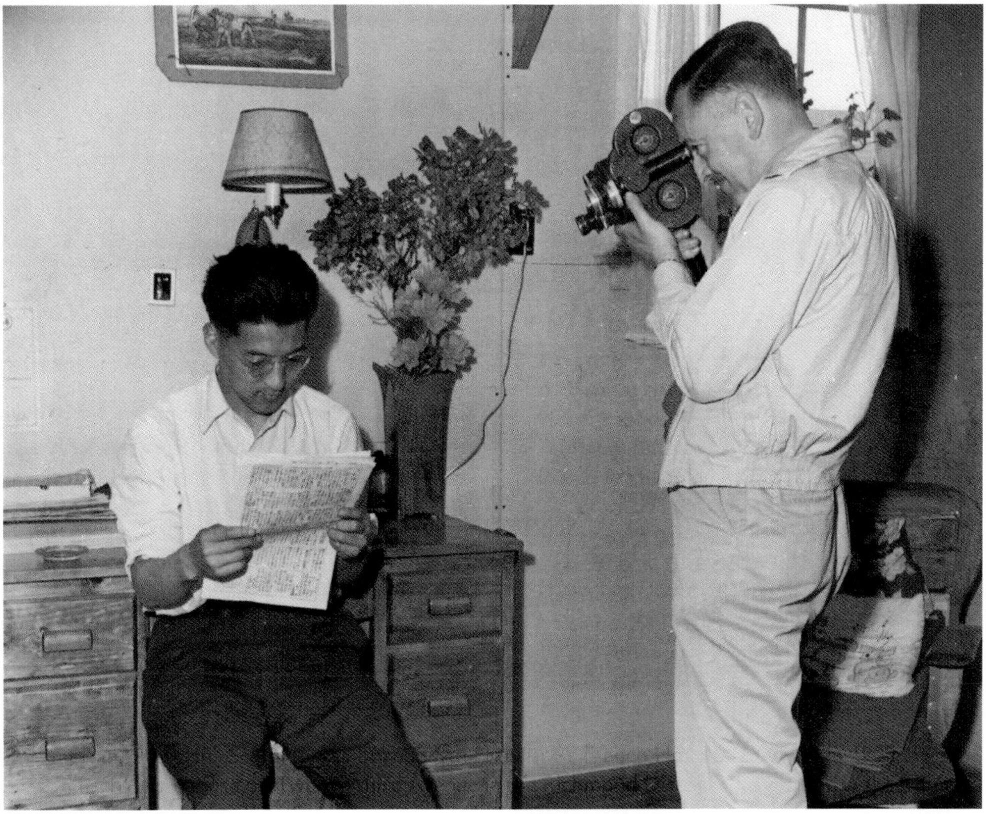

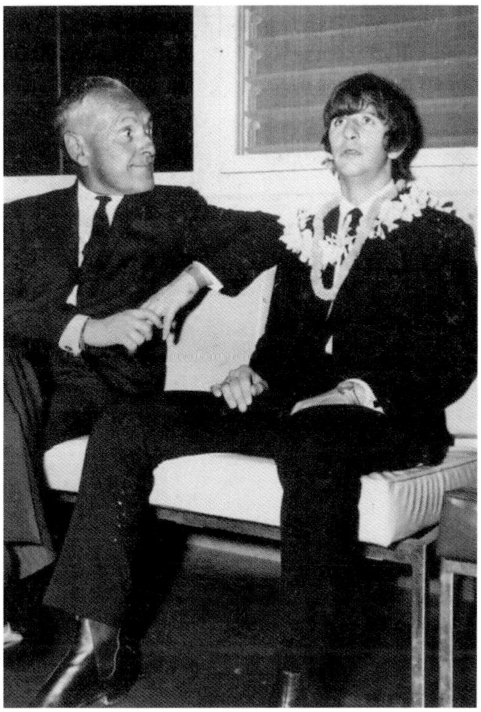

A Sunset Cinematographer

Frank Waverly Vail was born in 1896 in Healdsburg, and his family soon moved to San Francisco. As an adult, he lived on Sixteenth Avenue in the Sunset and was a respected cinematographer. While working at Pathé News (later Warner Pathe), Frank filmed the construction of Mount Rushmore and the building of the Golden Gate Bridge. In this photograph, Frank is seen filming everyday life at a Japanese relocation camp, Tule Lake Relocation Center, during World War II. According to former colleague John Carlson, Frank is using a Bell & Howell camera that he later gave to John. In the 1950s, Warner Pathe made a film with company filmmakers worldwide, including Frank, individually wishing people a Merry Christmas; the film is now on YouTube. Frank died in Saratoga, California, in 1998 at the age of 101. (Above, courtesy Bancroft Library, University of California, Berkeley; right, courtesy Christopher and Patty Diner.)

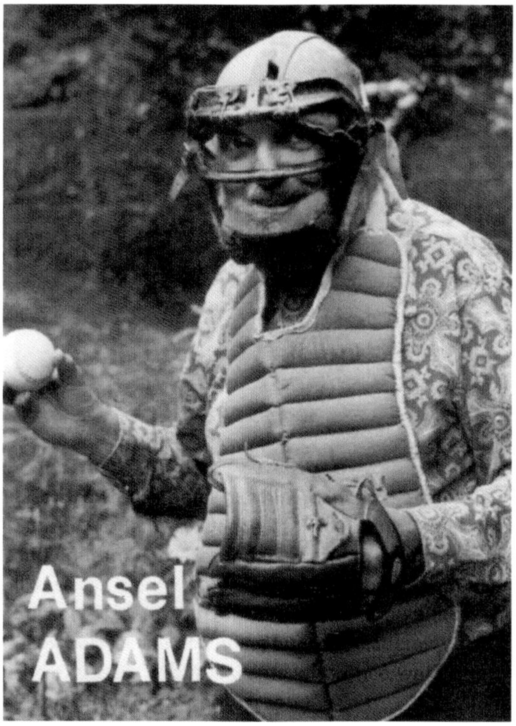

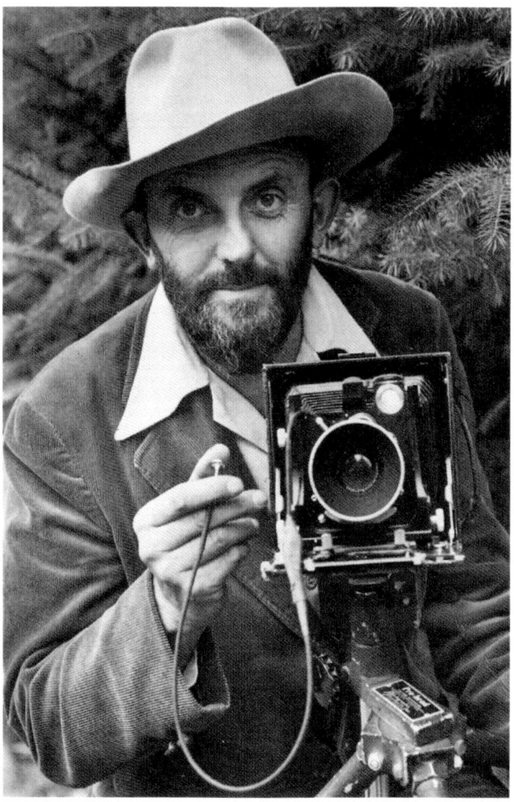

Changing the World View of Photography

Photographer Ansel Adams was born in February 1902 and grew up on Twenty-fourth Avenue in the Richmond District. On Ansel's 13th birthday, his father gave him a year's pass to the Panama Pacific International Exposition in San Francisco. He later wrote, "I visited every exhibit many times during that year." When Ansel was 14, his father gave him his first Box Brownie camera during a family visit to Yosemite. Ansel helped people see that photography was an art, not just "taking some pictures," and his photographs are among the most famous in the world. Ansel later became an active member of the Sierra Club, serving for 30 years on the board of directors. In 1975, photographer Mike Mandel made cards showing famous photographers in baseball poses (see right). (Above, courtesy Marilyn Blaisdell; below, courtesy San Francisco History Center, San Francisco Public Library.)

Teaching All Kinds of Dance
Lisa Brown has been teaching dance to all ages for more than 27 years. She opened her own studio, Sunset Academy of Dance, at 1337 Irving Street in October 1997. Sunset Academy offers dance training and education classes in tap, jazz, hip-hop, and children's classes—all in a small studio environment. "I like to inspire my students while helping them improve their technique," says Lisa. All the students at Sunset Academy of Dance perform at an annual show in June. One parent of a teenager says that her daughters began attending Sunset Academy when they were three years old and still look forward to their classes. In fact, parents who once were Sunset Academy students now bring their children in for classes. (Author's photograph.)

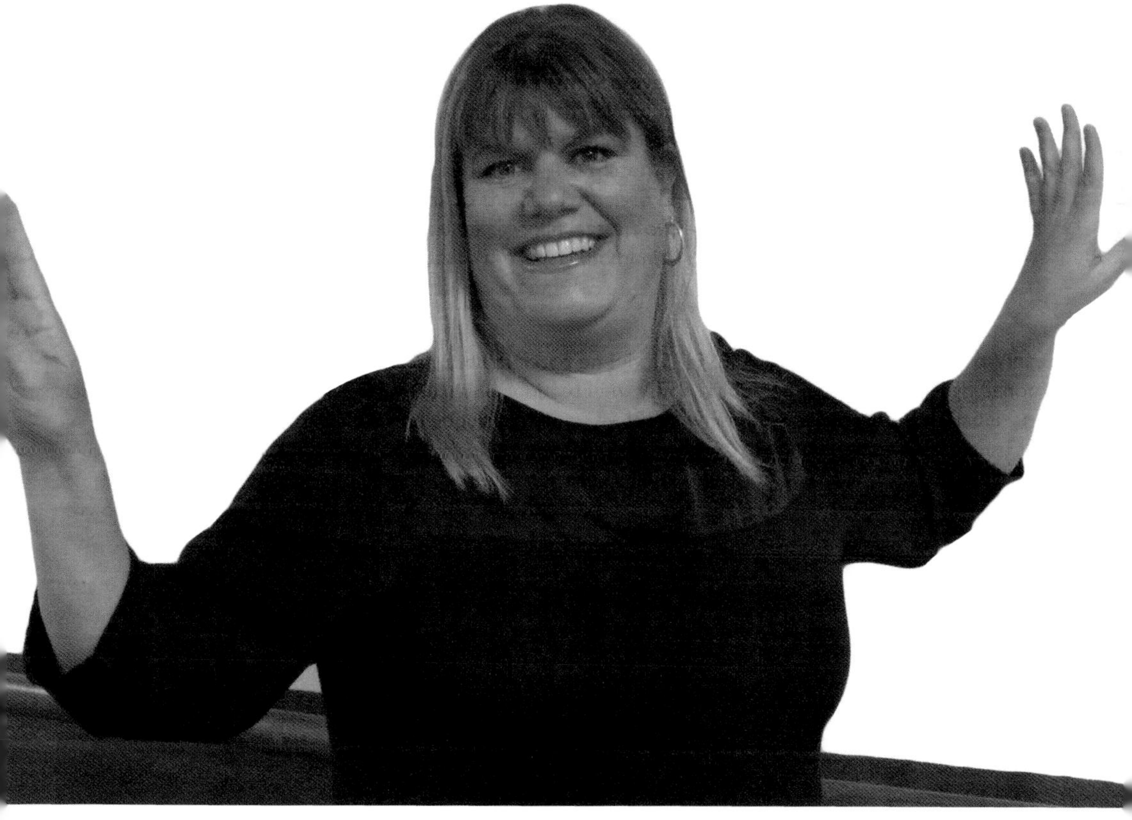

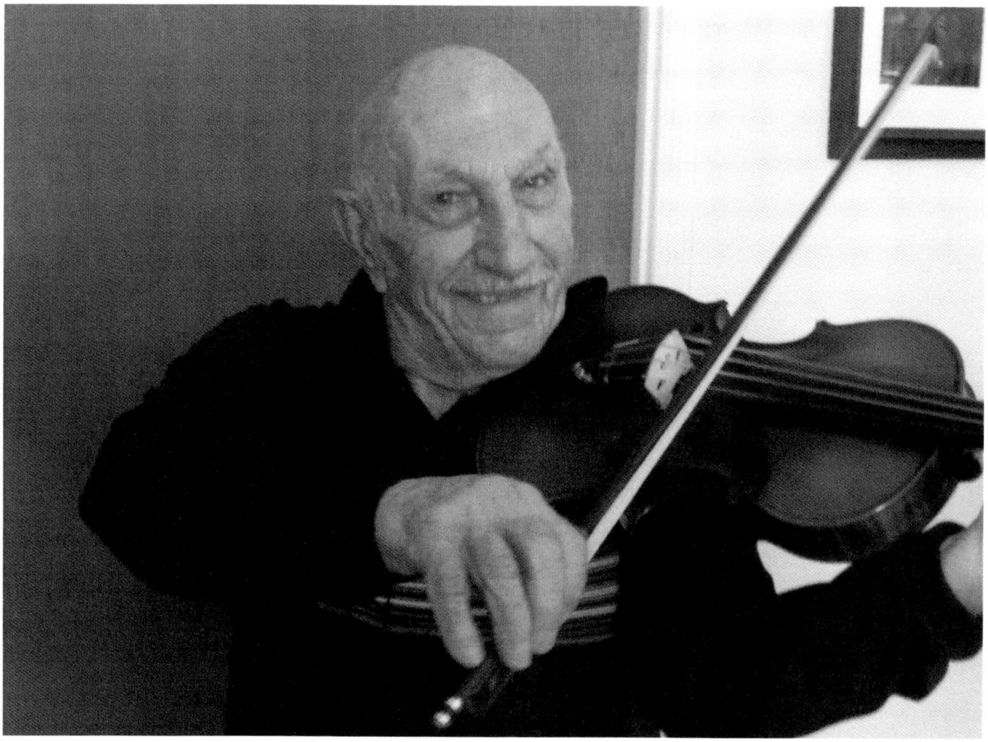

Playing and Making Violins
Remo Del Tredici was born in 1920 in Italy, and his family moved to San Francisco's Richmond District two years later. He graduated from Washington High School in 1937, and, in 1952, he moved to the Sunset. Although he played the violin when he was young, he stopped making music for 60 years. At age 80, he began taking violin lessons again, and, a few years later, he started making violins. He has since made more than 100, donating 20 violins to the San Francisco Unified School District, donating 20 to veterans, and selling others. At 94, he still takes violin lessons every Tuesday. On Thursdays, he plays in a string quartet, which gives free concerts to the local community. (Above, author's photograph; below, courtesy Remo del Tredici.)

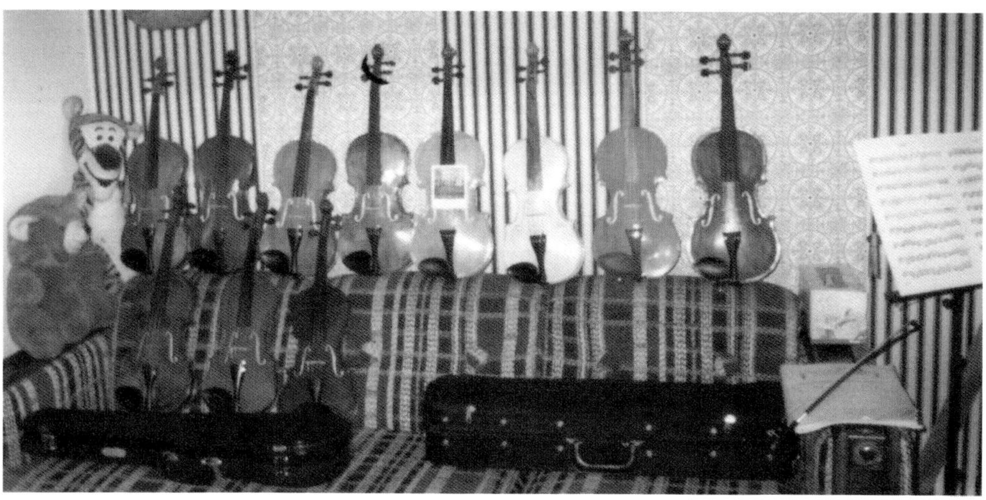

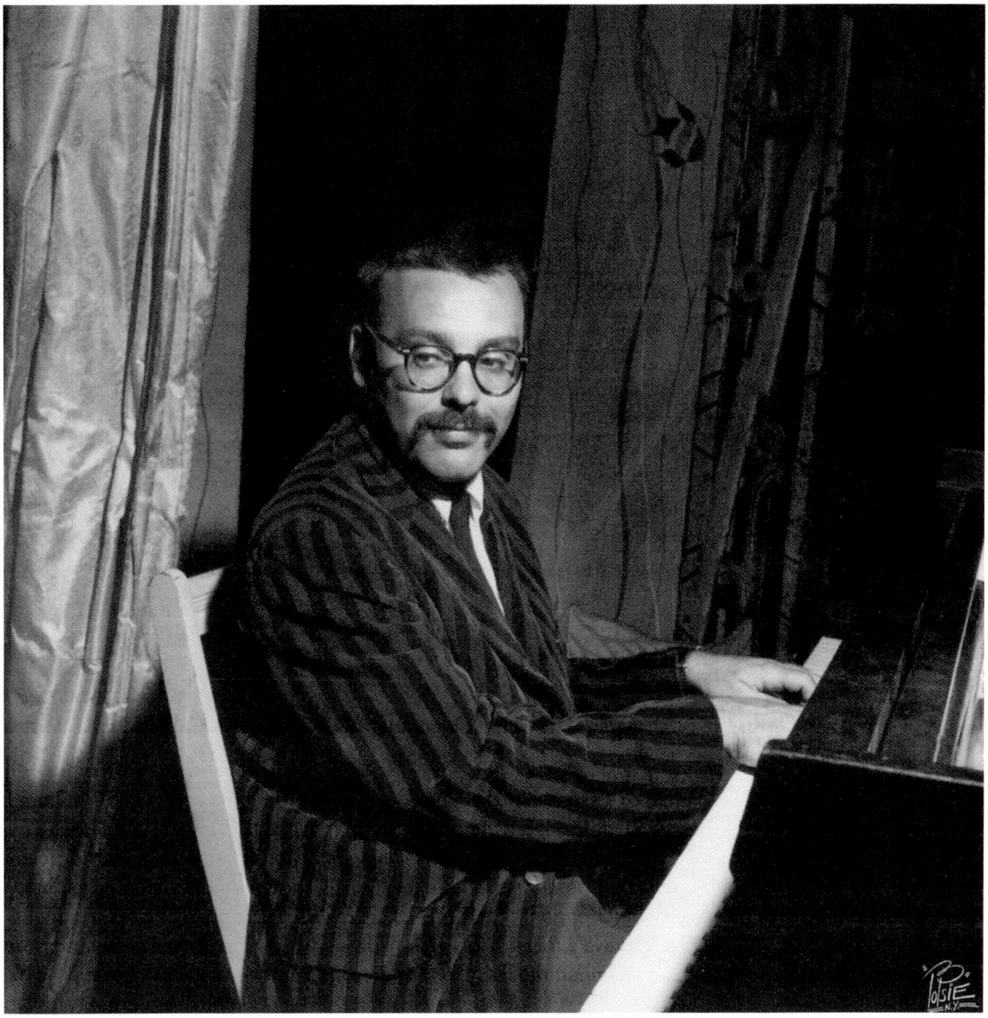

Good Grief, Charlie Brown!
Vincent Anthony Dellaglio was born in San Francisco on July 17, 1928. His name was changed to Vince Guaraldi when his stepfather, Tony Guaraldi, adopted him. Vince graduated from Lincoln High School in 1946, and his piano playing became popular in the early 1950s when he worked with Cal Tjader and Woody Herman. Vince is best known for composing the Grammy Award–winning song "Cast Your Fate to the Wind" and writing and playing the music for the *Peanuts* television specials. (Courtesy Michael Randolph; photograph by William "PoPsie" Randolph.)

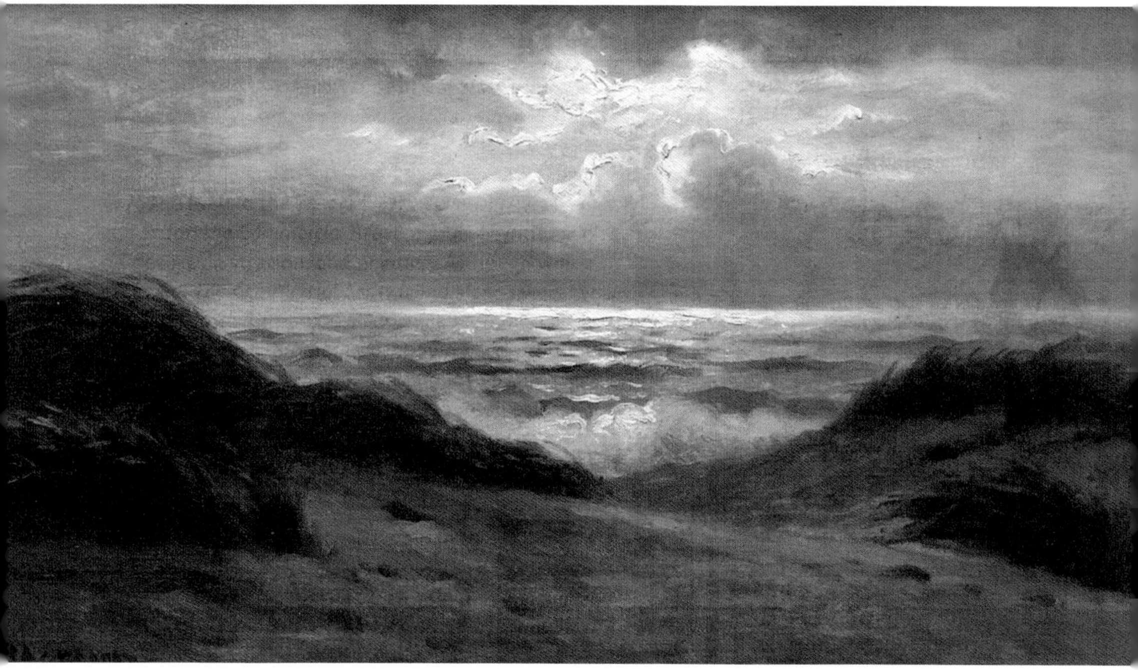

An Ocean Beach Artist

Nels Hagerup created more than 6,000 stunning seascapes, mostly of the San Francisco coast. He was born in 1864 in Norway and studied art in Berlin as a teen. Working as a merchant shipman, he came to America at age 18. He settled in Portland, Oregon, in 1882 and married Harriet Marie Hageman in 1851. The couple moved to San Francisco in 1892 and established a home at 1224 Forty-sixth Avenue in the Sunset District, less than a block from Golden Gate Park and three blocks from Ocean Beach. To support his family, Nels worked as a stevedore. When not at work, he often walked to the beach and painted; he is known for his sand dunes, ships, marine scenes, and sunsets. Nels Hagerup died in 1922. ("Dune Grasses" photograph courtesy Bodega Bay Heritage Gallery.)

Sharing Fine Art and Ideas

Louis "Lou" Lauck was one of the first commercial artists on the San Francisco design scene. Born in 1887 in Indianapolis, Lou was an artist for the *Indianapolis Star* before he moved to San Francisco in 1918 and began studying at the California Guild of Arts and Crafts. By 1925, he lived in the Richmond District. He was an early editor for *The Commercial Artist*, a journal with articles on design, illustration, and printing. Although well received, *The Commercial Artist* failed after several years. Lou later formed the Louis A. Lauck Commercial Art and Photographic Studio. Lou, shown here at his work table alongside his son Jack, was a photograph engraver, photographer, advertising designer, and oil painter. His paintings were primarily portraits and California landscapes. He died in 1972. (Courtesy June Lauck.)

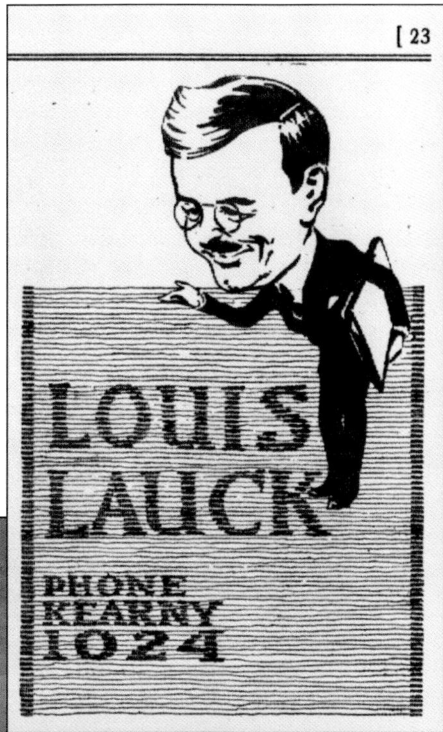

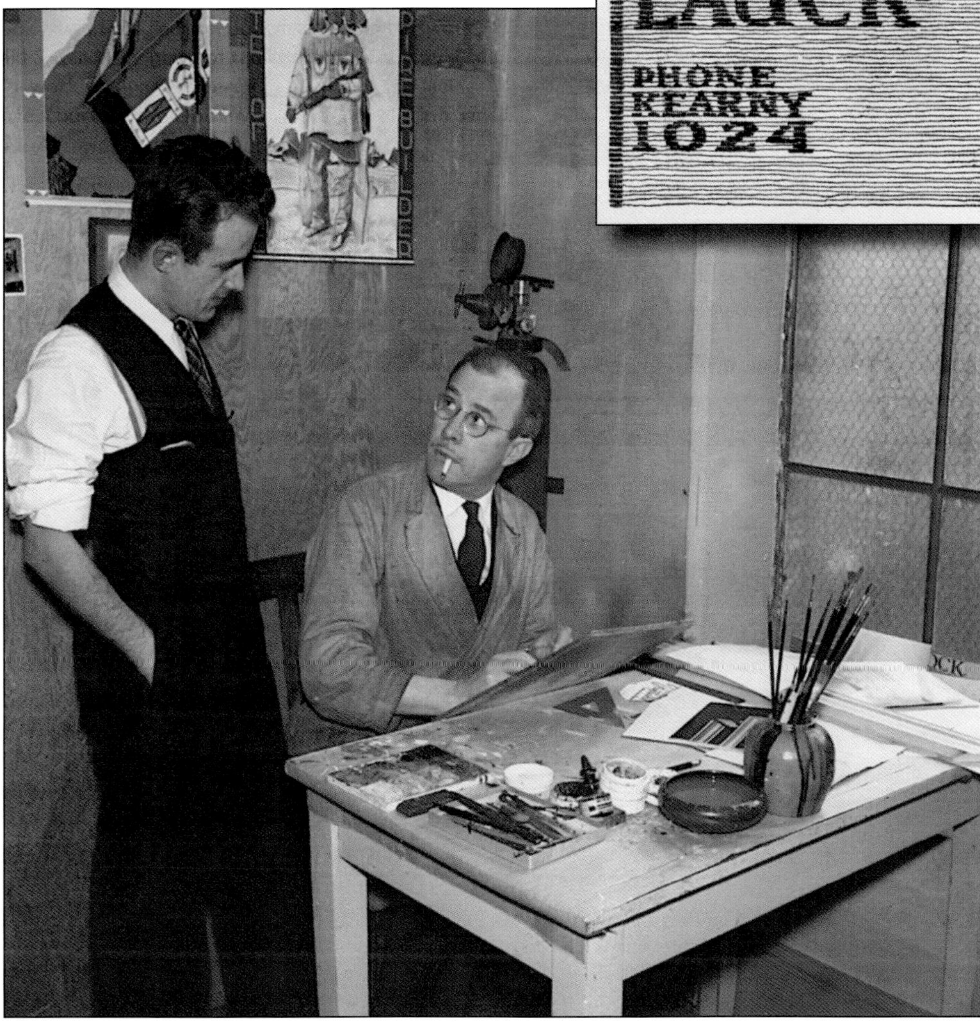

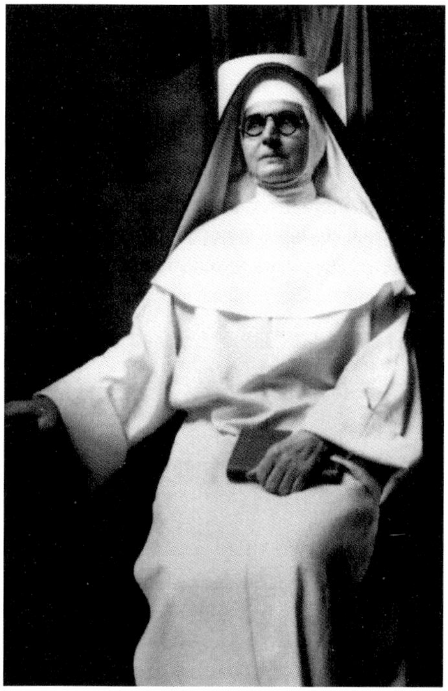

The Sculptor in the Convent

Sister Mary Justina, OP, was born Anna Niemierski in 1879 in Wietrienen, East Prussia (now Poland). She studied at the Berlin Academy of Fine Arts, and her friends and family assumed she would be an artist. Instead, she became a Dominican nun. In 1931, when Sister Justina was living at Mission San Jose in Fremont, California, she created the frieze on the front of San Francisco's new St. Anne of the Sunset Church. The sculpture shows 80 characters depicting the scriptural account of salvation history. Sister Justina created other religious sculptures in her long life and died on September 8, 1960. "She took part in the religion but was alone in her work," said Sister Mary Mark of the convent. "You could see her work was part of her prayer." (Right and facing page, courtesy the Dominican Sisters of Mission San Jose Archives; below, author's photograph.)

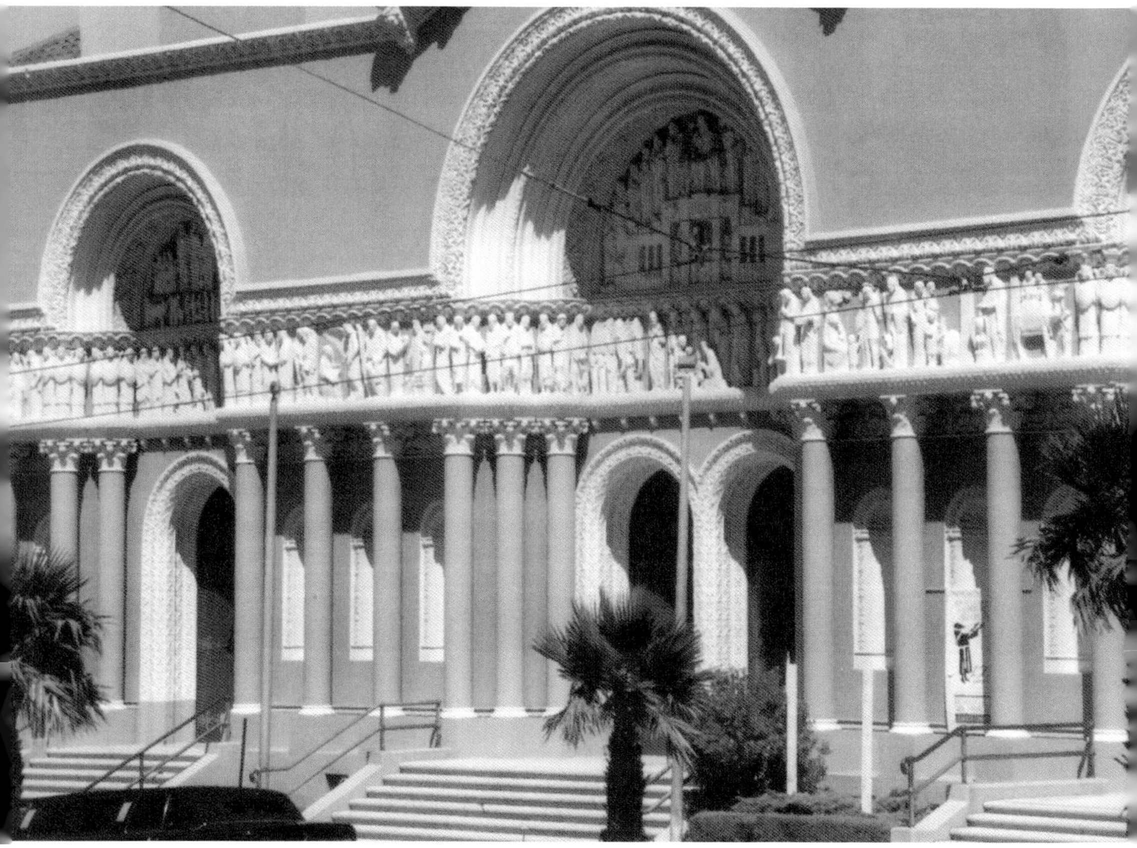

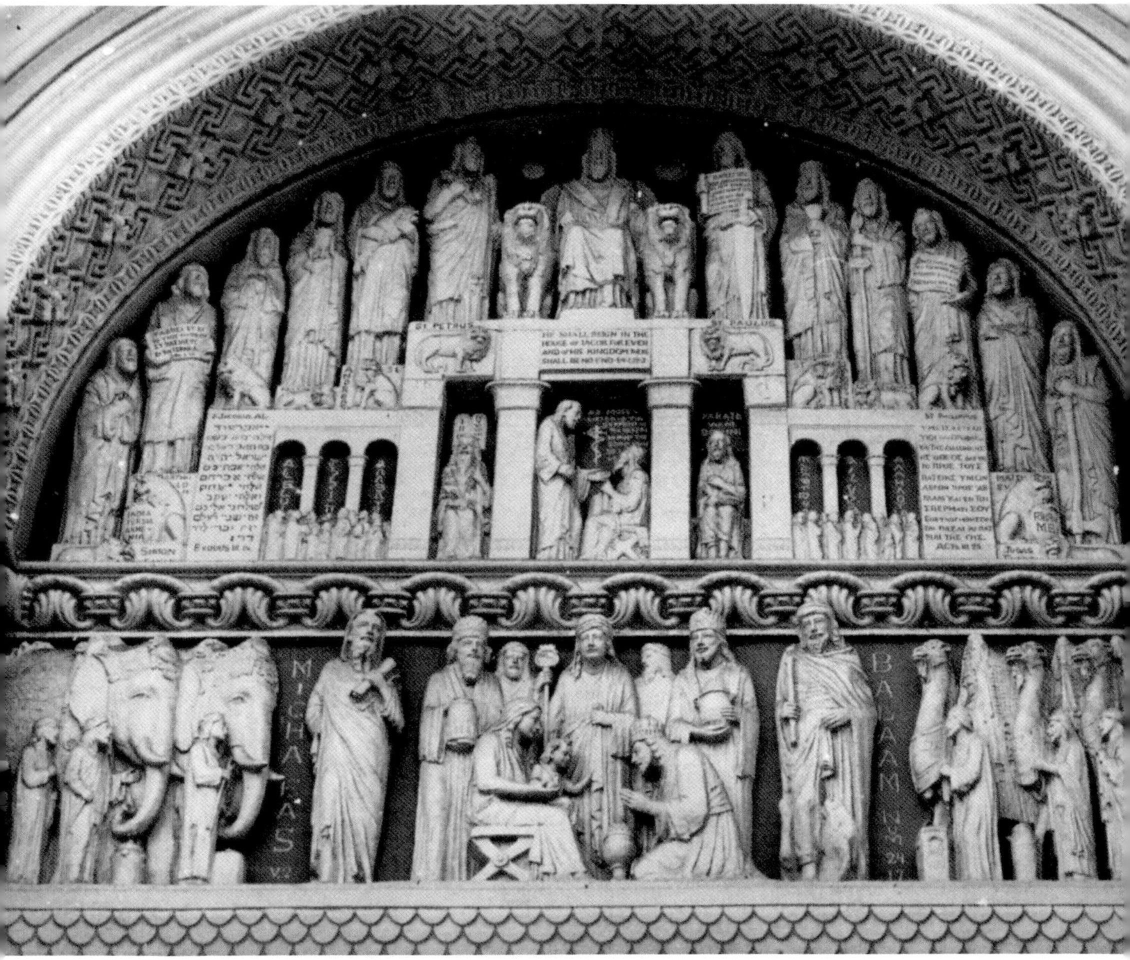
ST PETRUS
ST PAULUS
BALAAM

High School Murals

Visitors to George Washington High School in the Richmond District are astounded by the colorful detailed murals that grace the hallways. Victor Arnautoff, who was born in 1896 in Ukraine and came to the United States in 1925, lived in the Richmond District. Arnautoff was invited to paint the frescoes at the new George Washington High School as part of Pres. Franklin Roosevelt's Public Works Administration in the 1930s. The murals depict the life and times of the first president of the United States, George Washington. In the 1960s, some students and faculty protested that the murals showed African Americans only as slaves and should be painted over. Instead, a compromise was reached and new murals (see facing page, below) were painted elsewhere in the school. (Below, courtesy San Francisco History Center, San Francisco Public Library; facing page, author's photographs.)

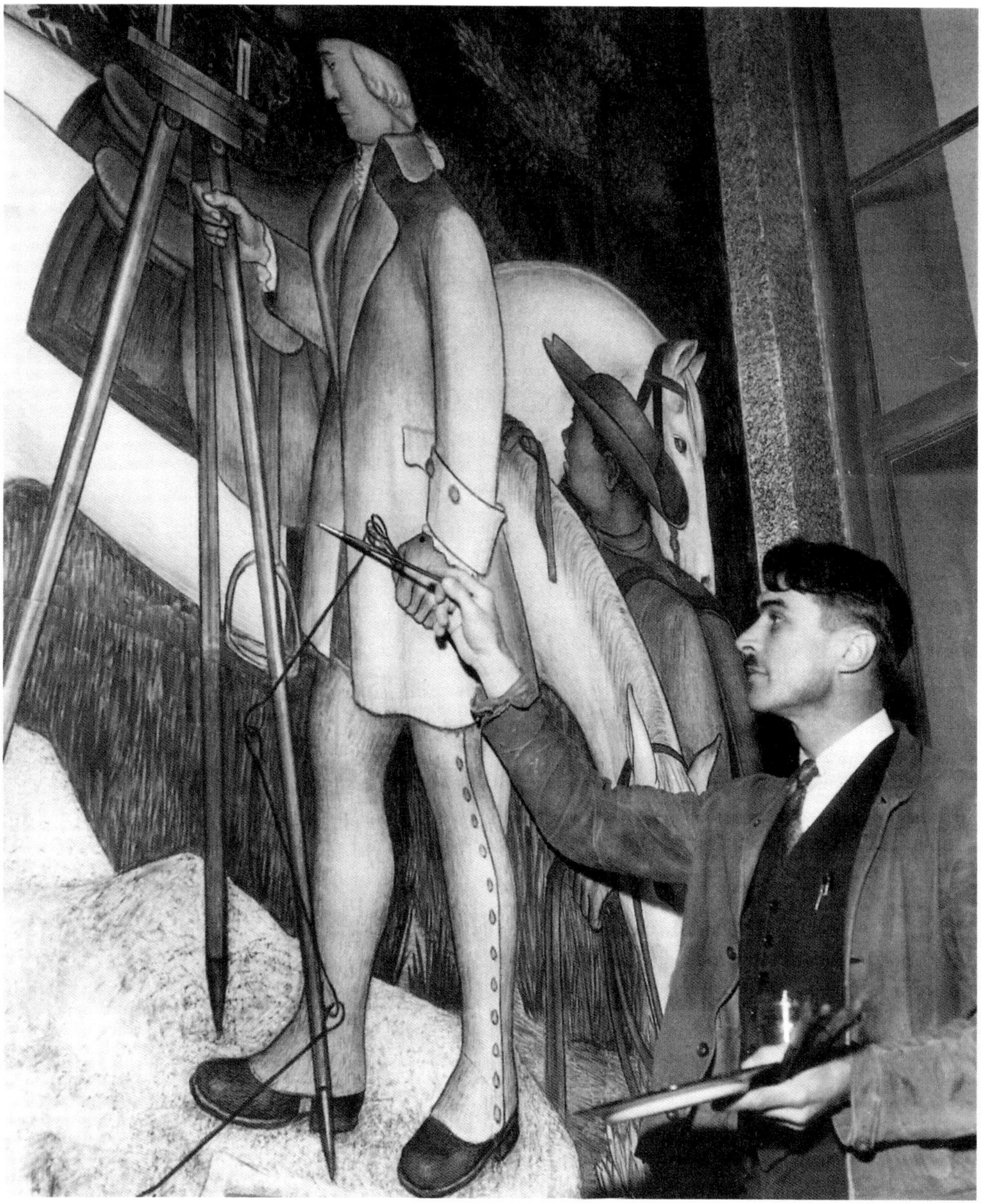

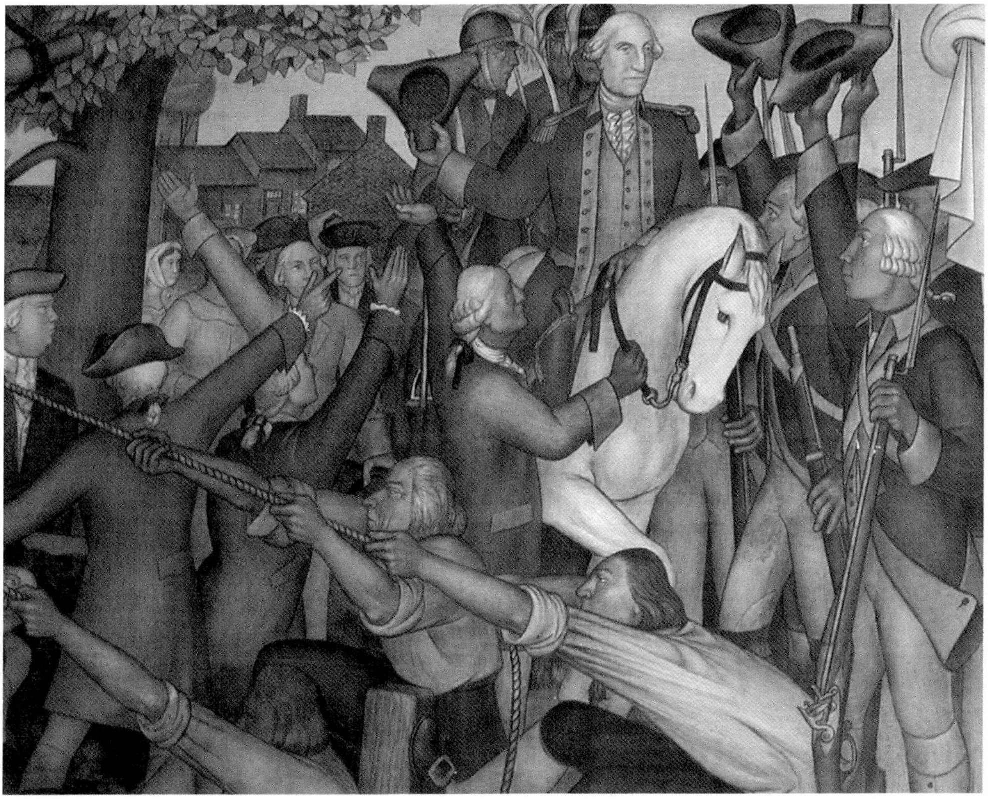

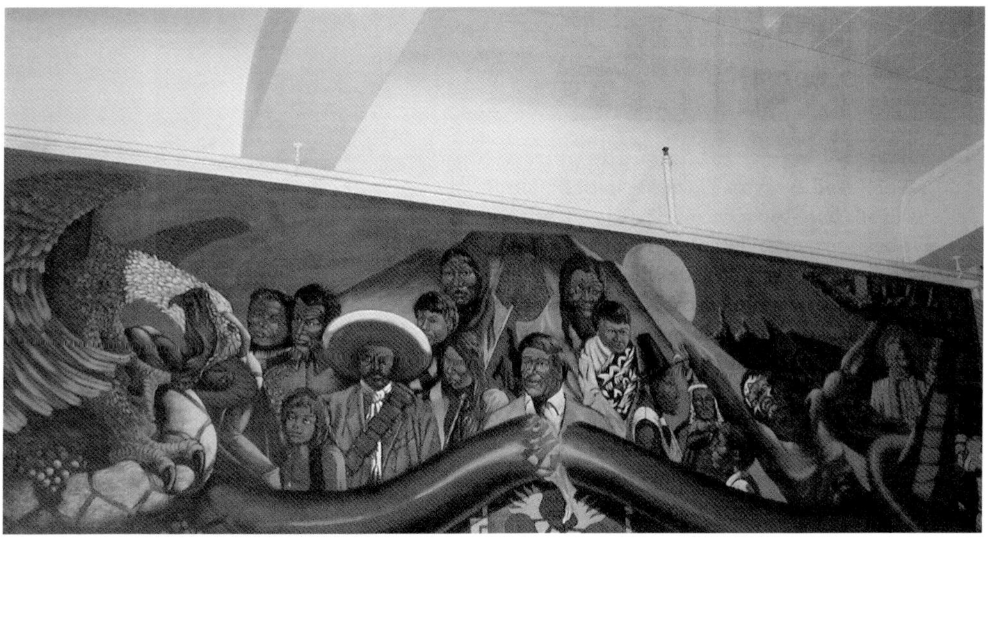

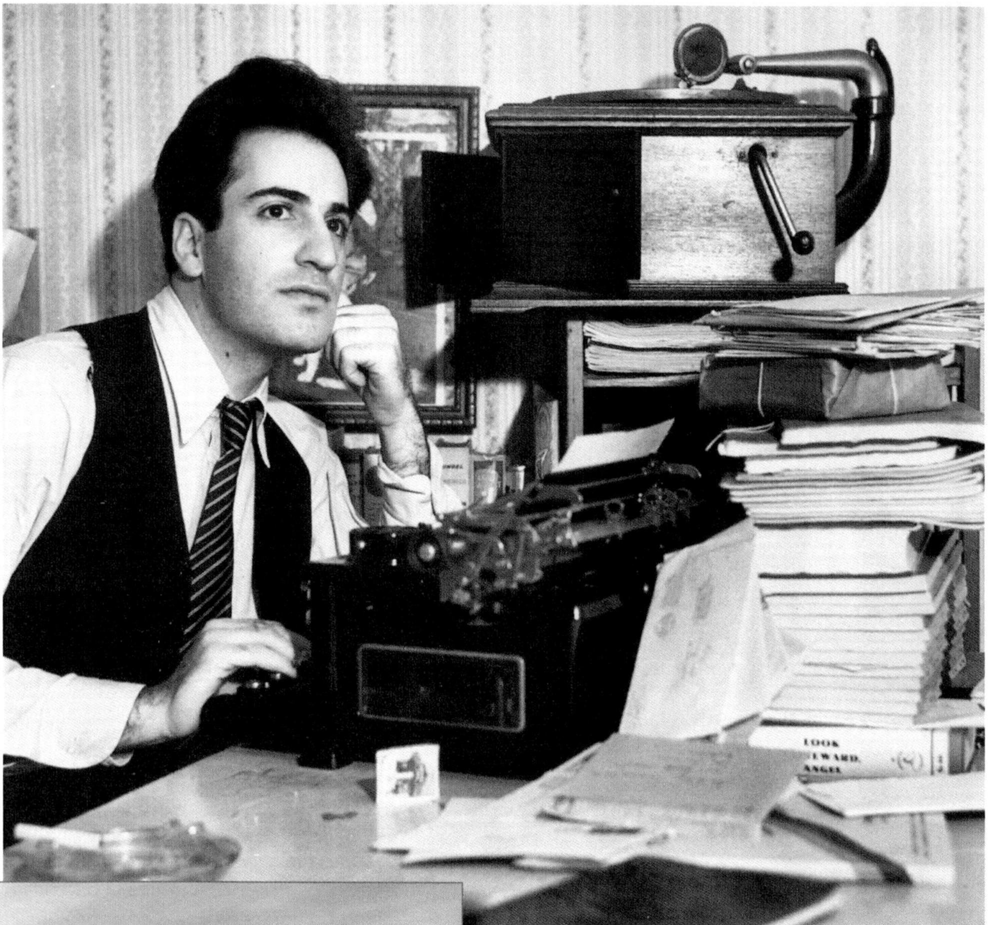

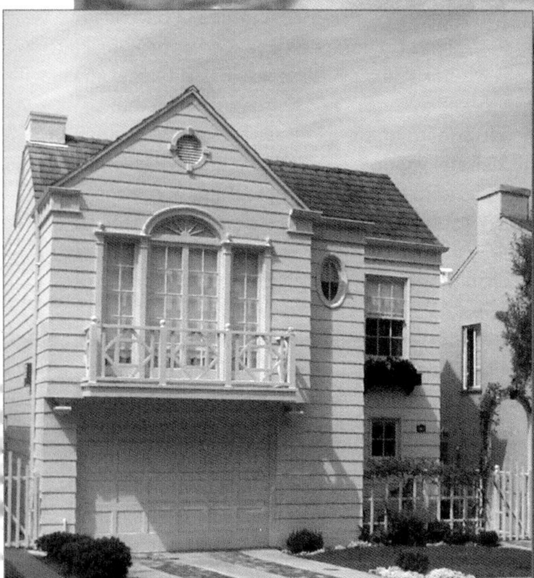

Writing about Life
Prolific author William Saroyan is best known for the novel *The Human Comedy* and the play *The Time of Your Life*, for which he received the Pulitzer Prize in 1940. The play was set in a saloon in San Francisco. Saroyan often wrote about Armenian-immigrant life in Fresno, California, where he was born in 1908. In the 1930s, builder Henry Doelger (see page 34) built a house for Saroyan's sister and mother on Fifteenth Avenue, near Noriega Street, in Golden Gate Heights. Saroyan had his own study and writing room downstairs with a view across the Sunset District toward the ocean. He once said, "Everybody has got to die, but I have always believed an exception would be made in my case." No such exception was made; Saroyan died of prostate cancer in 1981. (Above, courtesy San Francisco History Center, San Francisco Public Library; left, author's photograph.)

Illustrating a Beloved City

Ted Lewy was born in Germany in 1912 and escaped from Germany during Hitler's reign in 1936, moving to China. He arrived in San Francisco in 1940 and enlisted in the US Army during World War II, working as a military artist. After the war, he began working at the Emporium, a downtown San Francisco department store, creating watercolor illustrations for shopping bags and store boxes (see photograph). In the 1950s, he moved to the Sunset and opened a small business creating souvenirs for the increasing number of tourists who were coming to San Francisco. His brightly colored images of cable cars, downtown flower stands, bridges, and buildings showed his love for San Francisco. During his career, he painted murals, paper napkins, greeting cards, and postcards. He died in April 1963. (Author's photograph.)

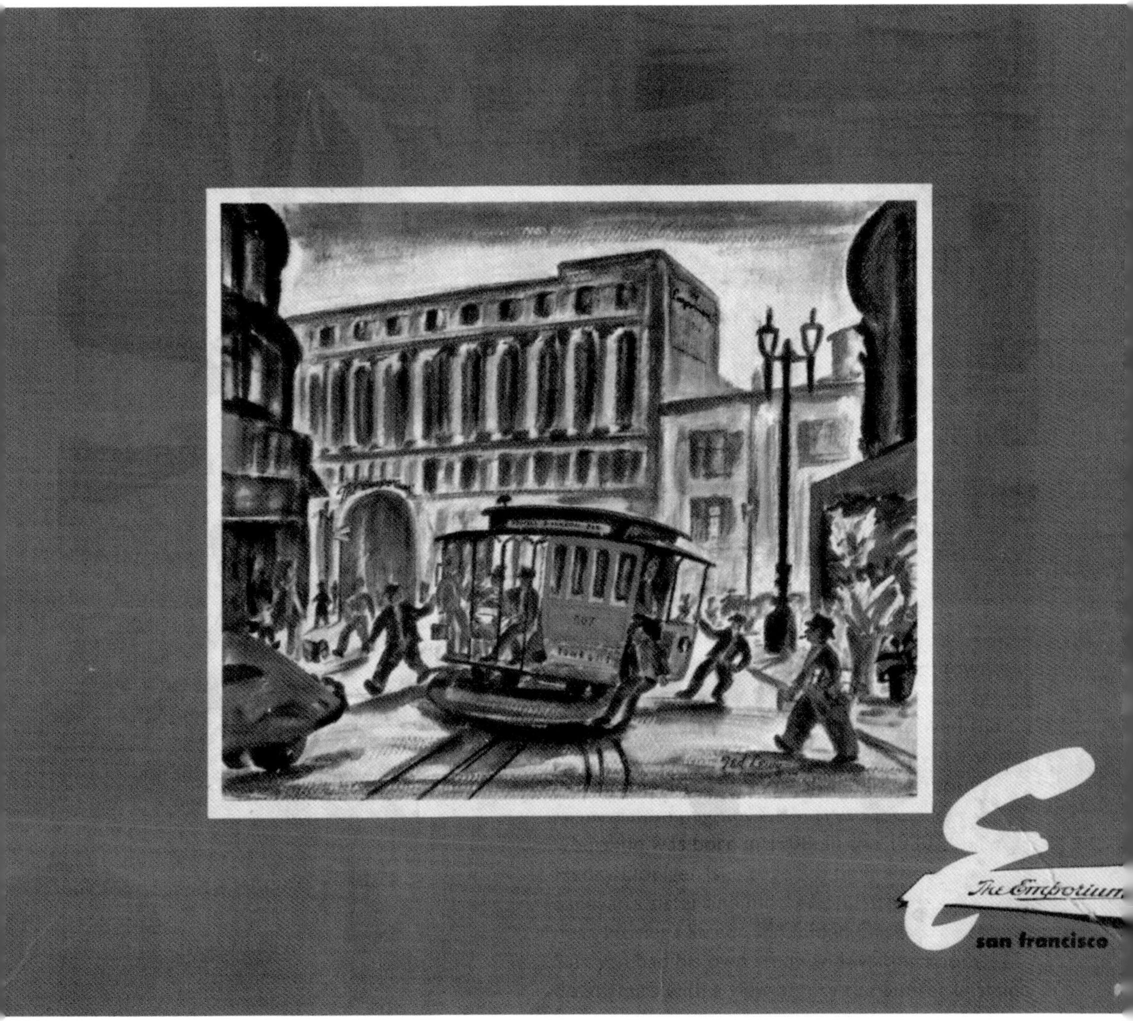

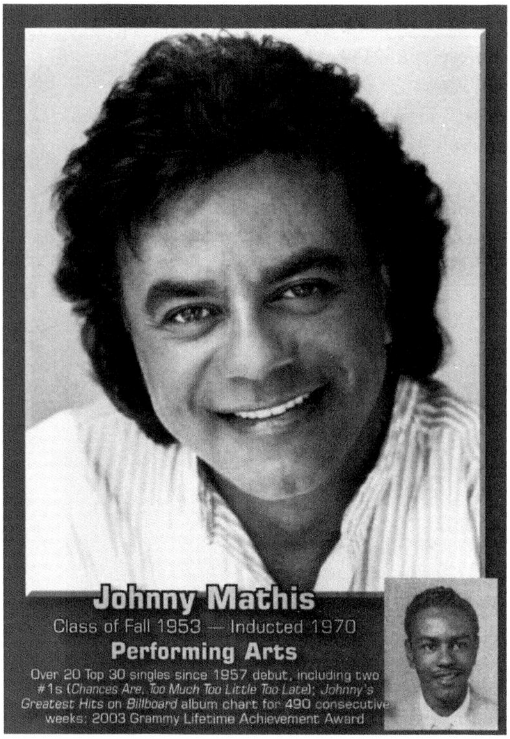

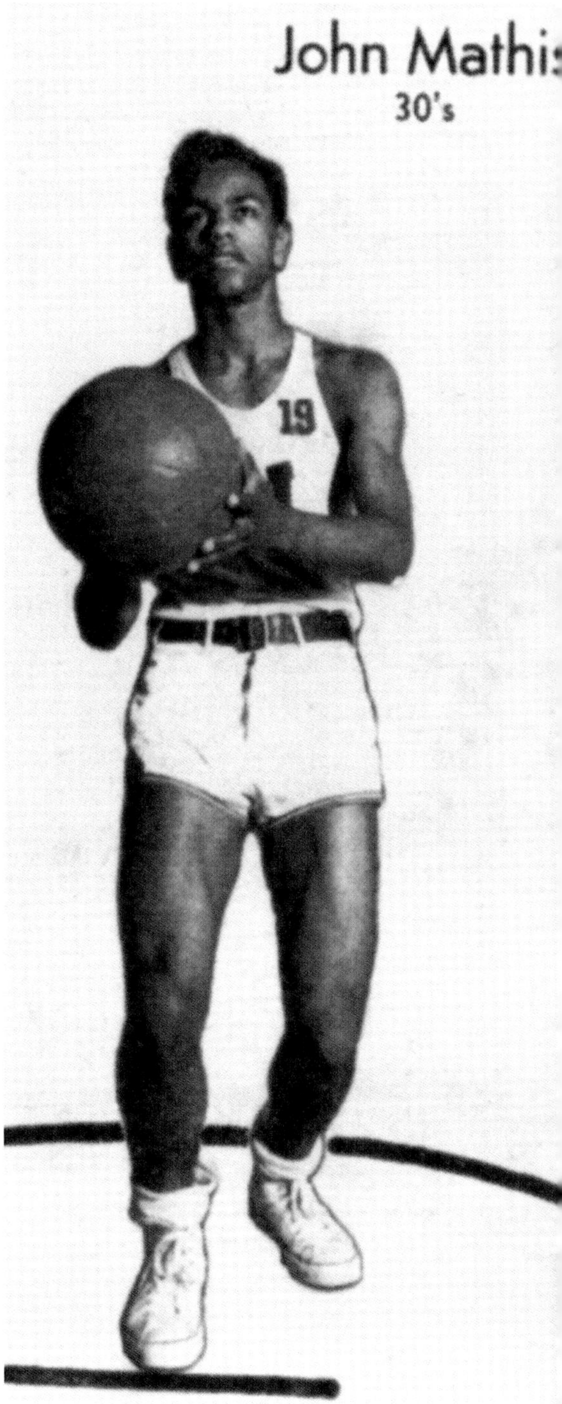

World-Renowned Singer
John Royce "Johnny" Mathis was born on September 30, 1935, in Texas. When he was a child, his family moved to San Francisco's Richmond District. At George Washington High School, he was known for his singing voice and his athletic ability in track and basketball. He attended San Francisco State College, where he set a high-jump record of six feet, five and a half inches. Johnny left San Francisco when Columbia Records offered him a recording session. He is known for early hits, including "Chances Are," "Misty," and "It's Not for Me to Say," and later hits like "Too Much, Too Little, Too Late" (with Deniece Williams) and "The Last Time I Felt Like This." Johnny has won numerous awards, including a Lifetime Achievement Award from the Academy of Recording Arts and Sciences, the Ella Award from the Society of Singers, and induction into the Hit Parade Hall of Fame. He currently lives in Beverly Hills. (Courtesy George Washington High School.)

A Regular at the Little Shamrock

In 1978, mystery writer John Lescroart moved to Thirty-fourth Avenue in the Richmond District. When he first moved there, he went to the Little Shamrock (see page 98), a pub founded in 1893 in the Sunset District. "I loved the place at first sight," he explains. "I loved the jukebox, I loved the light, I loved the darts." Lescroart set some of his books' scenes inside the pub. (Courtesy John Lescroart.)

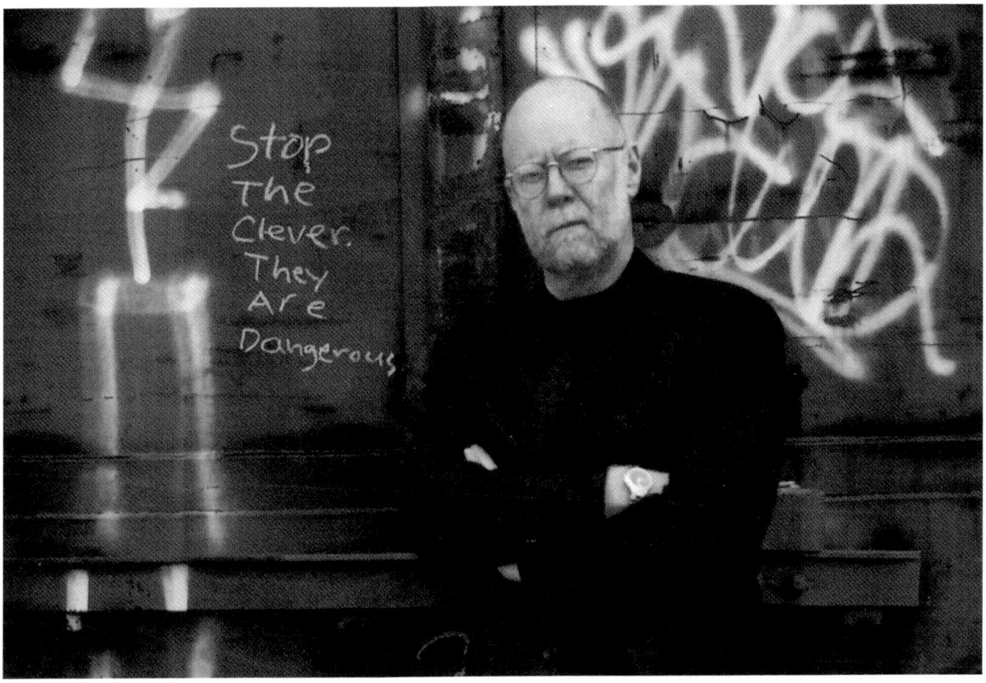

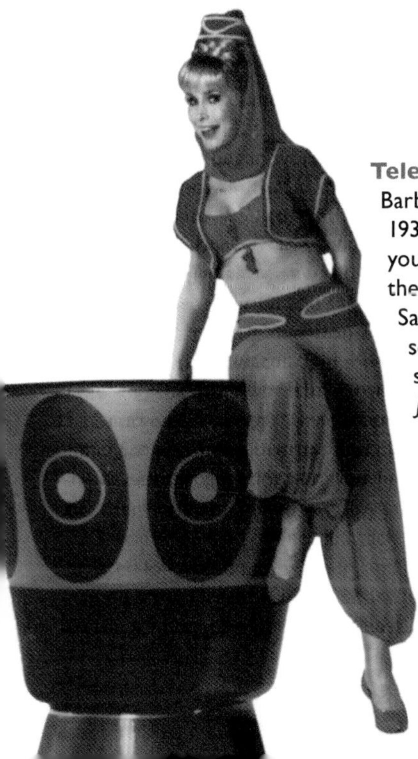

Television's Jeannie

Barbara Eden was born Barbara Jean Morehead in Tucson, Arizona, in 1931. She moved to Forty-fifth Avenue in the Sunset when she was very young. Barbara graduated from Lincoln High School in 1949, studied at the San Francisco Conservatory of Music, and, in 1951, won the Miss San Francisco pageant. She is best known as Jeannie in the television series *I Dream of Jeannie*. She has appeared in movies and television shows and worked on behalf of numerous charities. Her memoir, *Jeannie Out of the Bottle*, was published in 2010. (Courtesy Tangible Dreams Entertainment.)

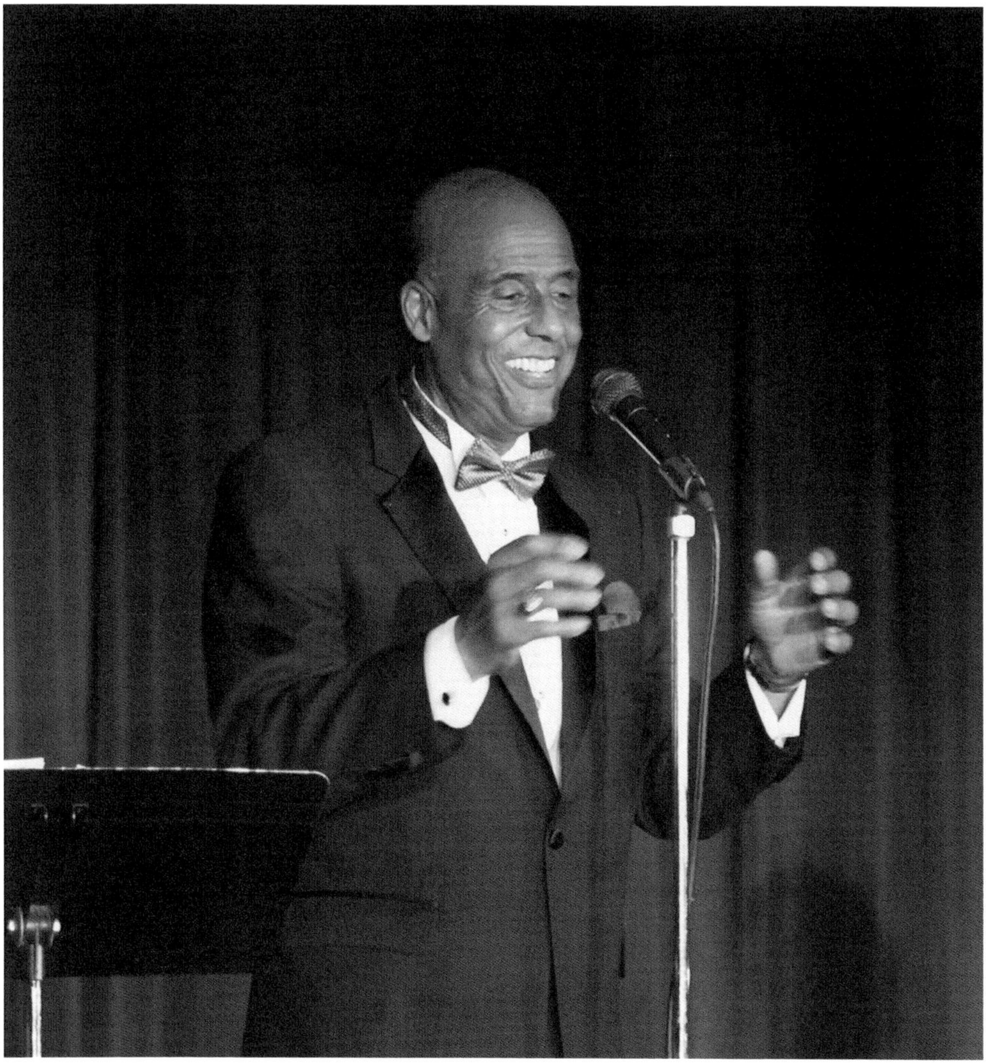

A Man of Many Talents
Noah Griffin's father was a civil rights pioneer. He and his wife moved to San Francisco in the 1940s to help found a branch of the National Association for the Advancement of Colored People (NAACP). Noah was born in 1946, and the family moved in 1952 to the Richmond District, where Noah attended Washington High School. After graduating from Harvard Law School, Noah returned to San Francisco, where he was appointed to the Mayor's Council on Criminal Justice and later to the Juvenile Delinquency Prevention Commission. He also wrote for the *San Francisco Examiner* and the *Independent* and worked as a radio talk show host. He wrote the lyrics for the song "San Francisco Giants" and the official ballad of the Golden Gate Bridge. He is known for establishing the Cole Porter Society, as well as singing, writing, lecturing, acting, and speaking. (Courtesy Noah Griffin.)

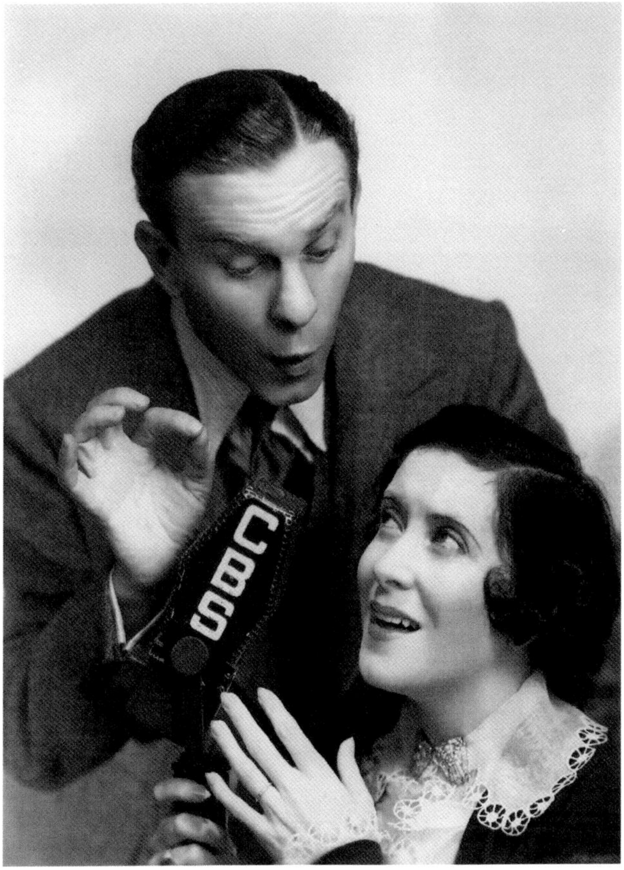

A Funny Lady

Born Grace Ethel Cecile Rosalie Allen on July 26, 1895, in San Francisco, Gracie Allen grew up on Fourth Avenue in the Richmond District. She attended Star of the Sea High School on Ninth Avenue. After graduating in 1914, she moved to New York to work in comedy. She met comedian George Burns in 1922, and they began working as a vaudeville comedy team. They were married in 1926. They had their own radio show in the 1930s and 1940s, and *The George Burns and Gracie Allen Show* was broadcast on television from 1950 to 1958.

In his 1988 book *Gracie: A Love Story*, George wrote about their act together, attributing their success to Gracie. Originally, she was the "straight man" and George was the comedian. However, their audiences laughed at whatever Gracie said and did not laugh at George's jokes. He quickly changed the act. Onstage, George just asked a question and gave Gracie a chance to talk. He wrote, "In one of our vaudeville routines, I asked Gracie, 'Did the maid ever drop you on your head when you were a baby?' 'Don't be silly, George,' she'd answer in an astonished voice . . . 'We couldn't afford a maid. My mother had to do it.'"

George also wrote, "Gracie certainly wasn't the first comedienne in vaudeville . . . What made Gracie different was her sincerity. She didn't try to be funny. Gracie never told a joke in her life, she simply answered the questions I asked her as best she could . . . All I had to do was say, 'Gracie, how's your brother?' and she talked for 38 years."

Gracie Allen died of a heart attack in 1964. The Gracie Awards, given annually for exemplary programming created for women, by women, and about women by the Alliance for Women in Media Foundation, were named after Gracie Allen. She never forgot her first school, Star of the Sea in San Francisco, donating to the school and attending at least one reunion. (Courtesy Jack Tillmany.)

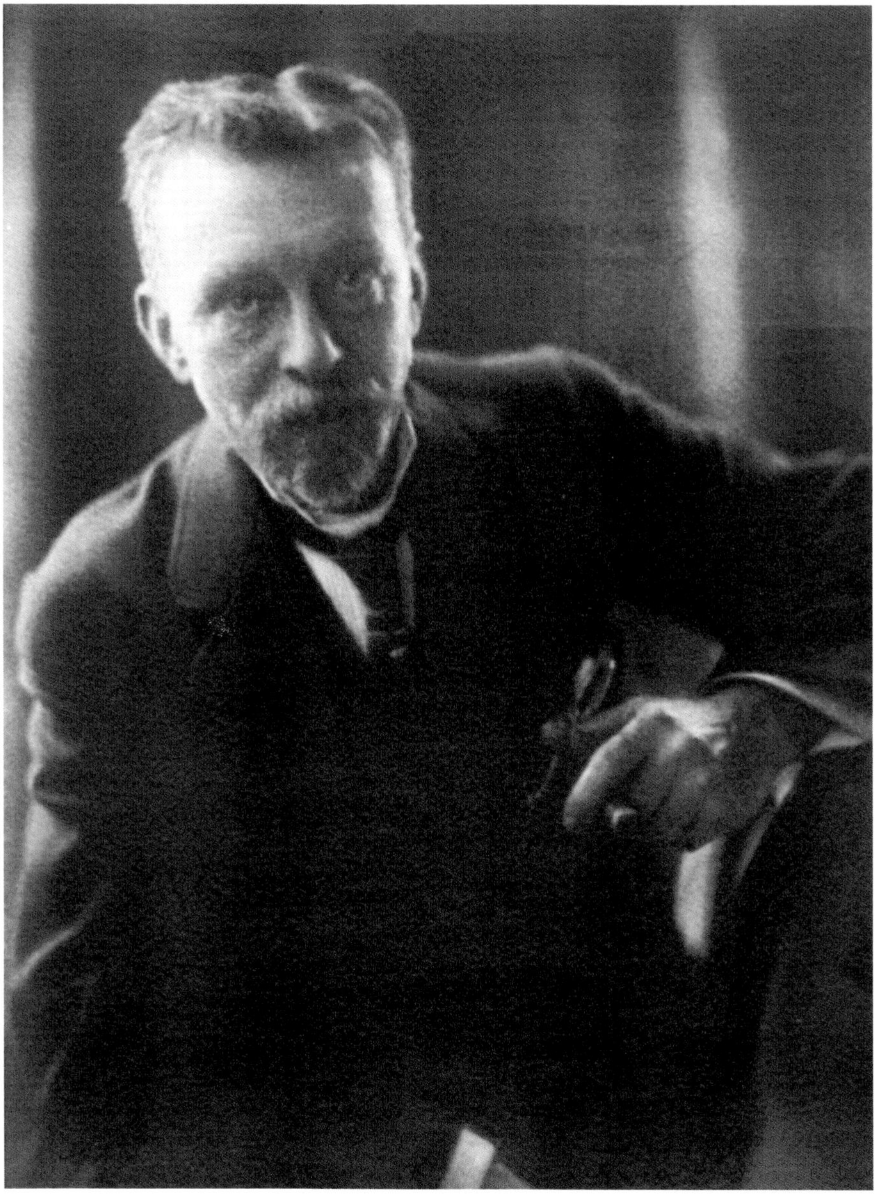

Source of the Richmond Name

George Turner Marsh was born in Australia in 1857. When he was 15, his family visited Japan en route to the United States. Fascinated by Japanese culture and art, George later opened the store Geo T. Marsh and Company: Japanese Art Repository in San Francisco. He built a home at Twelfth Avenue and Clement Street, calling it the Richmond House (see facing page) after the area of his birth. Later, when the board of supervisors was naming that section of San Francisco, property owners suggested "the Richmond District" to honor George Marsh and his pioneering Asian-art business; in 1890, the name was adopted. George later designed an Asian exhibit for the Midwinter Fair of 1894, and that area of Golden Gate Park still survives today as the Japanese Tea Garden. (Above, courtesy Annabelle Marsh Piercy; facing page above, courtesy Annabelle Marsh Piercy; facing page below, from *Midwinter Fair and Sunset Scenes*, 1894.)

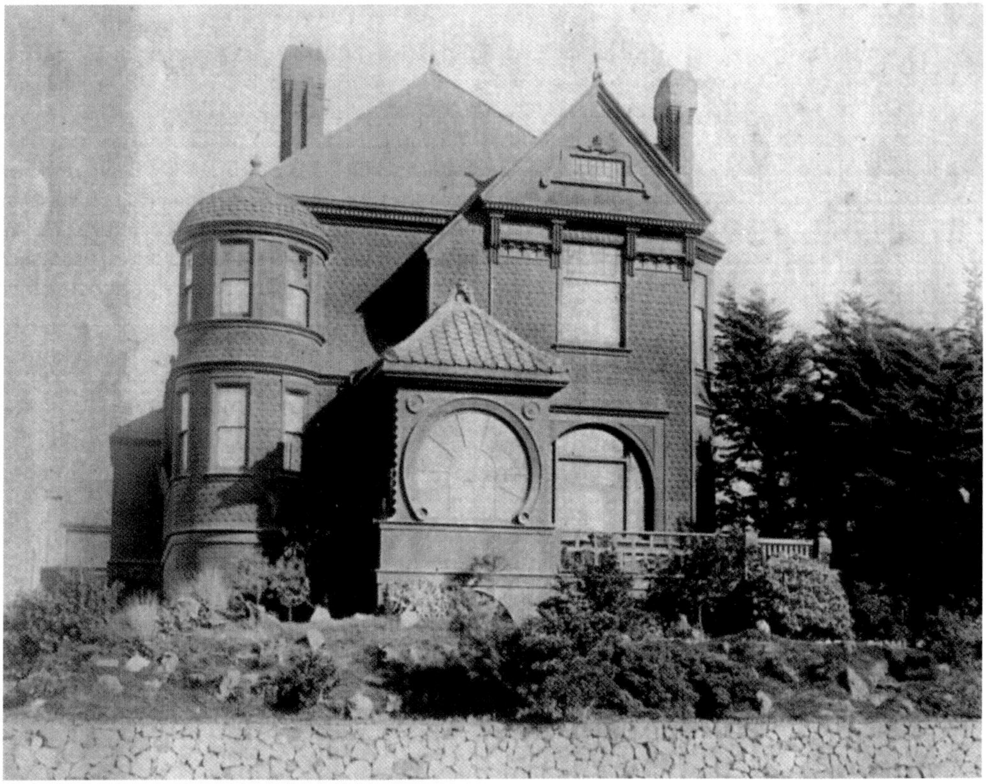

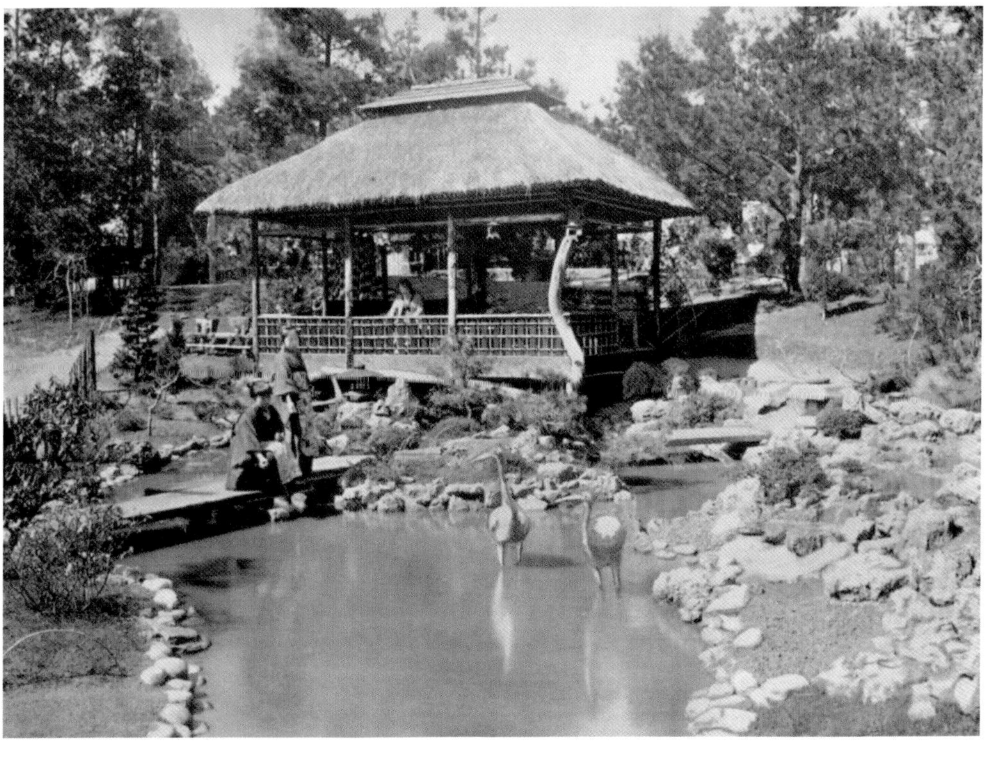

California Palace of the Legion of Honor

Alma Spreckels was known as the driving force behind a museum in the Richmond District's Lincoln Park. Alma Emma Charlotte Corday le Normand de Bretteville was born in the Sunset District in March 1881. She married the wealthy Adolph Spreckels in 1908. Alma Spreckels, shown here with her daughter Alma, was a temperamental woman with a passion for French culture. She convinced her husband and other donors to build a memorial to the 3,600 California soldiers who died in World War I. The California Palace of the Legion of Honor Museum (facing page) opened on November 11, 1924, and it still stands as one of San Francisco's beautiful museums. When Alma Spreckels died in 1968, her funeral was held in the main gallery of the Legion of Honor. (Below, courtesy San Francisco History Room, San Francisco Public Library; facing page above, courtesy Emiliano Echeverria; facing page below, courtesy Mark Adams.)

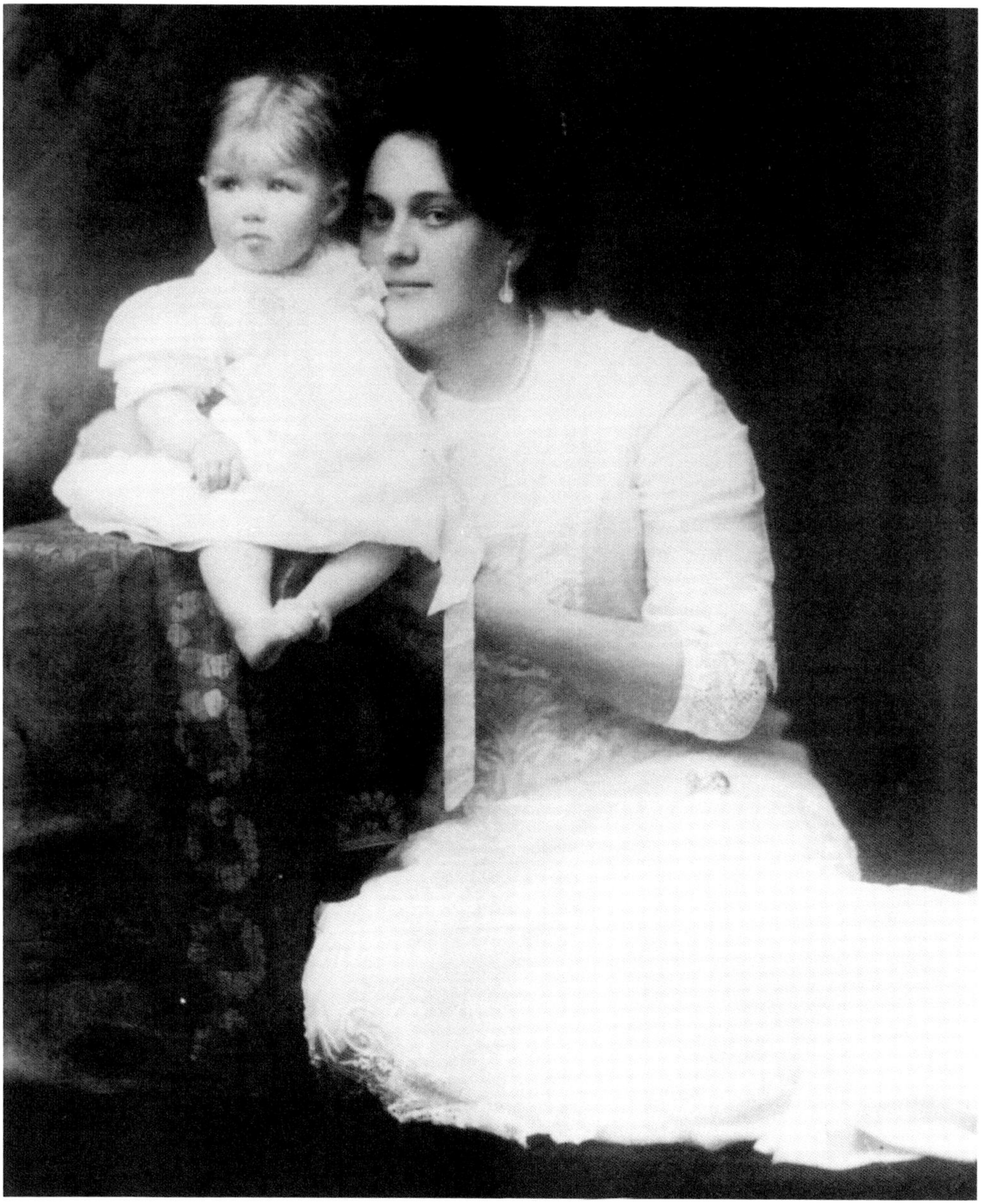

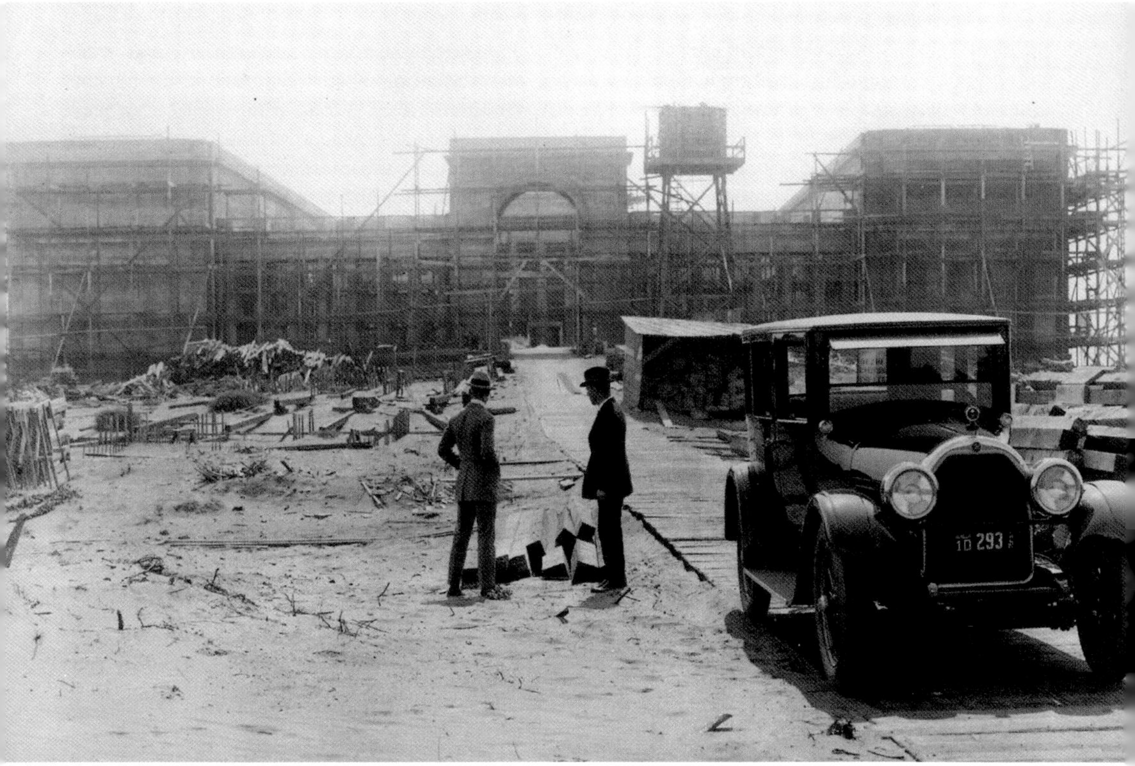

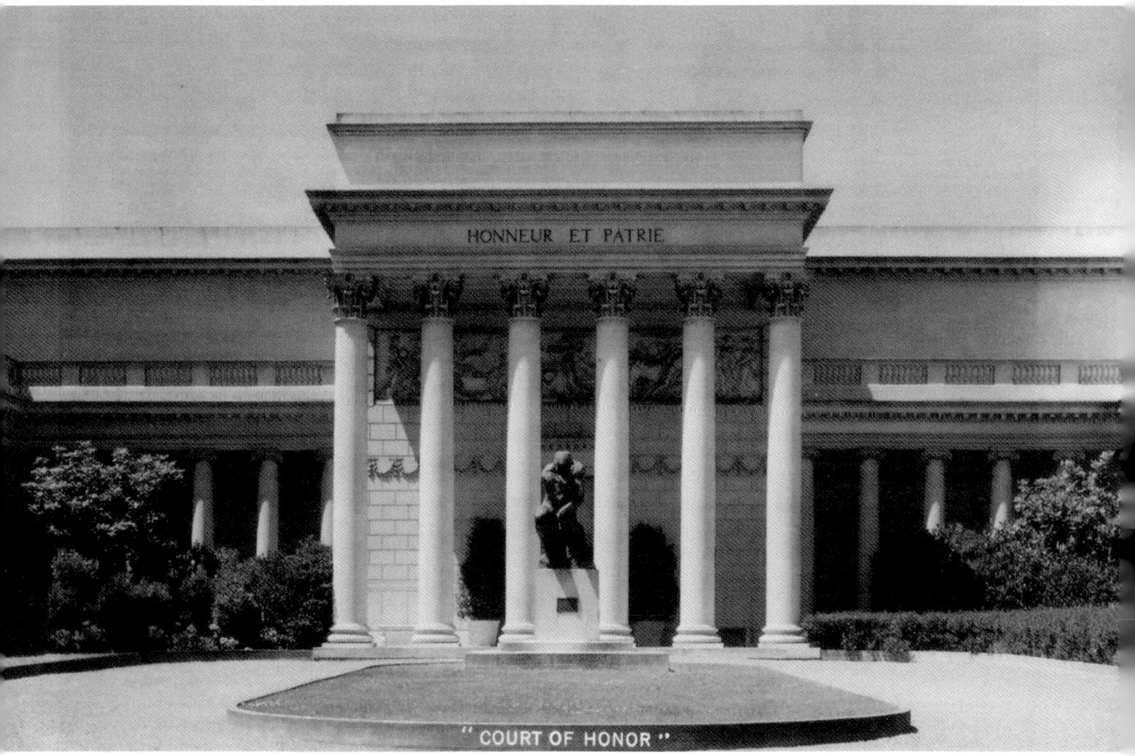

" COURT OF HONOR "

Pioneering Surfer

Born in 1929, Fred Van Dyke attended St. Anne's School through eighth grade and, in 1946, graduated from the new Abraham Lincoln High School "with a D average," he says. Van Dyke's memoir, *Once upon Abundance: Coming of Age in California and Hawaii*, describes growing up in the Sunset District and then moving to Hawaii. Over time, Van Dyke became a legendary pioneer in the sport of riding huge waves. He helped found and later wrote for *Surfer* magazine and was senior editor at *Ocean Sports International* magazine. He appeared as a surfer in two 1960s Hollywood movies and was part of the 2001 video documentary *Surfing for Life*, which highlighted surfers in their 70s, 80s, and 90s. Van Dyke now lives in Hawaii and Montana. He still writes and gives public presentations. (Author's photograph.)

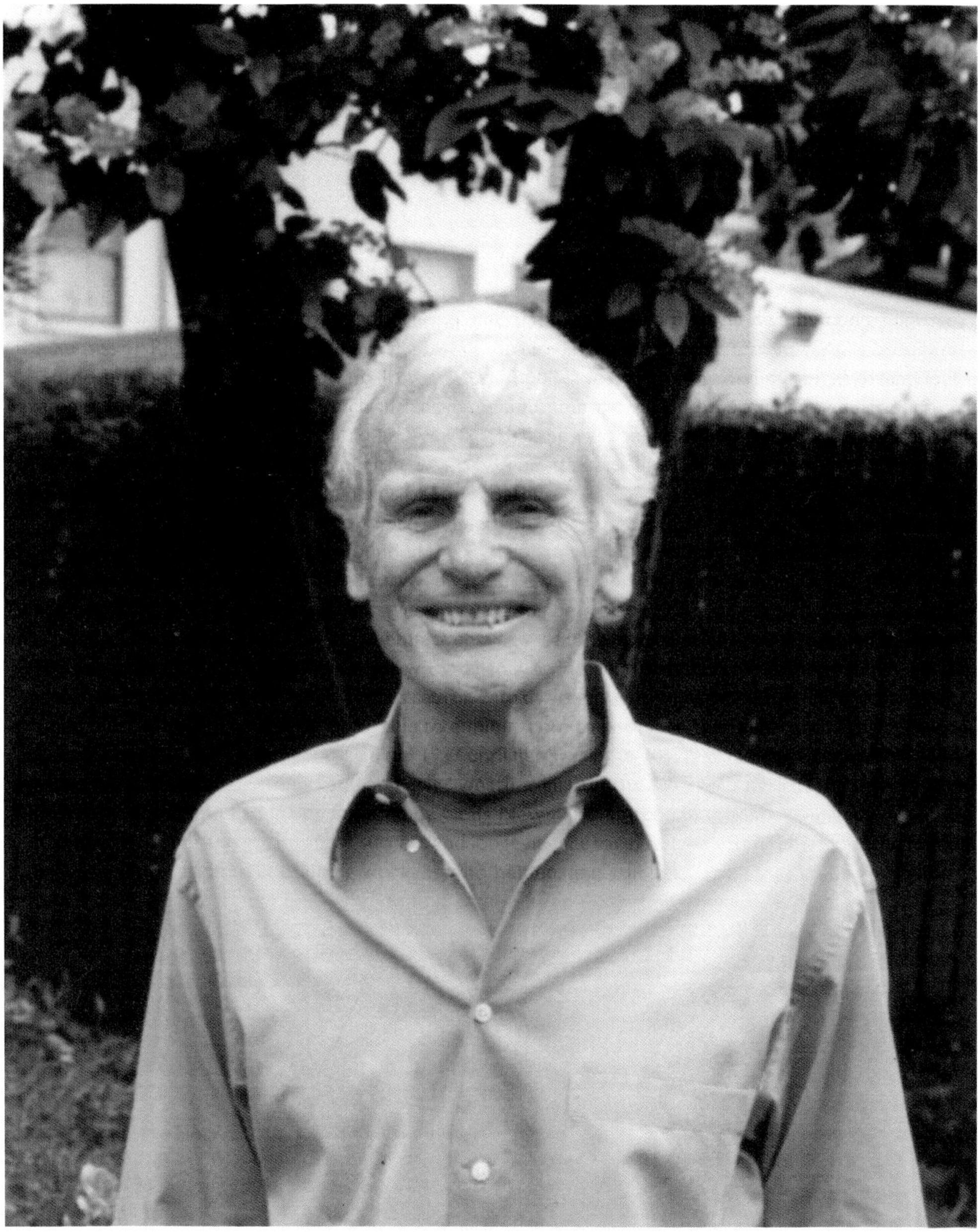

CHAPTER SIX

Businesses

Businesses form the core of any neighborhood, and the people who own or have owned businesses in the Sunset or Richmond Districts have made a difference to area residents and visitors.

Some businesses in this book no longer exist but were parts of growing neighborhoods. For example, Carl Larsen's Chicken Ranch thrived in the Sunset in the early 1900s but has since been covered by hundreds of houses. Adolph Sutro and George Whitney worked hard to develop the western edge of the Richmond District, giving San Franciscans Sutro Baths and Playland-at-the-Beach. All that stands today of these destinations are the ruins of Sutro Baths.

Some of the businesses in this book were founded long ago but still thrive in the modern neighborhood. For example, in 1893, Julia Quigley founded the Little Shamrock, the oldest continually running business in the Sunset District. This saloon has survived various owners and even Prohibition. Green Apple Books, which recently received the *Publisher's Weekly* award for best bookstore, opened in 1967. Since 1999, it has been operated by three long-term employees: Kevin Hunsanger, Pete Mulvihill, and Kevin Ryan.

This chapter also highlights individuals with unusual or interesting talents. They may or may not have opened formal businesses, but their legacies remain with us. Johnnie Williams, known as Johnny-the-Birdman, trained birds to do tricks and set up a table to exhibit them to people in the Richmond. Evelyn Wilson, a Sunset resident, was a parliamentarian from 1937 until her passing in 2012. As a young woman, Terry Lowry was a pioneer in television news and an early "weather girl" in the 1970s. Craigslist, the internationally known online classified ad listing founded by Craig Newmark, started in the Inner Sunset.

Companies come and go. Business success and longevity are rare. But we often remember the founders who had a vision and the continuing workers who helped, and still help, bring that vision to reality.

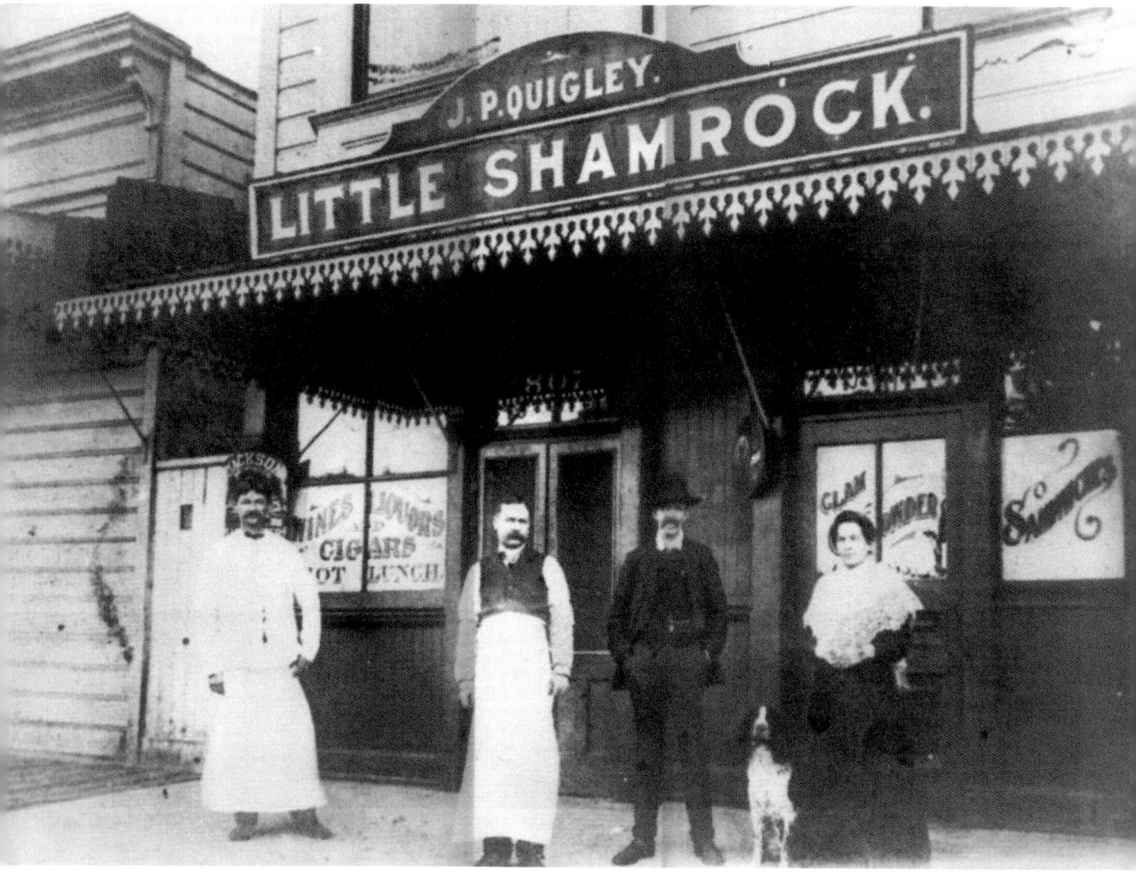

A Strong 1800s Businesswoman

Julia Herzo Quigley was a successful entrepreneur at a time when few women were. Born Julia Seery in Ireland in 1860, she came to this country when she was 14 years old. With her first husband, Antone Herzo, Julia started the Shamrock Saloon at Seventh Avenue and Fulton Street in the Richmond District. After her husband died, Julia sold the pub, and then this 33-year-old mother of three children opened The Little Shamrock on Fifth Avenue in the Richmond and The Little Shamrock on H Street (now Lincoln Way) in the Sunset. Julia (believed to at the far right in this photograph) married James Patrick Quigley. She died in 1929 at the age of 68. The Little Shamrock is the oldest continually running business in the Sunset District. (Courtesy The Little Shamrock.)

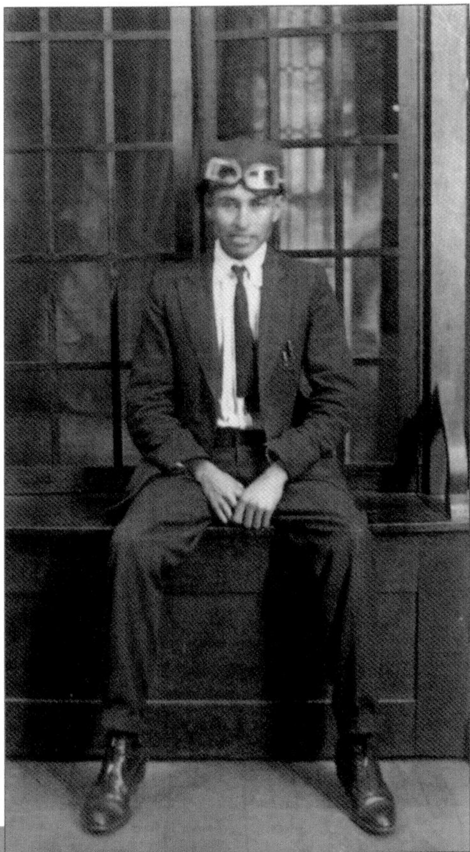

Flying over the Richmond
As the wind blows in from the Pacific Ocean, the Richmond District offers updrafts that are ideal for flying. Back in 1912, when much of the area was sand dunes, 15-year-old twin brothers Arthur (shown here) and Willy Gonzales designed a biplane and built it in the backyard of their home on Sixteenth Avenue. According to the Richmond District blog, the "Gonzales No. 1 Tractor Biplane" was constructed mostly of pine, with some spruce; wing supports were attached "with bicycle spokes and spoke adjusters . . . It was powered by a 35-horsepower, four-cylinder, air-cooled Kemp inline engine." When Arthur and Willy brought the biplane out to the sand dunes, children would come out to watch the boys work on it and then fly it above the neighborhood. (Courtesy the Hiller Aviation Museum.)

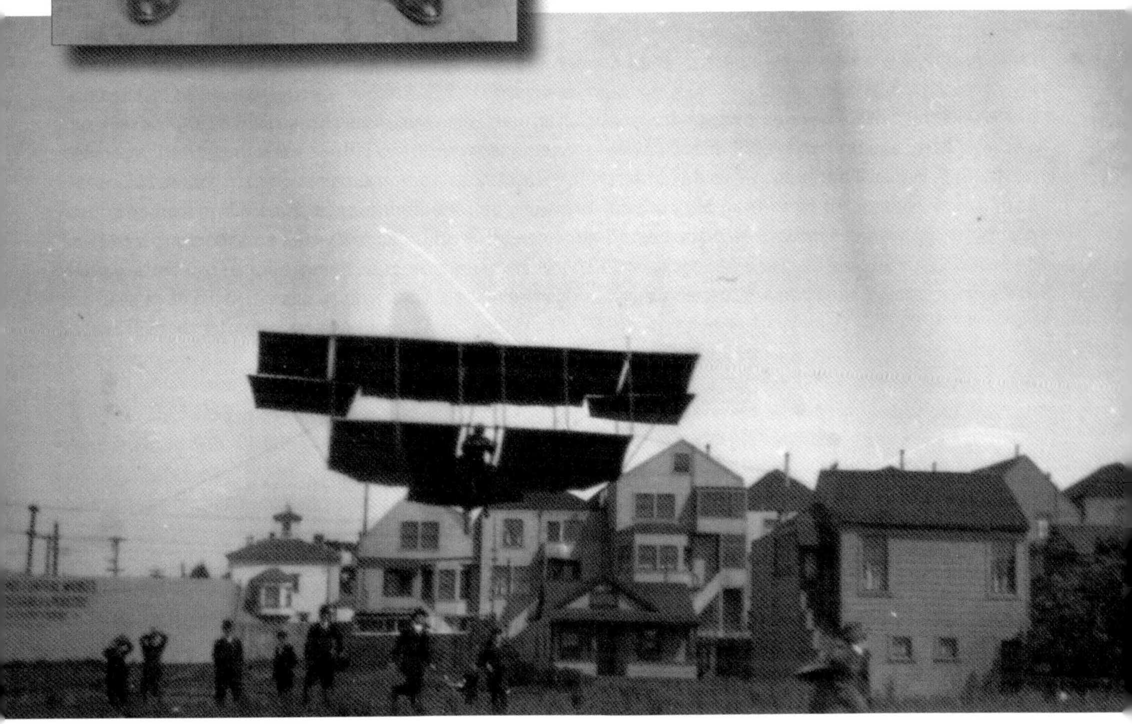

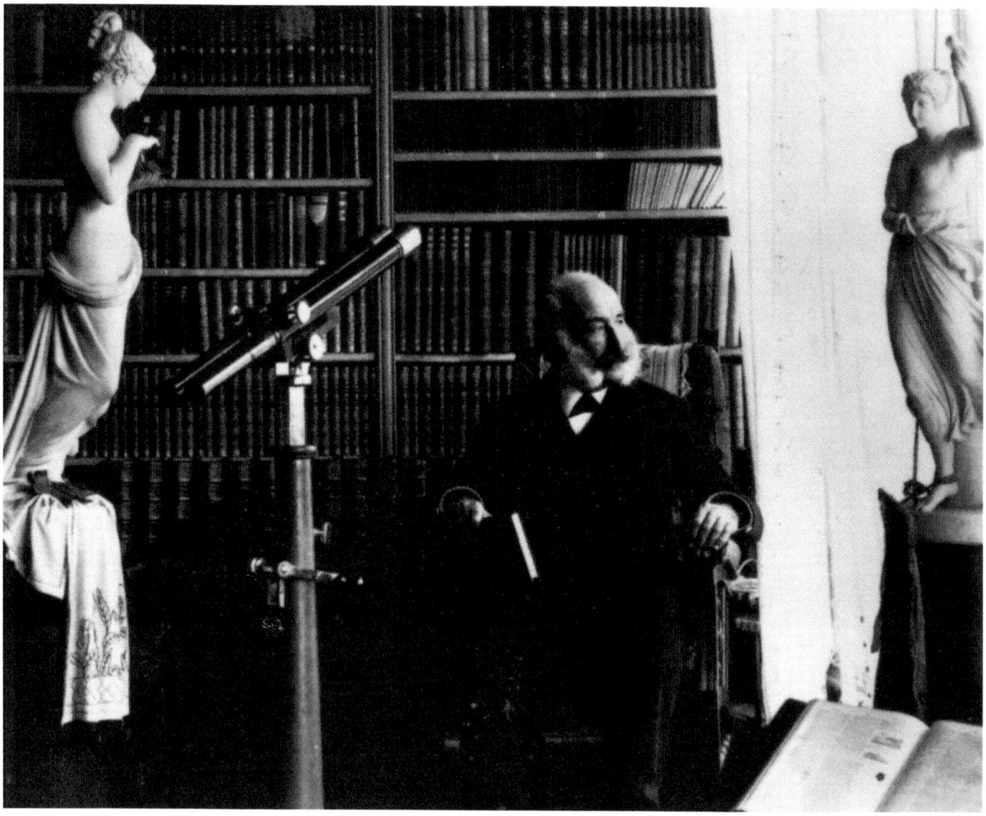

A Unique Philanthropist

Probably no one has had a greater influence on the history of the Richmond and Sunset Districts than Adolph Sutro. He was born in Prussia in 1830 and immigrated to California in 1850. When the Comstock silver strike hit in Nevada, he built a special tunnel to provide better ventilation and drainage for the miners. When he sold the tunnel in 1880, Adolph was a wealthy man.

Adolph shared his good fortune with other San Franciscans. He bought thousands of acres of land in San Francisco, mostly in the Outside Lands; at one time, he owned one-twelfth of all real estate in the city. He leased land at Ocean Beach to the people living in "Carville," a collection of obsolete cable cars and streetcars. He bought the Cliff House and remodeled it into the iconic castle structure (considered the "second" Cliff House) that burned down in 1907. (See facing page.)

On the bluff across the road from the Cliff House, Adolph built his own estate and invited people to visit the grounds. The land is now Sutro Heights Park, open to the public.

Perhaps what Adolph is best known for is Sutro Baths, a huge building with historical exhibits and six swimming pools, each with a different water temperature. When the Southern Pacific Railroad insisted on charging 10¢ for people to ride to Sutro Baths on a streetcar, Sutro built his own railroad line and charged only 5¢.

Sutro Baths burned down in 1966. For many years, the city tried to keep curious visitors away from the ruins, but now they are open to the public and are a popular spot for tourists and residents.

Sutro served as San Francisco's mayor from 1894 to 1896. In 1898, he donated land to found the Affiliated Colleges (now the University of California, San Francisco). He sponsored Arbor Day plantings on his property just south of the Inner Sunset, planting thousands of trees in "Sutro Forest." He donated his large private library for public use. Much of it was destroyed in 1906, and the collection is now housed at San Francisco State University. Adolph died in San Francisco on August 8, 1898. (Courtesy Marilyn Blaisdell.)

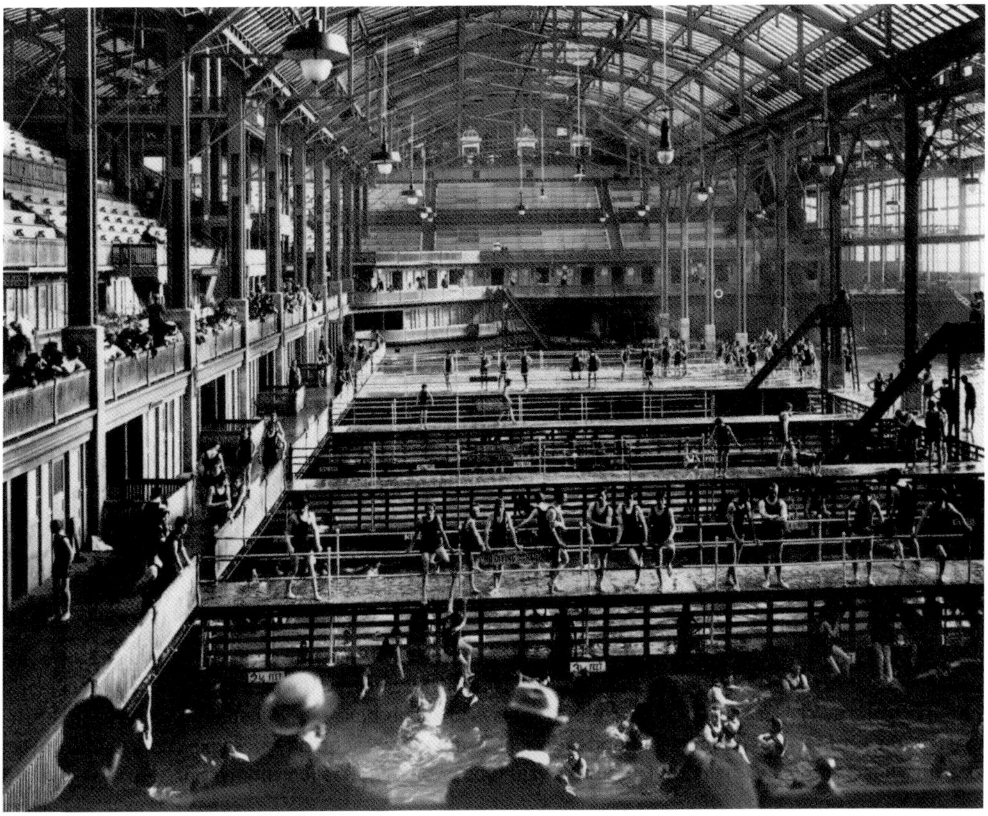

Sutro Baths

Adolph Sutro opened Sutro Baths (above) to great acclaim. Swimmers enjoyed six pools of differing temperatures. He loved statuary; some of the statues that lined his property can be seen in the photograph below of the Cliff House, which Adolph also owned. (Above, courtesy Marilyn Blaisdell; below, courtesy Ron Ross.)

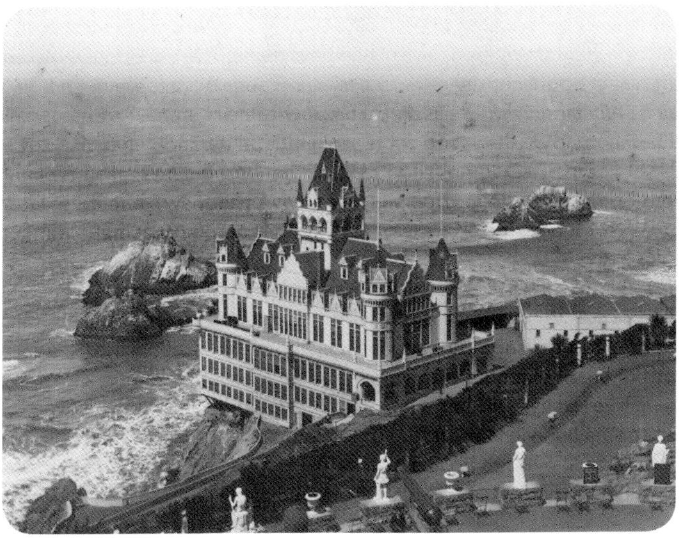

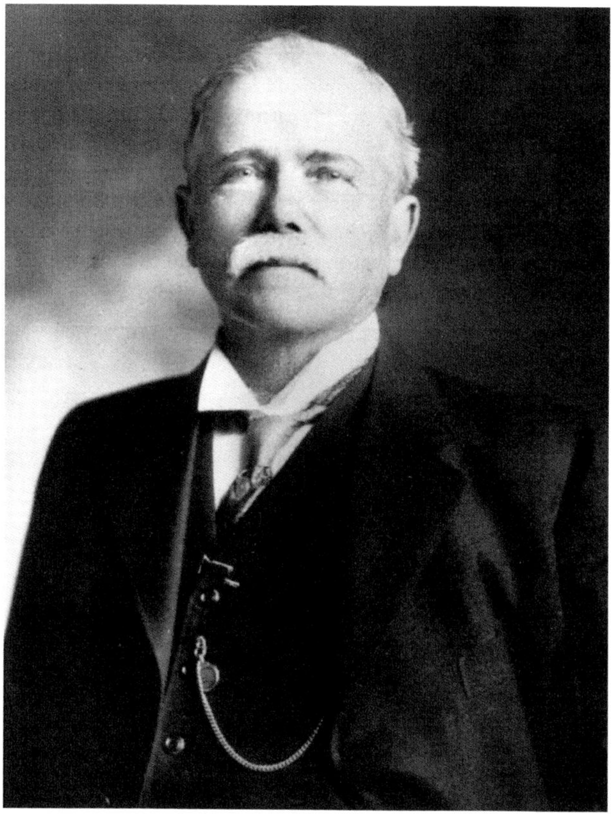

The "Gentle Dane"

Carl Larsen was one of the first people to see the potential benefit of owning land in the sandy Sunset District. He was born in 1844 in Odense, Denmark, and came to San Francisco in his late 20s. In 1879, he opened the popular Tivoli Café downtown. Carl began buying land in the Sunset and operated a chicken ranch (see facing page, above) on one square block bounded by Sixteenth and Seventeenth Avenues and Moraga and Noriega Streets. Each morning, a horse-drawn carriage took eggs from the Sunset chicken ranch to Larsen's Tivoli Café downtown.

Sometimes called the "Gentle Dane," Larsen lived downtown, but he was very involved in the Sunset. He was a member of the Nineteenth Avenue Boulevard Club, a neighborhood group that lobbied for a paved road along Nineteenth Avenue. He also worked for civic improvements and streetcar service to the area. Over the years, Larsen donated or sold most of his land. In 1926, he donated land for Golden Gate Heights Park. He is best remembered for his 1928 donation of Carl Larsen Park on two square blocks between Nineteenth and Twentieth Avenues. In the bottom photograph on the facing page, he is being thanked by Mayor James Rolph. In the 1960s, Larsen Park featured a Navy jet for children to climb over and sit in.

Carl Larsen died on November 5, 1928. He had never married and had no known children. Evidence indicates that Larsen planned to leave some of his estate to his adopted city. A handwritten will, dated July 27, 1909, gave money to friends, family members, and organizations, and gave the remaining funds to San Francisco for a museum in Golden Gate Park. Some of the people listed in the will never saw those funds. When the will was discovered, Larsen's signature and the signature of a witness had been "cut off." A judge declared the will invalid, and most of the estate was divided among Larsen's relatives in Denmark. Larsen's museum was never built in Golden Gate Park, but two Sunset parks, Golden Gate Heights Park and Larsen Park, stand as reminders of Carl Larsen. (Courtesy San Francisco History Center, San Francisco Public Library.)

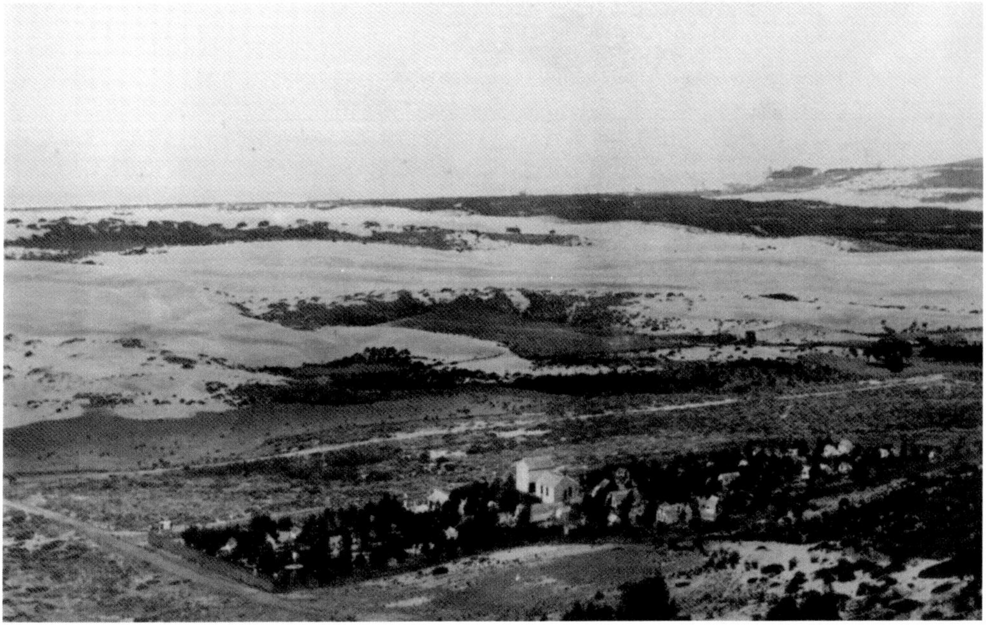

Larsen Park

Carl Larsen (see opposite page) was one of the early landowners in the Sunset District. His chicken farm (above) is surrounded by the sand dunes prevalent in the Sunset in the early 1900s. In 1928, the mayor (below, left) expresses his appreciation for Carl's donation of land in the Sunset for Larsen Park. (Above, courtesy anonymous collection; below, courtesy San Francisco History Center, San Francisco Public Library.)

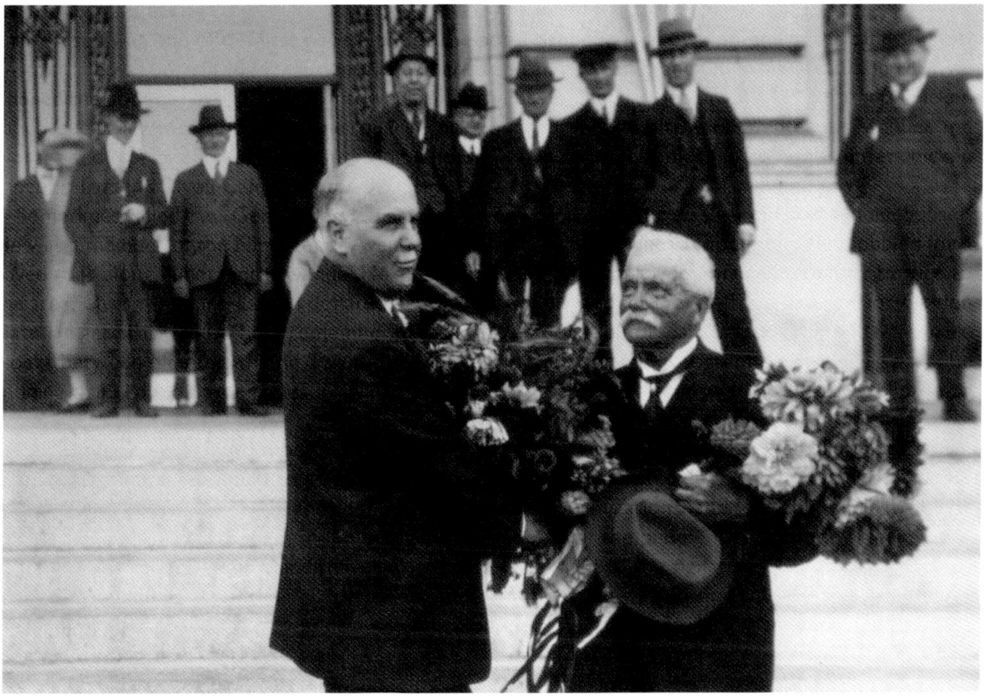

Amusing the Public

In 1926, George Whitney and his brother Leo took over and renamed an ocean-side amusement park in San Francisco. Many older residents remember Playland's attractions and rides, including the Fun House, the Big Dipper, Shoot the Chutes, Topsy's Roost, and the Diving Bell. George, shown here on the left with a business associate in front of one of the Fun House mirrors, was a collector, always looking for objects that might attract viewers. In 1937, he purchased the closed Cliff House and reopened it later that year. In 1952, he bought Sutro Baths and added many of the items he had collected to the museum. He once said, "Playland is a nickel-and-dime business, and we'll do well as long as people have nickels and dimes in their pockets." George died in 1958. Playland closed in 1972 and was replaced by condominiums. (Courtesy San Francisco History Room, San Francisco Public Library.)

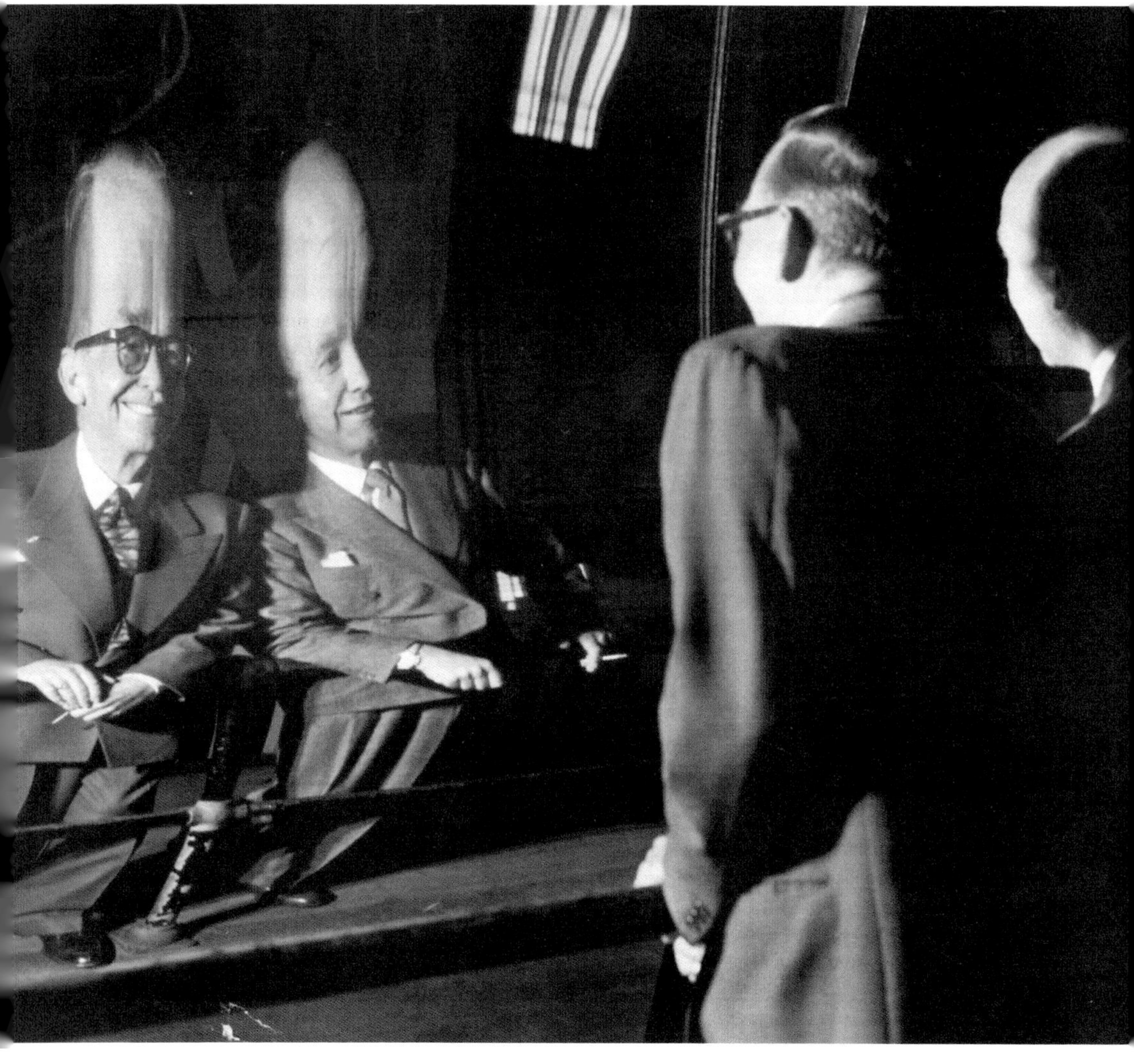

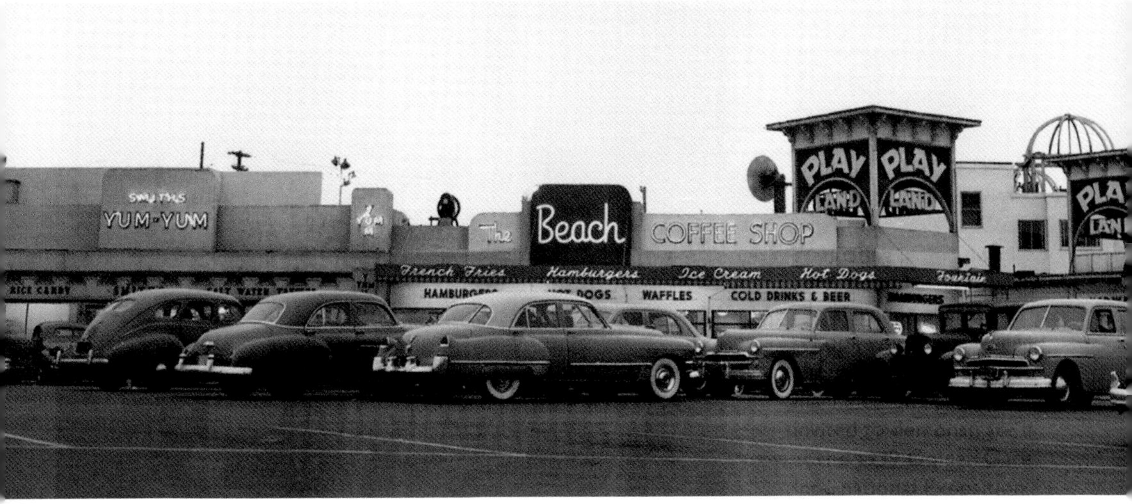

Playland-at-the-Beach

George and Leo Whitney's Playland-at-the-Beach was a popular destination, especially from the 1920s through the 1940s. (Above, courtesy Dennis O'Rorke; below, courtesy David Gallagher, photograph by Eugene E. Gallagher.)

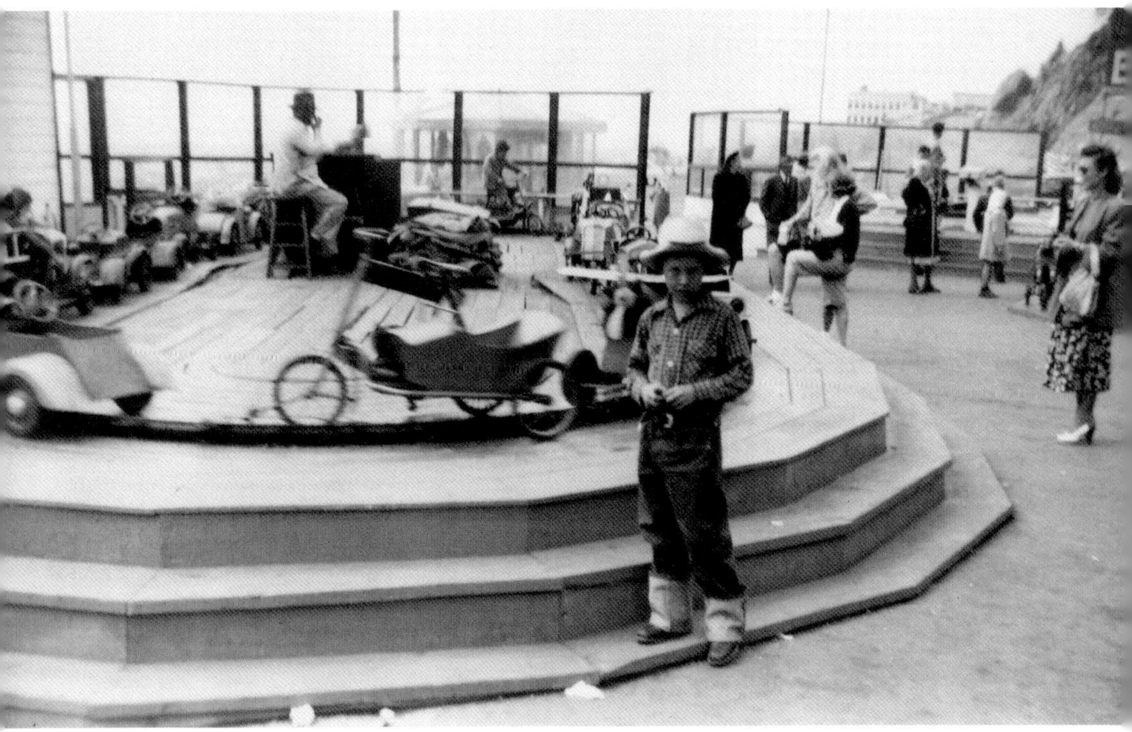

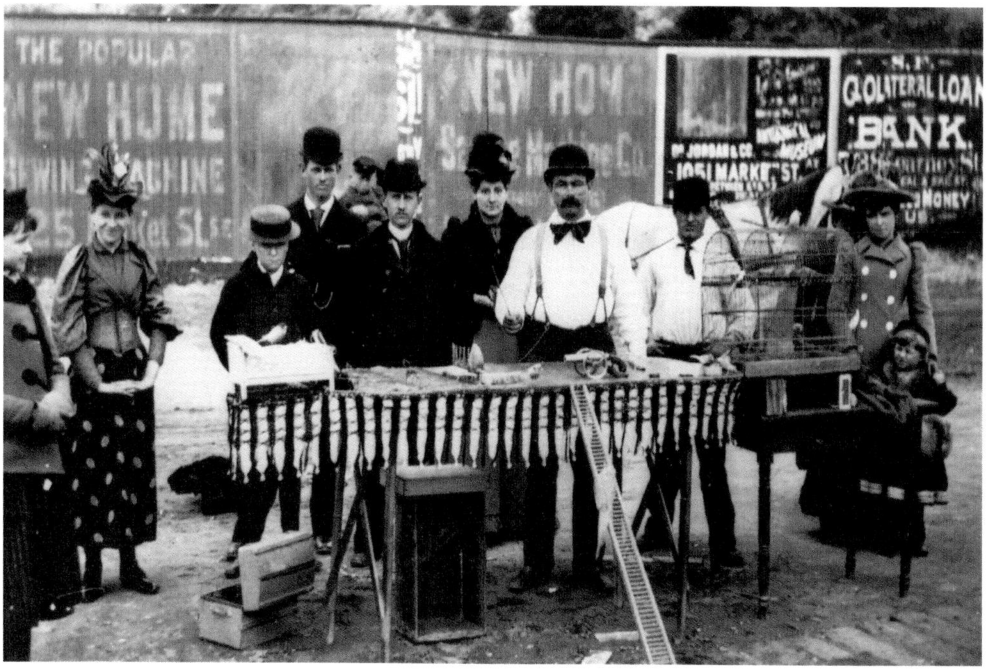

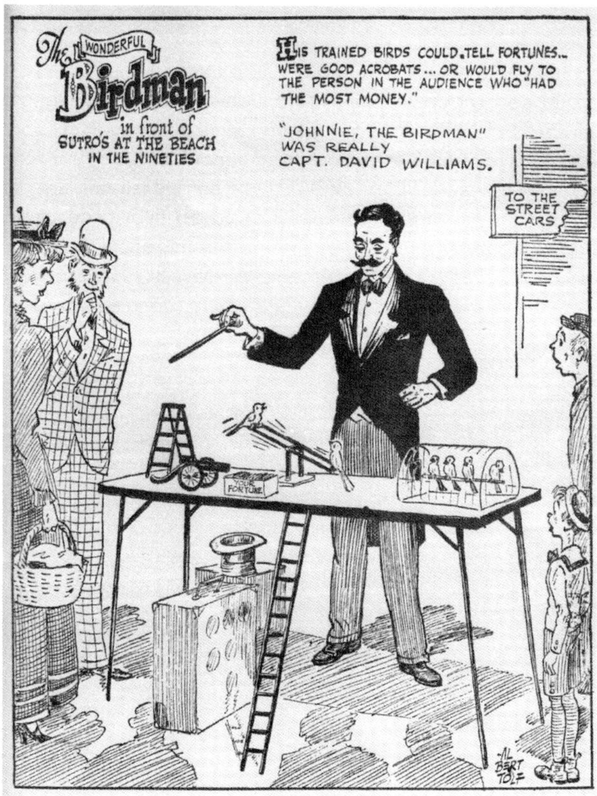

Johnnie-the-Birdman
For more than 20 years, John Williams entertained visitors to Ocean Beach and the Cliff House. He was best known as "Johnnie-the-Birdman," and his passion was training birds to do tricks. When he set up his table near Lands End, he turned on the charm and could nudge the nickels out of a crowd. The frugal Johnnie saved his nickels and bought adjoining lots with cottages on Eleventh Avenue in the Richmond. He did his trained budgie act from 1886 until the crowds dwindled after the Cliff House burned in 1907. Johnnie was a great entertainer, but he was reclusive in his private life, and his birds were his only companions. With his birds around him, he died suddenly of a brain hemorrhage in 1909 at age 60. In the 1950s, cartoonist Albert Tolf depicted Johnnie in the *San Francisco News*. (Courtesy Marilyn Blaisdell.)

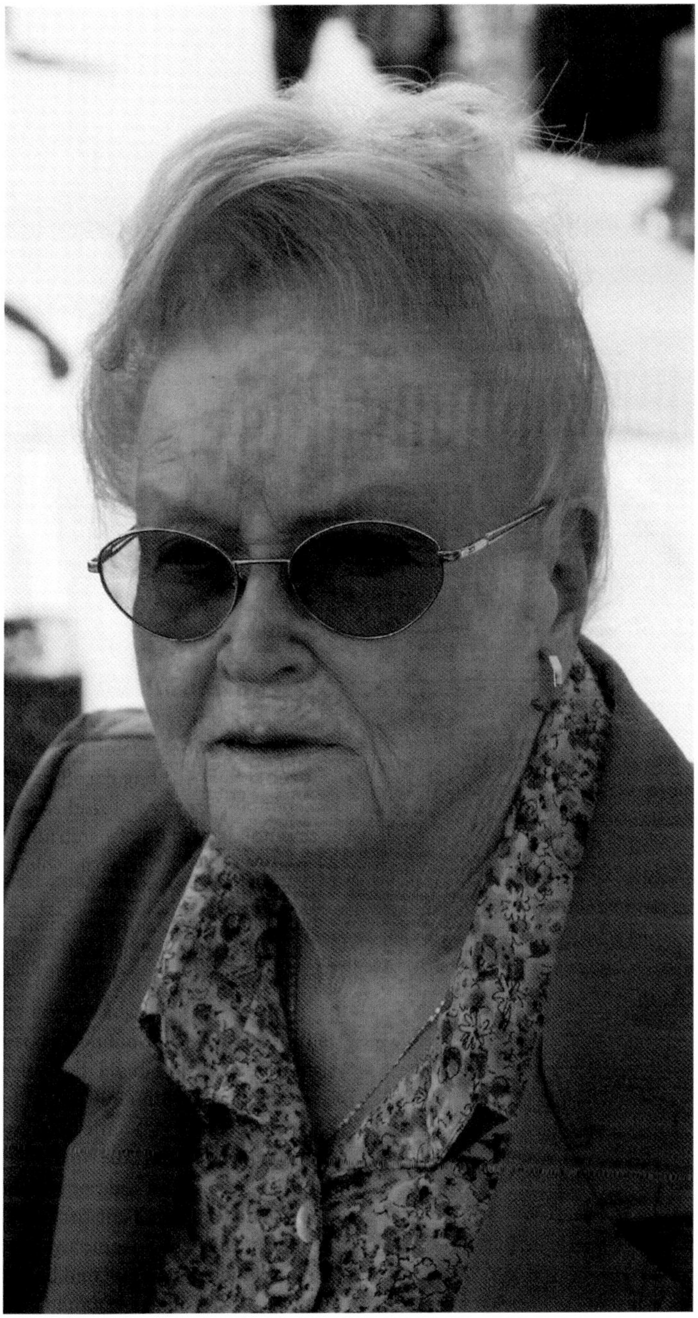

Keeping Groups on Track
Born in Wisconsin in August 1919, Evelyn (Avery) Wilson moved with her family to San Francisco's Sunset District when she was six. After graduating from Lowell High School in 1937, she attended secretarial school, where she learned about the new "Stenotype machine," and she was invited to demonstrate it at the 1939 Golden Gate International Exposition on Treasure Island. In her late 30s, Evelyn studied to become a professional registered parliamentarian, learning to ensure that group meetings followed the procedures in *Roberts' Rules of Order.* She was the official parliamentarian for various groups, including for 45 years for the San Francisco School Board. Evelyn volunteered for the Sunset Parkside Education and Action Committee (SPEAK) when it was founded in 1969. She served as the SPEAK board's president, secretary, treasurer, and, of course, parliamentarian. She was still active in SPEAK when she died in 2013 at the age of 94. (Courtesy the Wilson family.)

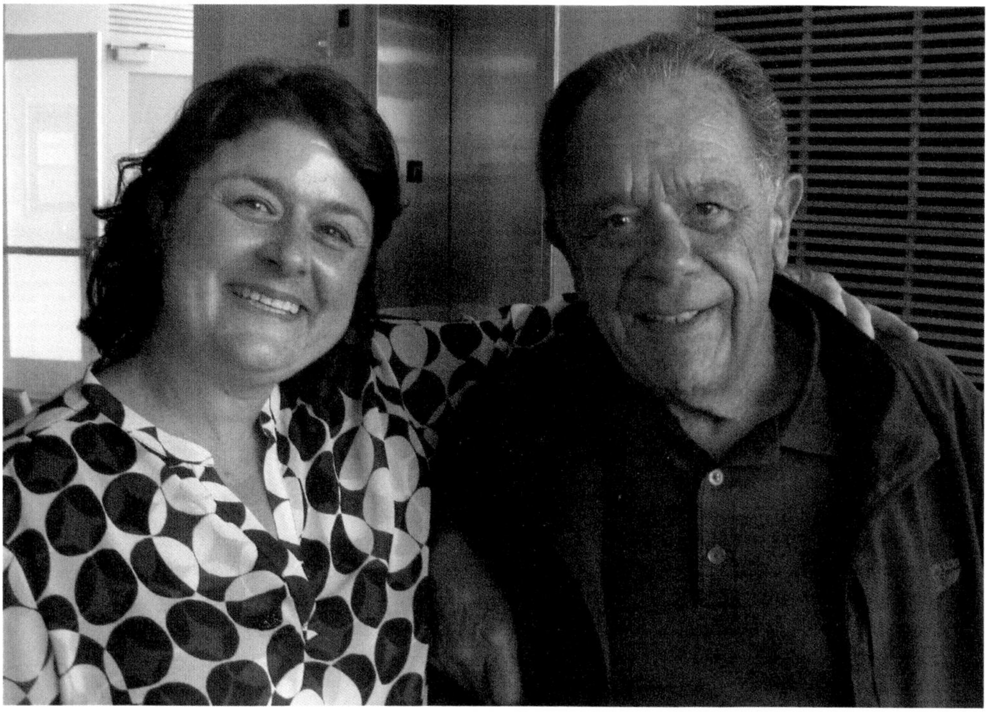

Famous Ocean-View Restaurant

At the northwestern edge of San Francisco, the Cliff House Restaurant provides a striking view of the Pacific Ocean. Dan Hountalas has made the Cliff House a family business for the past 40 years. Dan was born in 1935 in San Francisco and grew up on Forty-eighth Avenue between Geary Boulevard and Anza Street. He operated Cliff Chalet, a nearby restaurant that burned down in 1966. In 1972, George Whitney Jr. (see page 104) gave the then-closed and rundown Cliff House to Dan. After extensive renovations, Dan reopened the building to great acclaim. "Eighty-one percent of our clients are local," says Dan. He retired years ago, but he's often at the Cliff House. His daughter Vickie, shown here with him, and her husband, Ralph, now operate the business. (Author's photographs.)

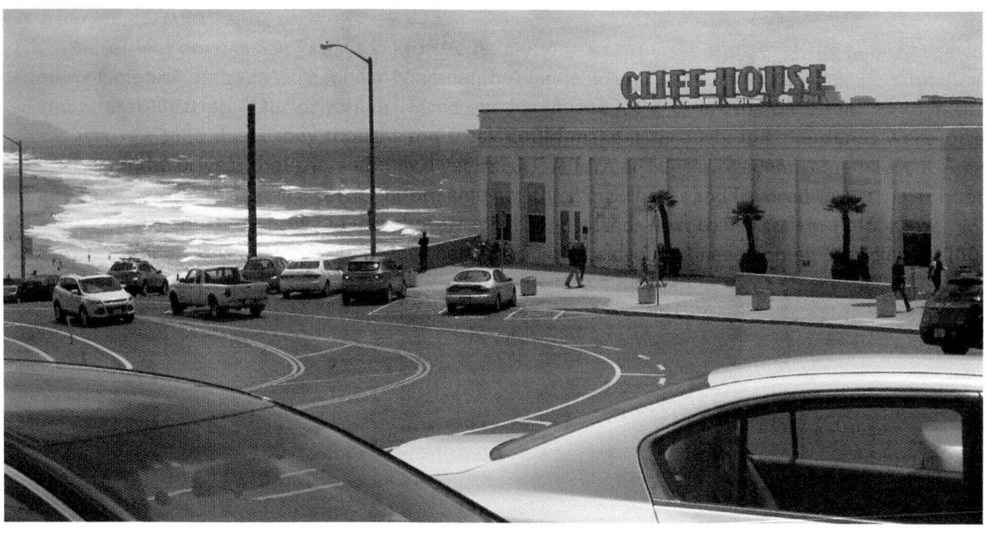

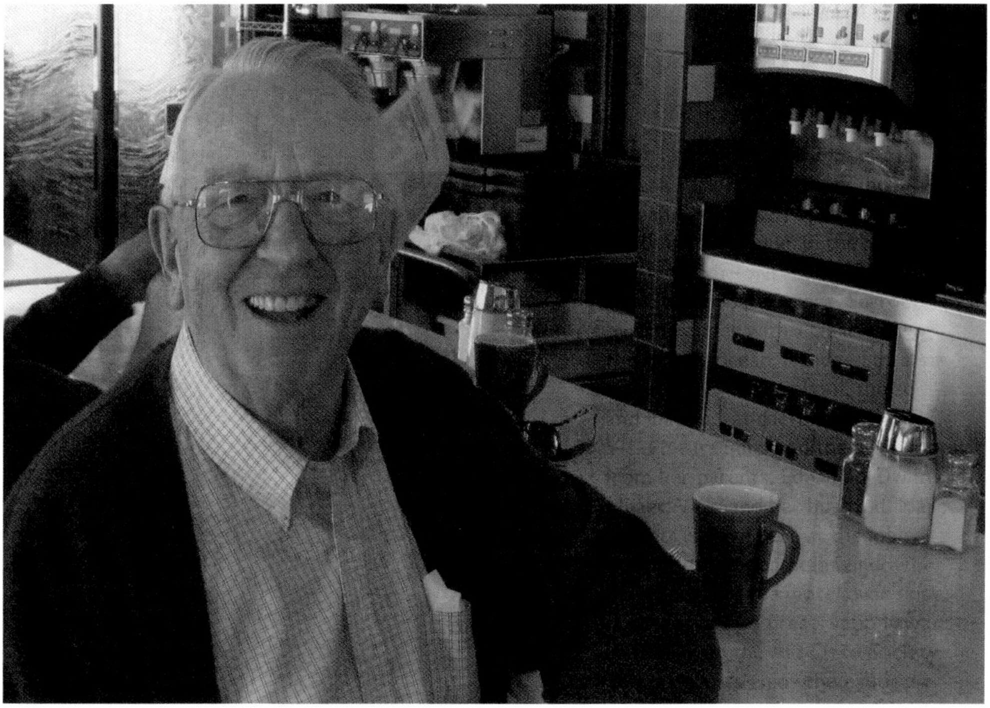

A Family Affair
When Louis Hontalas (same family as on facing page but with a different spelling) opened Louis' Restaurant in 1937, his son Jim Hontalas (above) did not realize that the restaurant (pronounced "Louie's") would be a permanent part of his life. Jim was born in San Francisco in 1930. He has always lived in the Richmond or the Sunset, and he graduated from Washington High School in 1948. From the time he was a boy, he helped out at the Richmond District restaurant, which has a beautiful ocean view, and was happy to take it over as a young man. It has continued to be a family affair; today, it is run by his two sons and his daughter. "Many of the people who eat here are returning customers," says Jim. "Some of them now bring in their grandchildren." (Author's photographs.)

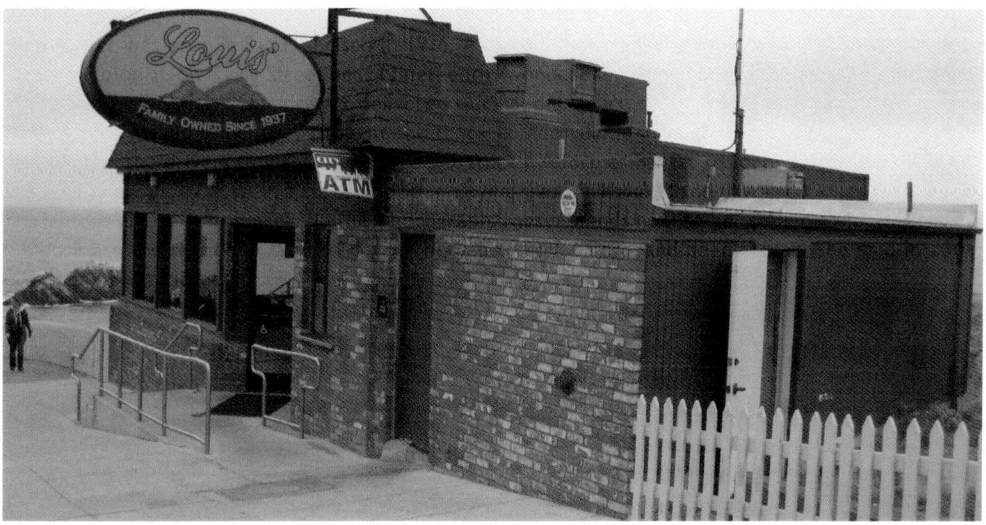

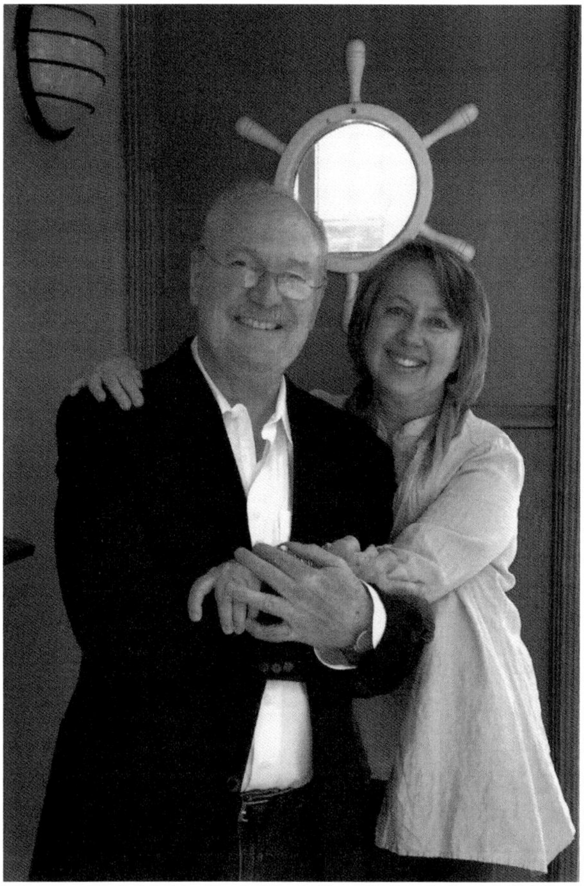

San Francisco's First Motel
Ocean Park Motor Court (now Ocean Park Motel) opened at 2690 Forty-sixth Avenue, in the Sunset, just weeks before the 1937 opening of the Golden Gate Bridge. Surrounded by sand dunes with a clear view of the nearby ocean, it lodged tourists visiting Fleishhacker Pool, the zoo, and Playland-at-the-Beach. In 1977, Vicki Mears inherited the aging motel from her parents, Edna and Owen Mears. Vicki and her husband, Marc Duffett (shown here at the lobby door with the porthole window), have operated the motel ever since, encouraged by a preservation award in 1987 from the Art Deco Society. Today's guests enjoy the nautical décor, the garden hot tub, and the short walk to the beach. Marc says, "It's the charm and the very history of the Ocean Park that we love so dearly." (Courtesy Vicki and Marc Duffett.)

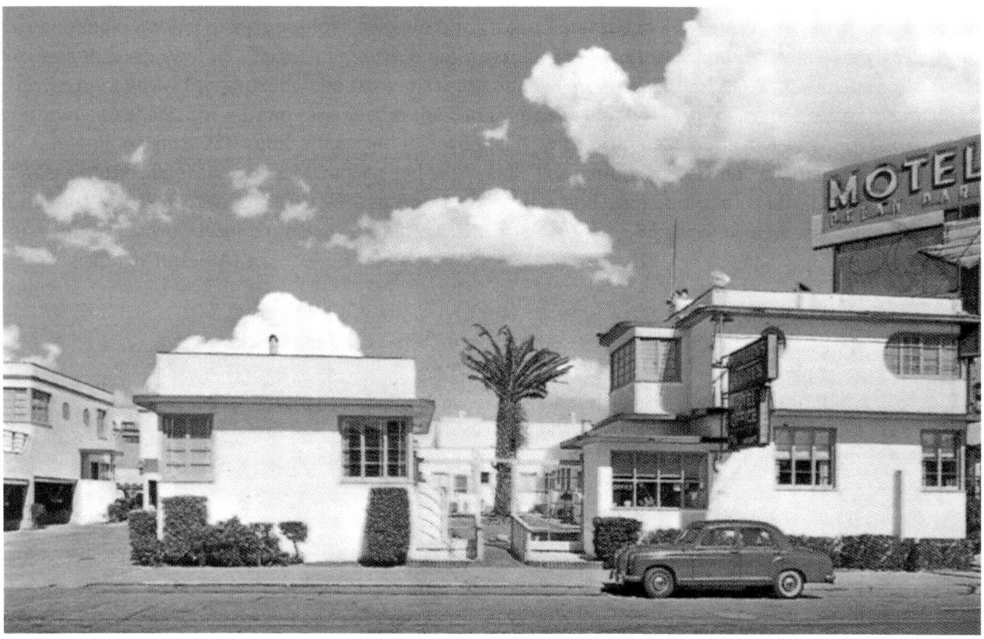

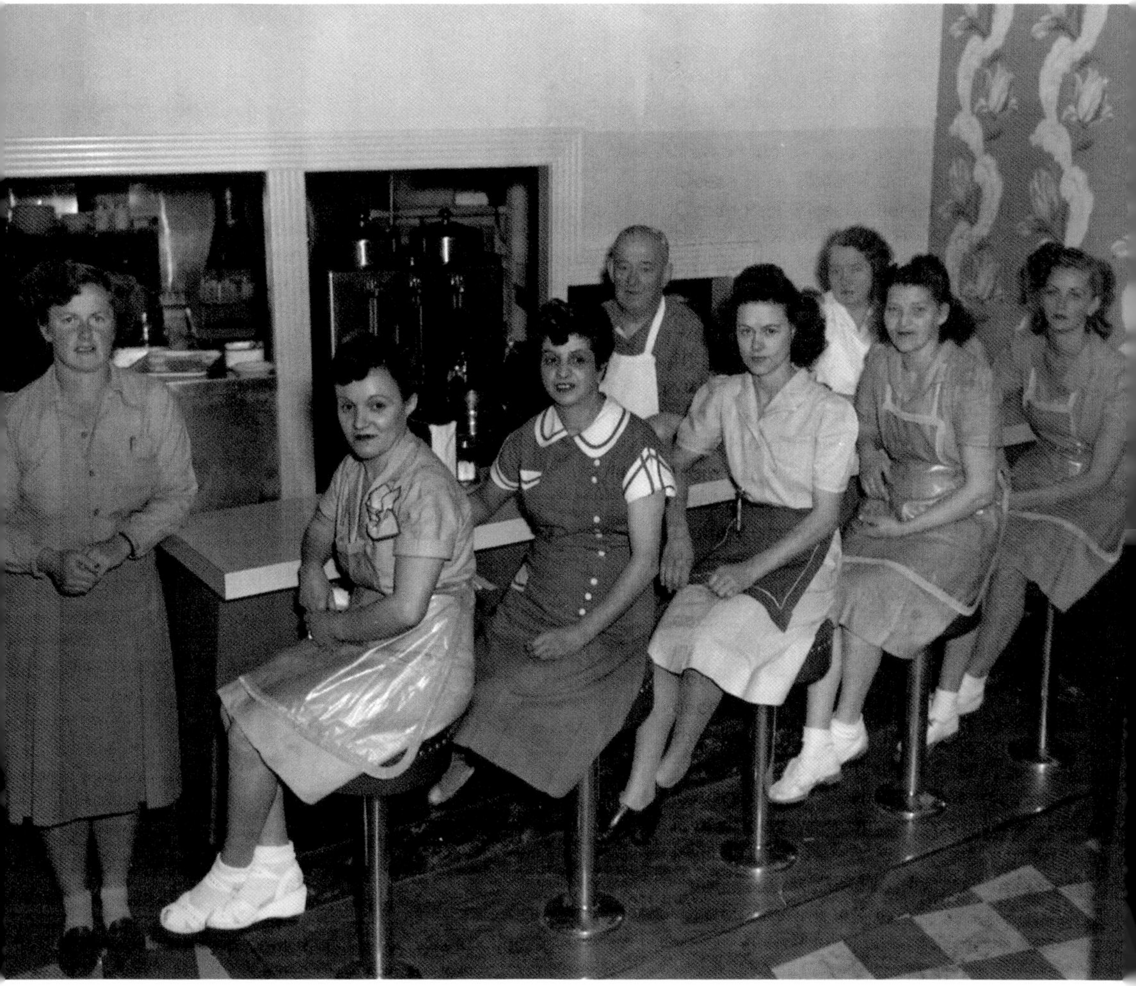

A Favorite Teen Hangout

Ellen Kieser was born in San Francisco in 1916. As a young woman, she took over the family business, Kieser's Colonial, on Irving Street near Nineteenth Avenue. Ellen remembered the massive sand dunes of the Sunset District. "Our drivers delivered our handmade ice cream," she once said. "When they came across a sand dune, they thought the truck could make it through. But the dunes were often deeper than the drivers thought, and they'd get stuck." A former Sunset resident remembers Kieser's as a teen hangout. "We sat in a corner booth enjoying thick milkshakes and flavored Cokes. That booth was famous all over the Sunset." In this photograph, Kieser stands next to her staff in 1946. Kieser sold the business and retired in 1978 to devote herself to golf, bridge, and needlepoint. She died in 2006. (Courtesy Ellen Kieser.)

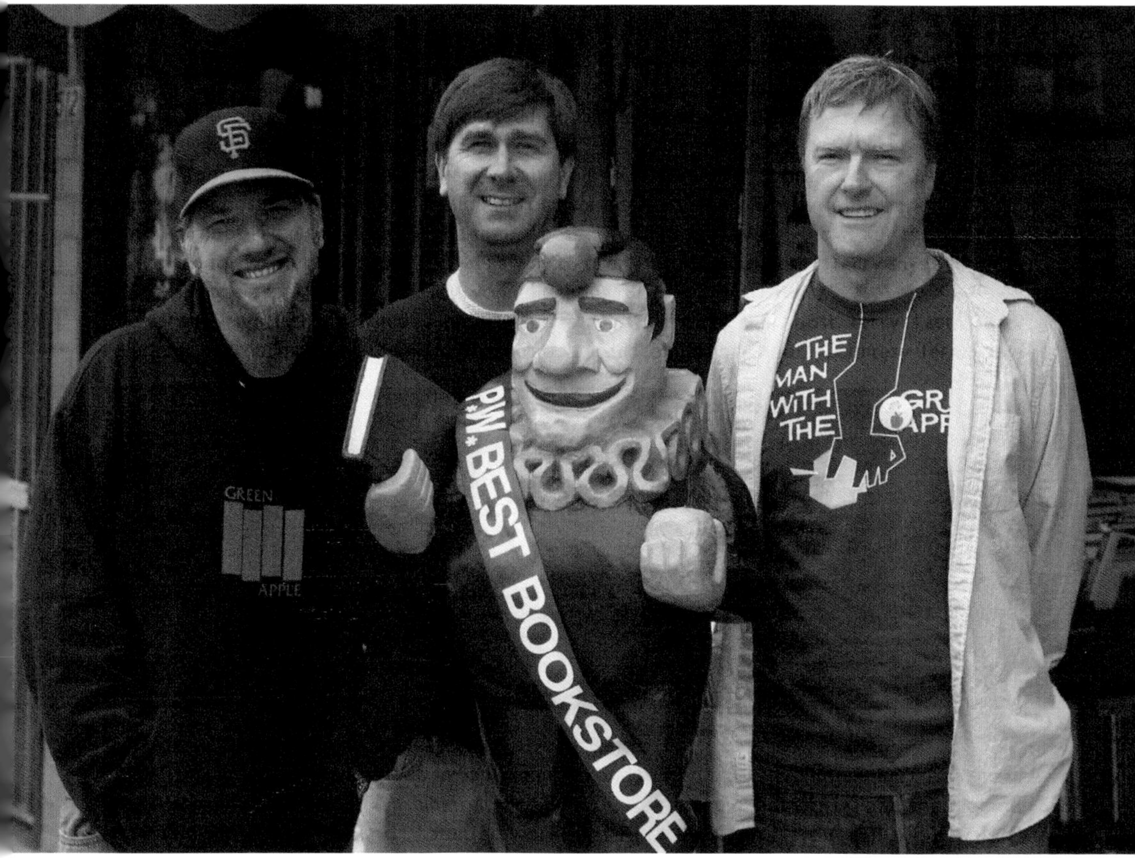

A Favorite Bookstore

Green Apple Books, many people's "favorite bookstore," started in 1967 near the corner of Clement Street and Sixth Avenue. Three long-term employees, Kevin Hunsanger, Pete Mulvihill, and Kevin Ryan (shown here with "Mergatroid," the store mascot), bought the store in 1999 and have made sure that it continues to adapt, thrive, and take part in the San Francisco community. Today, the shop covers about 10 times its original 750 square feet and is perennially voted the best bookstore in the Bay Area by readers of the *San Francisco Bay Guardian* and *SF Weekly*. The national magazine *Publisher's Weekly* named it the 2014 Bookstore of the Year. Green Apple offers new and used books, plus LPs, DVDs, magazines, cards, and gifts; yet, despite the many changes in the book industry, 85 percent of its sales are still books. (Photograph by Robin Allen.)

TV News and More

Terry Lowry, shown here as a young driver, was born in Oakland in 1947. Her family moved to Forty-seventh Avenue and Rivera Street in San Francisco, where she attended A.P. Giannini Middle School and Abraham Lincoln High School. She graduated from San Francisco State College with a teaching credential in Spanish and international relations.

After a short stint as a teacher, Terry was hired by KRON-TV/FM to translate the evening news into Spanish and host a bilingual public affairs program. Terry moved on to weather reporter, one of the few on-air jobs given to women at the time. These "weather girls" were known for their short, skimpy outfits and for writing backward. "It was a way to break into the business," Terry says. "It was a tough business, made especially tougher for women fighting for equal opportunity."

Over the years, Terry worked as news anchor, reporter, and talk show host. Terry is active on various volunteer boards, including the alumni association at Lincoln High School. (Courtesy Terry Lowry.)

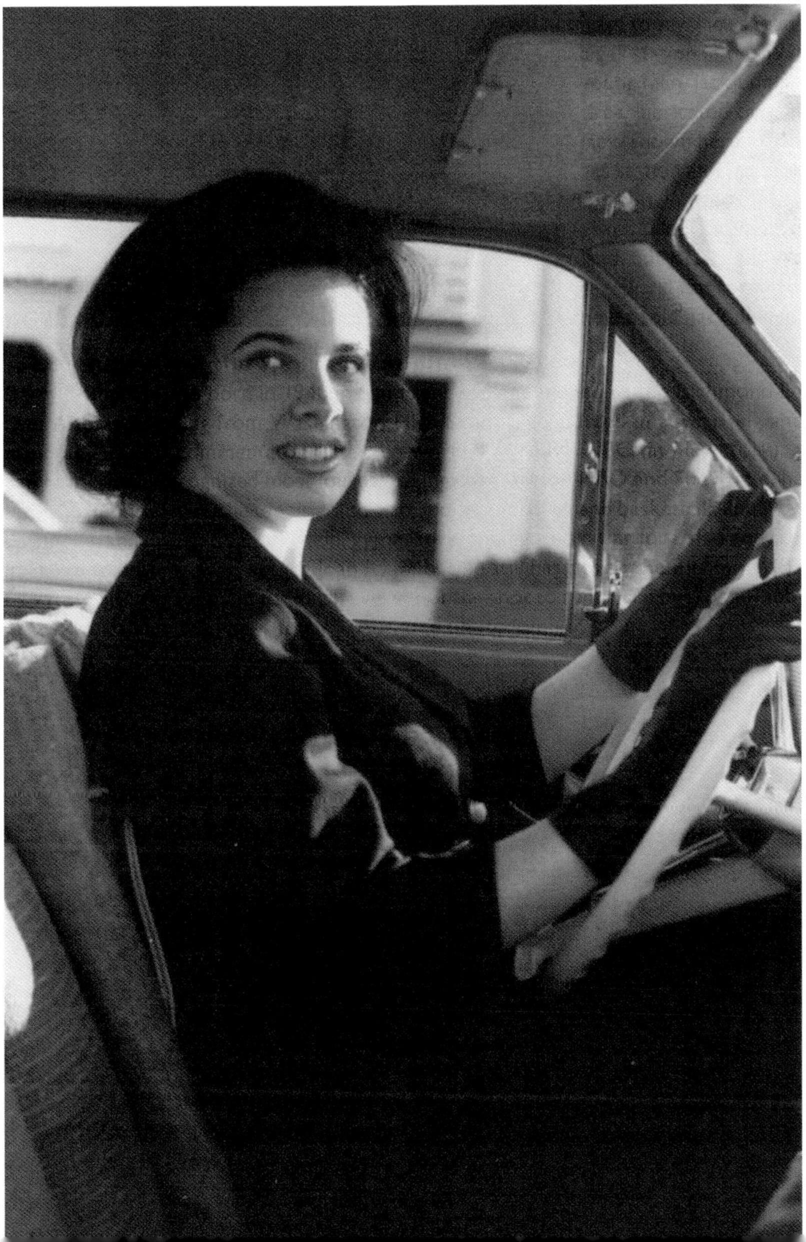

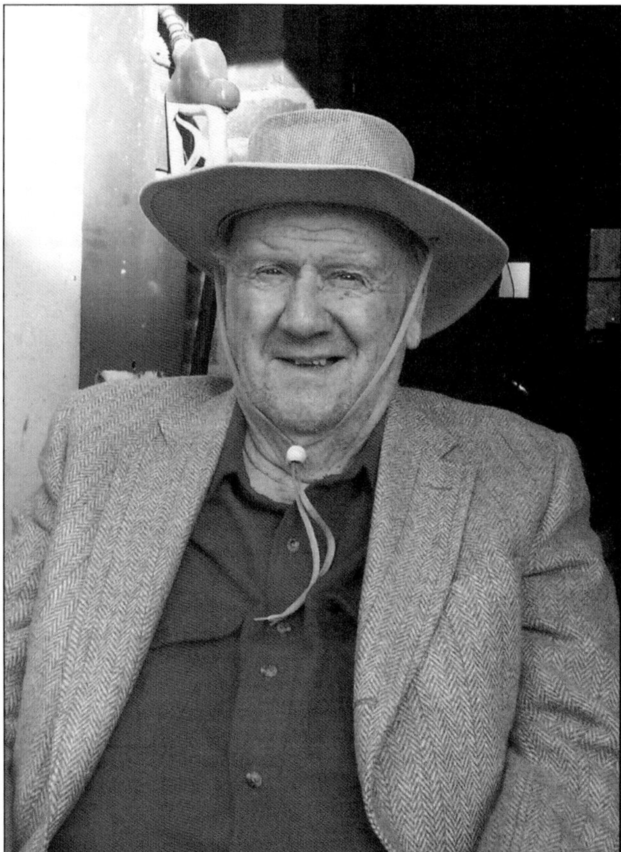

Keeping History Alive

Jack Goldsworthy was born in 1926 and raised in the Sunset District. "I can remember when there were sand dunes all the way up 16th to Judah Street," he used to say. Jack's grandfather opened a gas station in the 1920s, and, as a young man, Jack pumped gas, fixed flat tires, lubricated cars, and sold batteries. Jack, shown here in 2011, worked at the gas station and made sure it was not torn down over the years. In recent years, people have offered to buy the land, but Jack never wanted the station razed and the corner developed, so he never sold. Jack died in 2012; as of 2014, the gas station is still standing. (Left, courtesy Bruce Eng; below, courtesy private collection.)

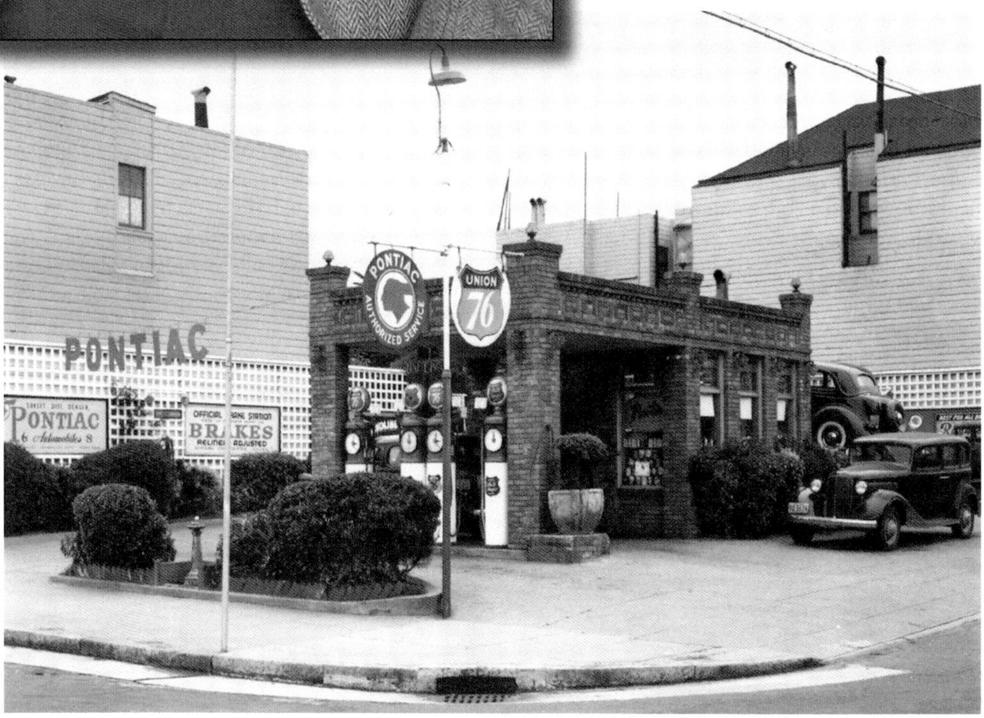

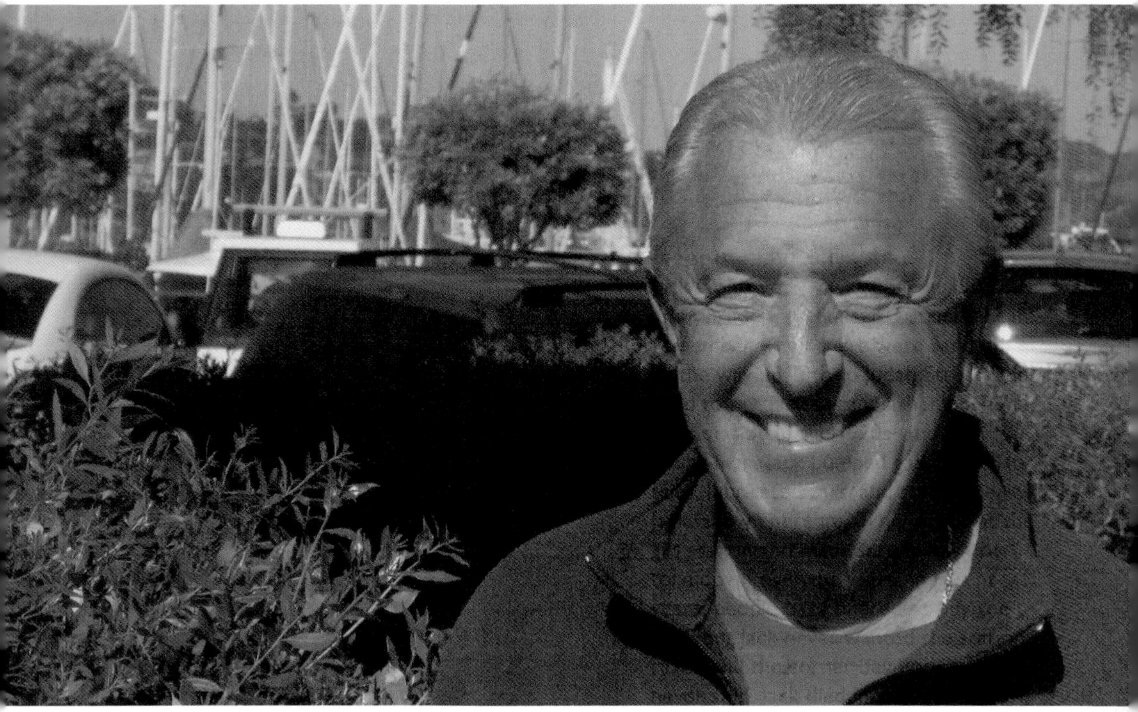

A Legend behind the Sports Microphone
Barry Tompkins was born in 1940 in San Francisco and moved to the Richmond District when he was five. After graduating from Washington High School, he started in advertising and then joined KCBS radio as a sports commentator. Later, he worked at KPIX, NBC (in New York), and KRON (back in San Francisco). Recognized most for his boxing coverage on HBO and Showtime, he has also broadcast eight Olympic Games, the tennis grand slam, college football and basketball, and world championships in swimming and diving, track and field, gymnastics, and figure skating for ESPN and Fox Sports. Barry lives in Sausalito with his wife, author Joan Ryan, but he still has ties to the Richmond. Barry says, "Thirty of us Washington grads meet for lunch every month—not to reminisce but to talk about what's happening in our lives and in the world today." (Author's photograph.)

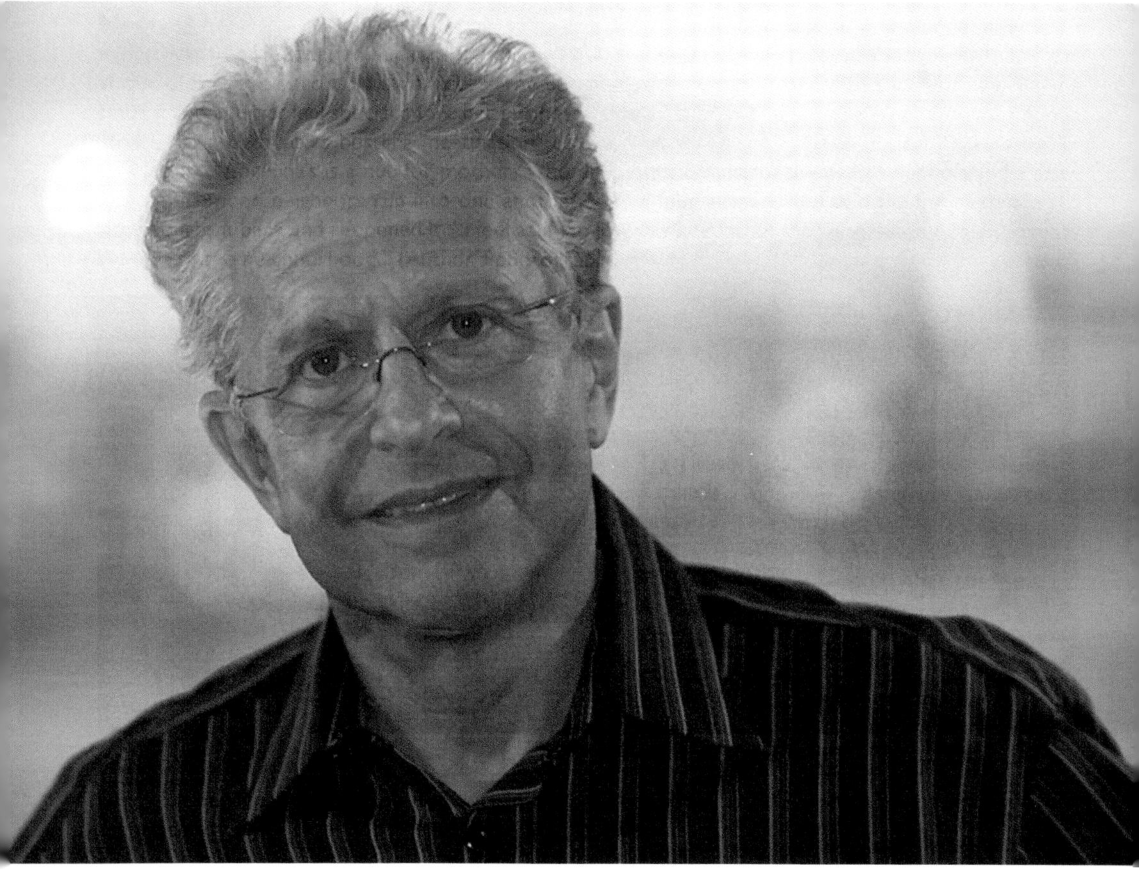

An Accomplished Lawyer
Laurence Tribe was born in Shanghai in 1941 and later moved to San Francisco, where he graduated from Lincoln High School when he was 16. At that young age, he entered Harvard University, and he later received an AB in mathematics from Harvard University and a JD from Harvard Law School. He has taught at Harvard since 1968 and is the Carl M. Loeb University Professor. A scholar of constitutional law, Tribe has argued before the US Supreme Court more than 30 times. He is the author of many books, including *The Invisible Constitution* and (with Joshua Matz) *Uncertain Justice: The Roberts Court and the Constitution*. (Courtesy Matt Teuten.)

Meeting Friends at Angelina's

When Angie Rando opened her café and deli in 1983, she had fond memories of shopping with her dad at one of San Francisco's old Italian delis. The butcher would welcome her with a slice of salami and a smile that made her feel special. Now, her business, Angelina's, at Twenty-second Avenue and California Street, has grown into a bustling "destination" café and full-service catering operation. One customer says fondly, "Angelina's is a hub for mothers who drop off their kids at the nearby schools and a place where Richmond neighbors run into one another." After four years, Angie sold the business, but she later bought it back and reopened it. "I feel as if I'm just the 'keeper' of the place," says Angie. "It really belongs to the neighborhood." (Author's photograph.)

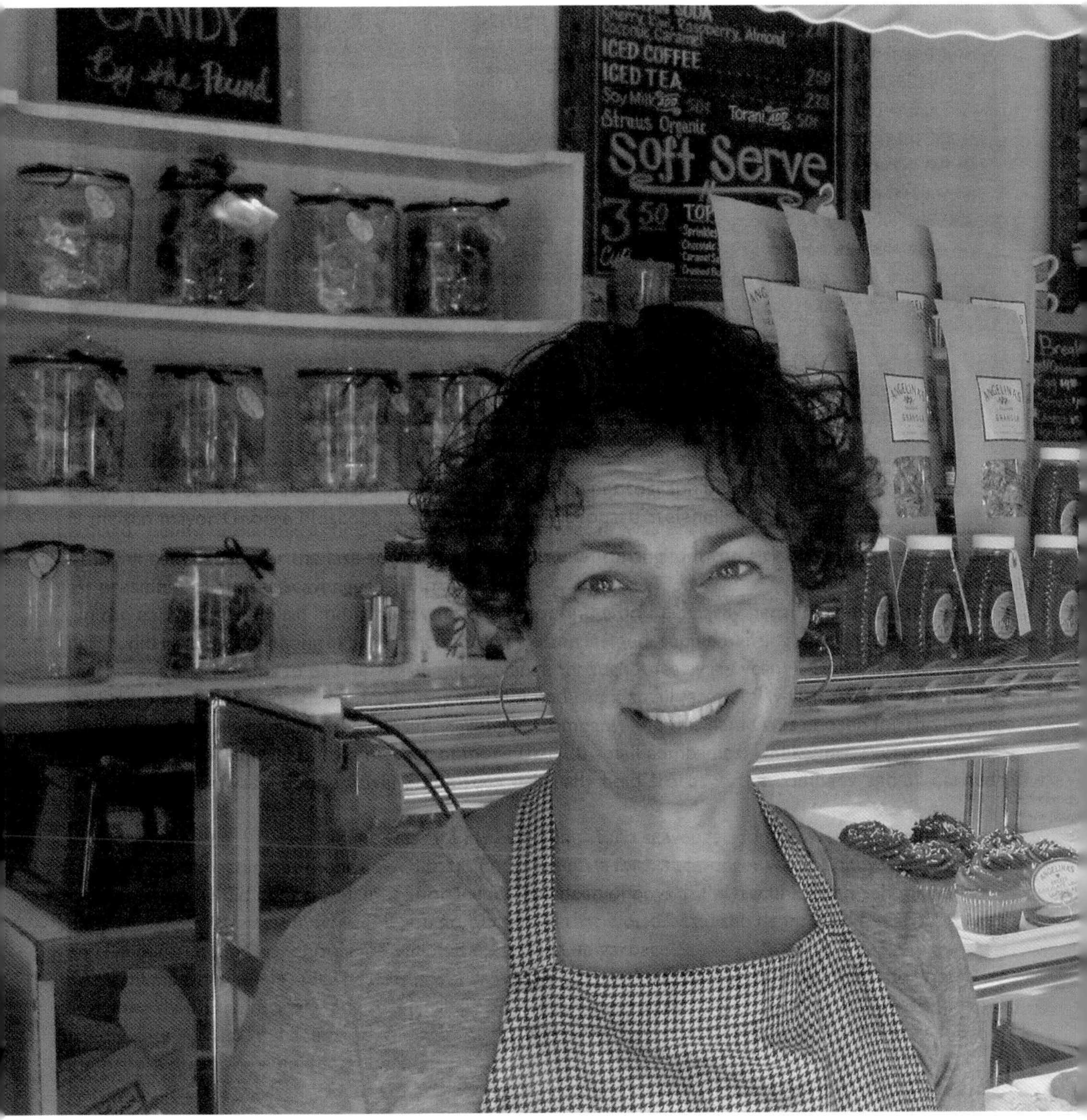

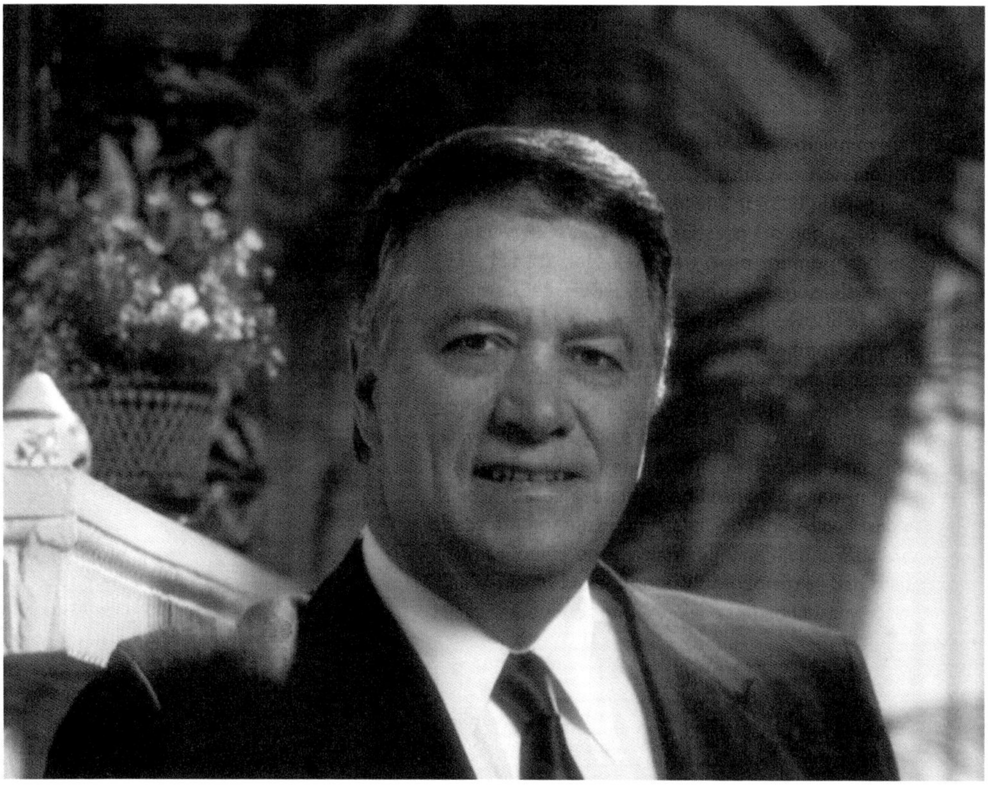

Doing the Work You Love

Leonard "Lenny" Stefanelli, a third-generation San Franciscan, was born in 1934. He has lived just south of the Sunset District for the last 46 years. Lenny is known throughout the city of San Francisco as the past president of Sunset Scavenger Company.

In the early 1900s, Italian immigrants who could not find work, primarily because they did not speak English, did garbage collecting in San Francisco. They often farmed, supplementing their incomes by using their horses and wagons to pick up trash and scavenge through it (early recycling). One early scavenger was Emilio Rattaro, who arrived from Italy in 1904 and ran a small farm at Twelfth Avenue and Judah Street. He called his company the Sunset Scavenger Company, and this name was chosen for the larger organization created in 1920 by a merger of more than 20 small companies. Unlike most corporations, Sunset Scavenger was a cooperative. Employees originally held shares in the company and all earned the same salary.

When Lenny was 10 years old, he was already "working" for a scavenger company—ringing customer doorbells and collecting the money owed to his uncle Pasquale for his scavenger work. Lenny worked hard at that job, but he did not do well in school. In fact, the dean of boys at Polytechnic High School warned Lenny that he had better improve: "If you go outside in that world," said the dean, "and f— around like you f—ed around in this school, you will end up picking up garbage!"

And that is what Lenny did! The dean's words were meant to be a warning that he should do "better," suggesting that it did not take any special skills or intelligence to be a garbage man. For 15 years, Lenny proudly rode a truck and collected garbage. At the age of 31, he became president of Sunset Scavenger Company, a position he held for 24 years.

At age 80 and now semiretired, Lenny is a senior adviser to Recology (the descendant of the Sunset Scavenger Company), an $800-million business that provides solid waste services throughout northern California, Oregon, and Washington. Like many others who have worked in the business, he is proud to be called a "scavenger." (Courtesy Leonard Stefanelli.)

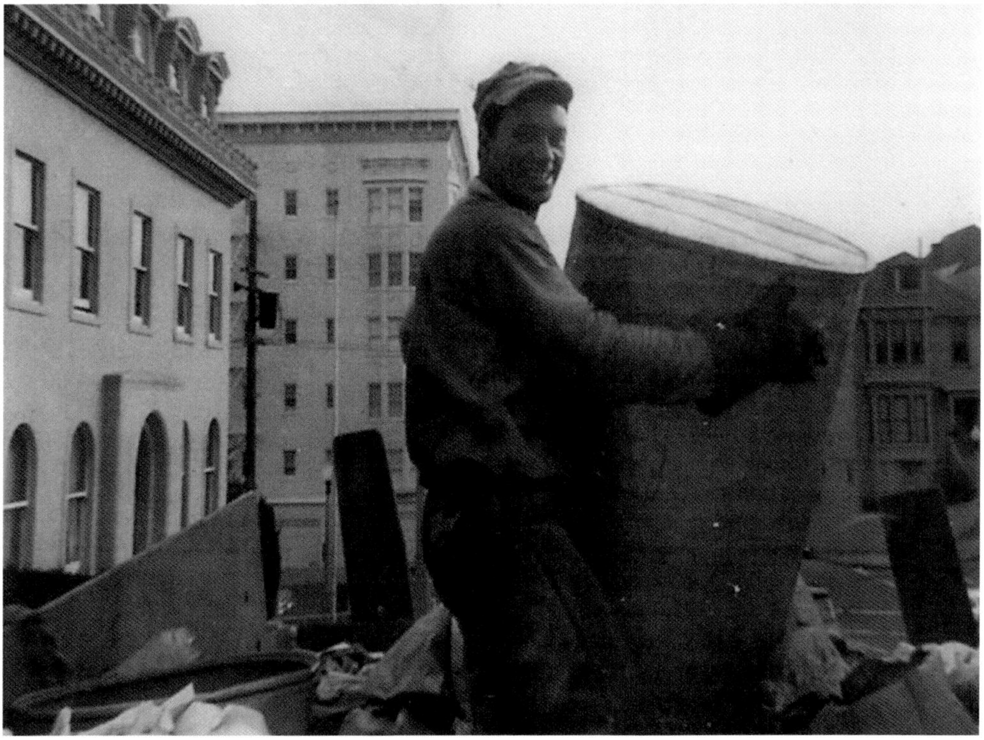

Lenny Stefanelli
Lenny Stefanelli is seen above hard at work in 1956. In the photograph below, he is having lunch with San Francisco mayor George Moscone in 1978. (Courtesy Leonard Stefanelli.)

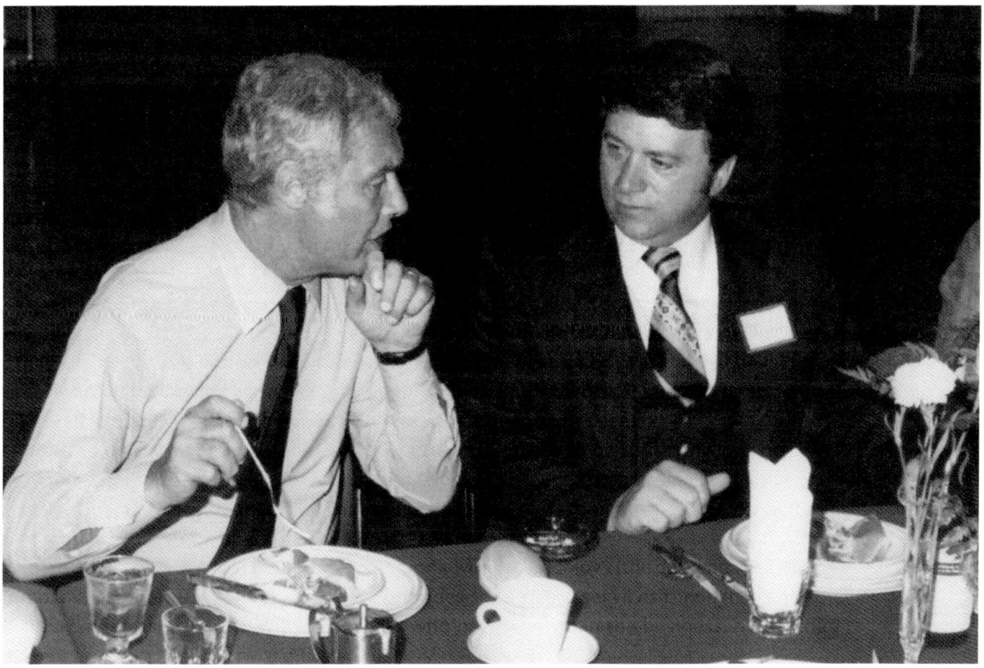

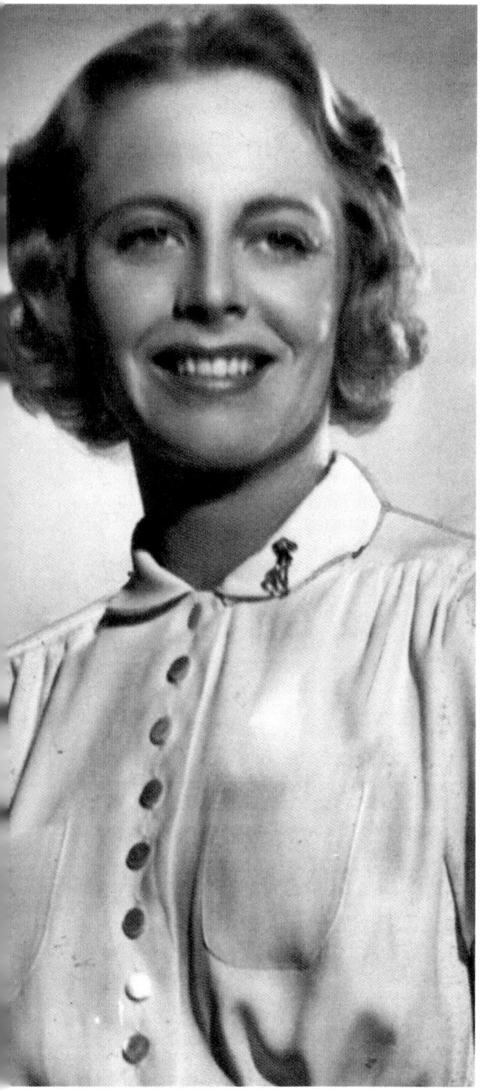

Famed Tennis Champion

Alice Marble was born in 1913. Her family moved to San Francisco's Inner Sunset when she was five. Her first love was baseball, but then she started playing tennis, practicing and playing matches in Golden Gate Park. In 1932, Marble began winning major tennis matches. She became the number-one women's tennis player in the United States and was ranked as the world's top woman tennis player from 1936 to 1949. The photograph below is a 1938 publicity shot of Alice Marble and baseball player Lefty O'Doul.

In the 1950s, Alice had a cameo role playing tennis in the Spencer Tracy and Katharine Hepburn movie *Pat and Mike*. Although she left San Francisco early in her career, she is memorialized in the city by the Alice Marble Tennis Courts on Russian Hill. She died in Palm Springs, California, in December 1990. (Courtesy San Francisco History Center, San Francisco Public Library.)

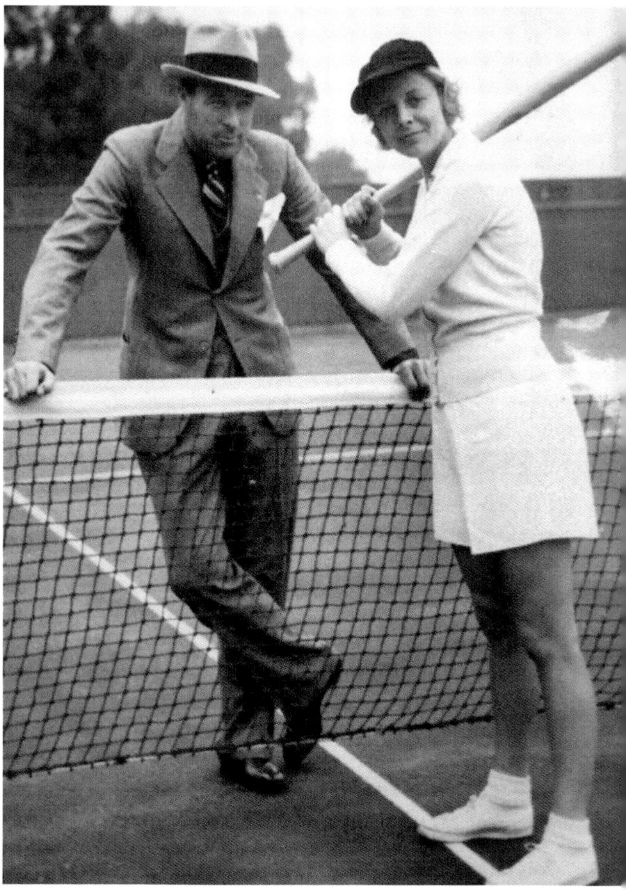

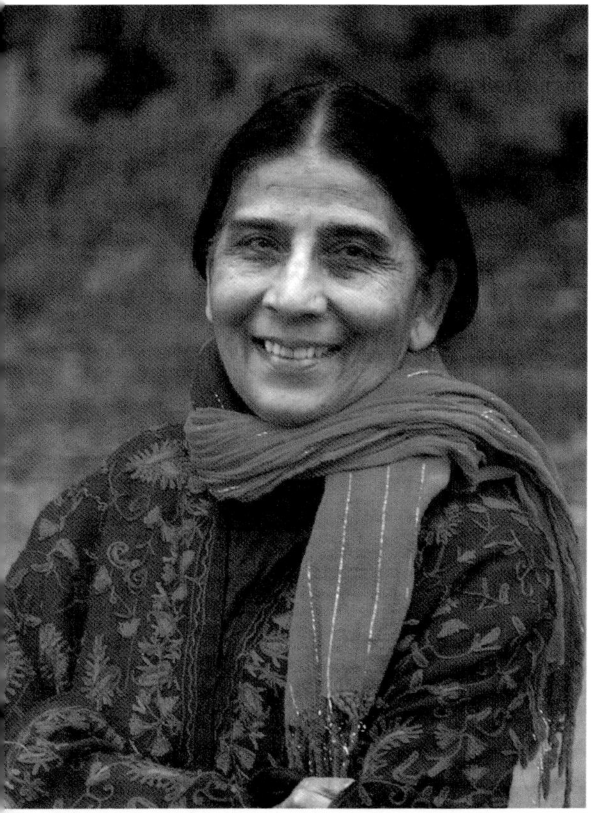

Loving the Work She Does
"Not many workers these days can say that they love their work," says Shanta Nimbark Sacharoff. "But I do. It is gratifying to be where the workers co-own, co-manage, and make business decisions together." Shanta has been a co-owner of the Other Avenues Food Cooperative for more than 30 years. Born in 1945 in a small village in India, Shanta moved to San Francisco in the 1970s, where she raised three children. She has studied nutrition, written recipes, published books, and taught cooking. Her journey in the food co-op movement is woven into her work in creating plant-centered recipes to share with shoppers. "I think Other Avenues has inspired and helped to revitalize the Outer Sunset community," reflects Shanta. "In the bigger picture, the co-op also helps the planet by providing healthy organic food to the community."(Courtesy Shanta Nimbark Sacharoff.)

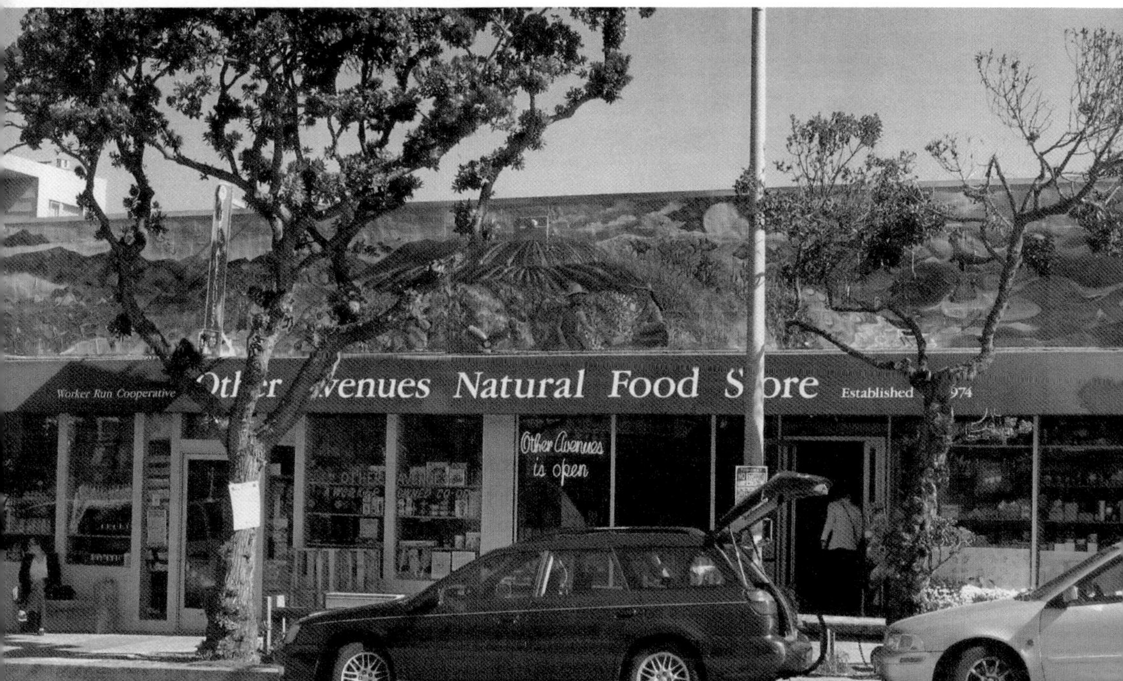

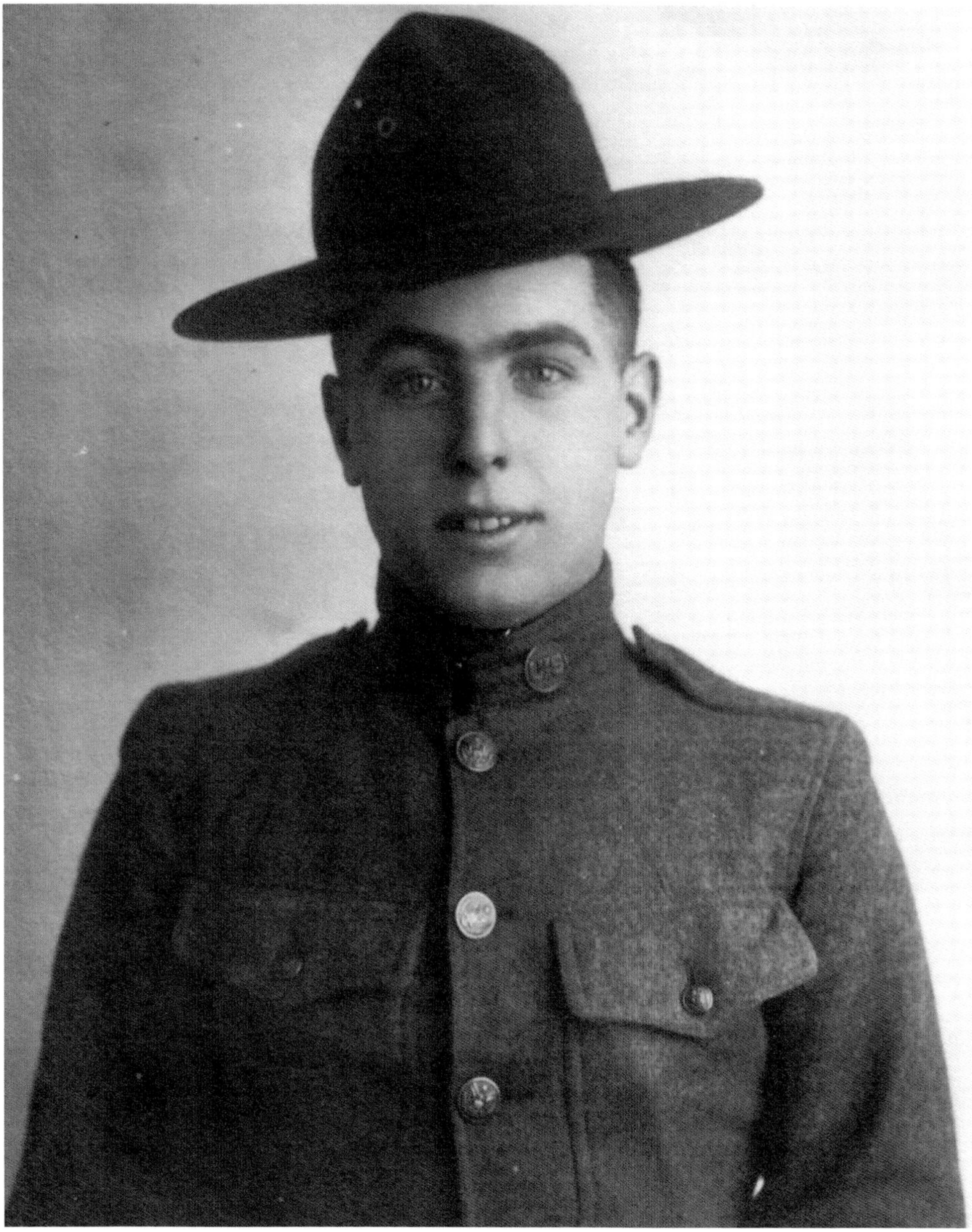

A Popular Bay Swim

On October 1, 1938, a horse named Blackie made history by swimming across San Francisco Bay. It all started at Roberts-at-the-Beach Restaurant (no longer there), operated by Richie "Shorty" Roberts. Roberts was *the* place to go from the 1920s to the 1950s. In September 1938, Shorty made a $1,000 wager with customer Bill Kyne that Shorty's horse, 12-year-old Blackie, could swim from Marin County to San Francisco. Shorty joined the bay adventure (see far left in the photograph above, on the facing page), even though he could not swim; he wore a life preserver and held onto Blackie's tail. The swim took just over 23 minutes. When the two reached land, oats and hay were waiting for Blackie, but he turned around and began to head back toward the water. The evening after the swim, Shorty hosed a huge party at the restaurant to celebrate Blackie's accomplishment. (Courtesy the Spotorno family.)

Shorty Roberts

Shorty Roberts held onto Blackie the horse's tail in the swim across San Francisco Bay (above). He often cooked at the large stove at Roberts-at-the-Beach Restaurant (below). (Courtesy the Spotorno family.).

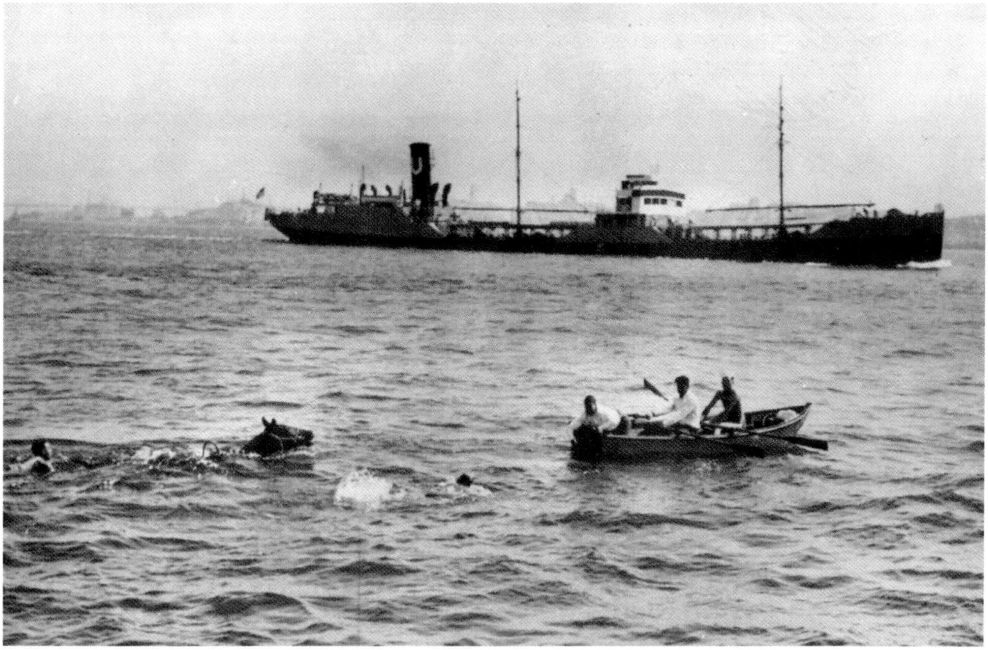

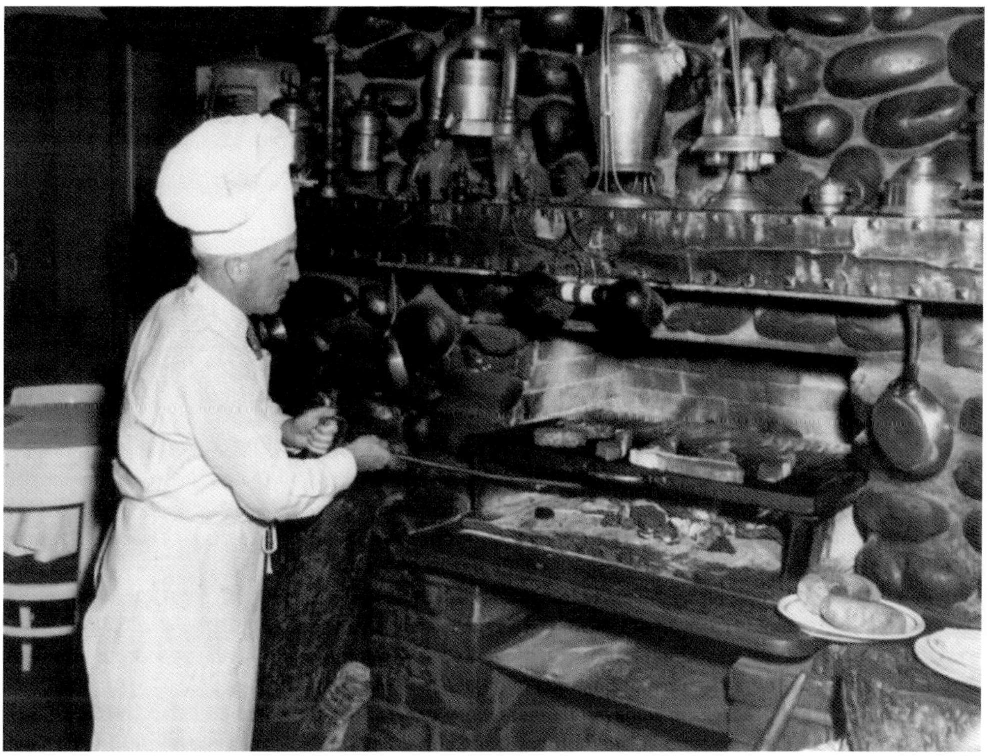

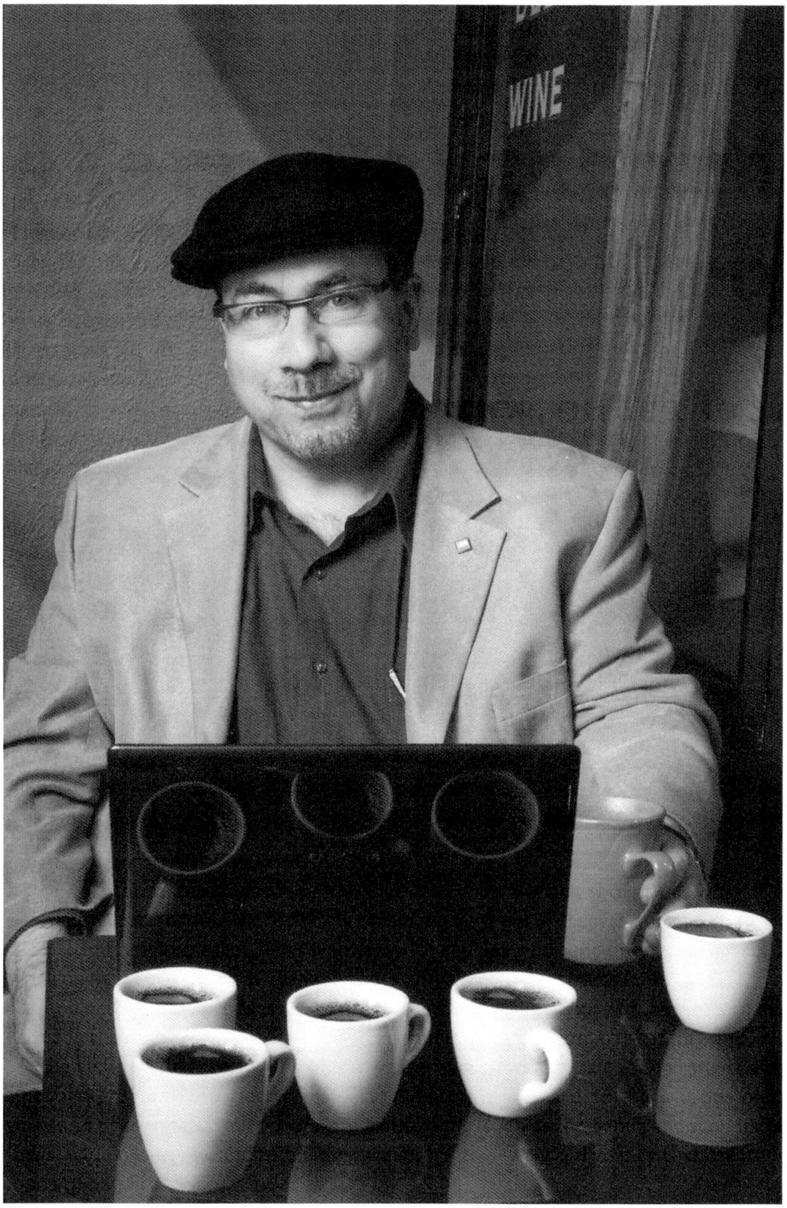

Craigslist in the Sunset

Craig Newmark is a self-described nerd, web pioneer, speaker, philanthropist, and advocate of the use of technology for the public good. He is the founder of craigslist, started in 1995 and now one of the world's most visited websites. Craiglist's office was located on Ninth Avenue in the Inner Sunset District until it moved downtown in 2010.

Today, Craig's primary focus is craigconnects, which he launched in March 2011. The mission of craigconnects in the short term is to promote and enhance the use of technology and social media to benefit philanthropy and public service. Craig communicates regularly through his own blog on www.craigconnects.org and through Huffington Post, Facebook, LinkedIn, and Twitter. He also travels the country speaking on various issues, appearing on behalf of organizations he supports, and delivering his craigconnects message to audiences nationwide. (Courtesy Stephanie Canciello, Unali Artists.)

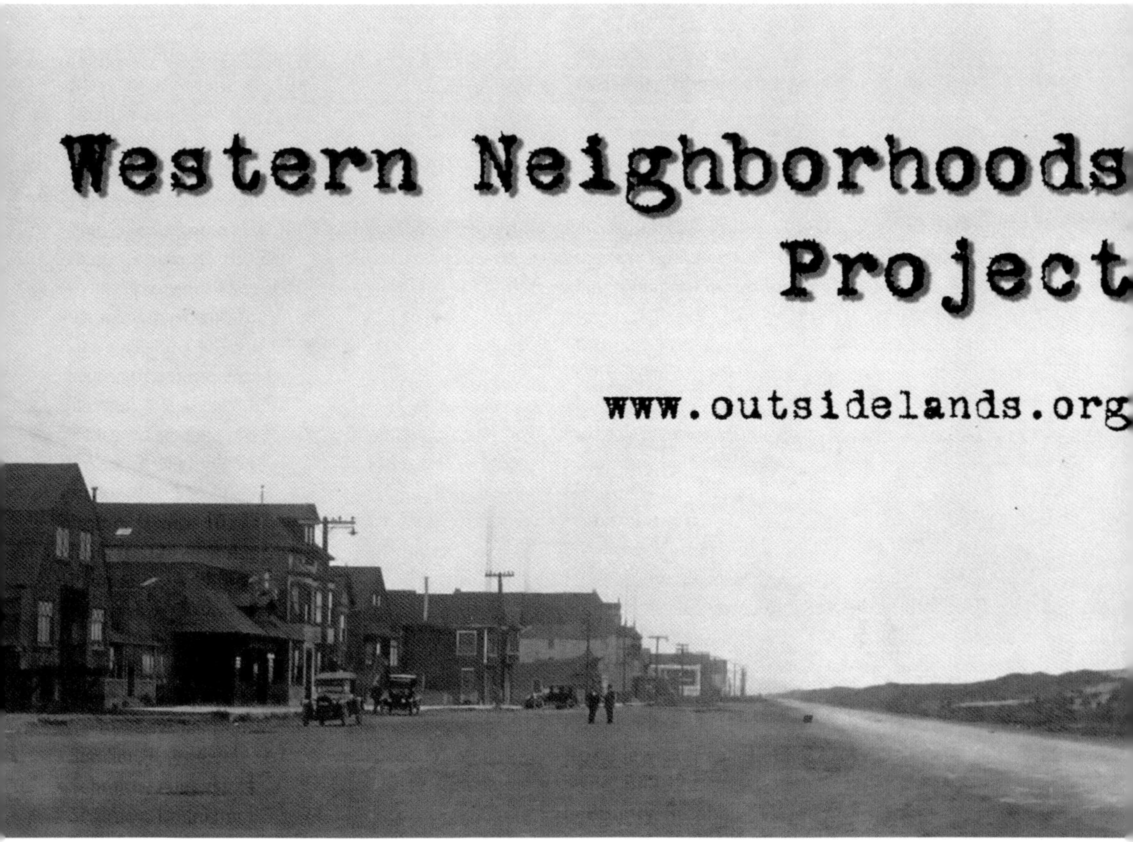

Western Neighborhoods Project (WNP)

Only one history organization is focused on the Outside Lands, the neighborhoods west of Twin Peaks in San Francisco. The Western Neighborhoods Project (see page 69) preserves and promotes the history of the west side of San Francisco through its website, with articles, announcements, podcasts, and message boards, and through special member walking tours and a quarterly newsletter.

The primary objectives and purposes of WNP are: to research the history of the western neighborhoods of San Francisco in the interest of preservation and community education; to promote and make accessible to the public the rich and diverse stories of the western neighborhoods of San Francisco; to solicit oral histories, photographs, and historical items pertaining to the western neighborhoods of San Francisco for cataloguing and preservation in appropriate institutions (such as the San Francisco History Center at the San Francisco Main Library); and to build awareness of the cultural diversity that created the western neighborhoods of San Francisco.

Find out more at www.outsidelands.org. (Logo courtesy Western Neighborhoods Project; photograph by Jesse Brown Cook.)

INDEX